Notes on Doctrinal and Spiritual Subjects
Volume 2

NOTES

ON

DOCTRINAL AND SPIRITUAL SUBJECTS.

VOL. II.

NOTES

ON

DOCTRINAL AND SPIRITUAL SUBJECTS.

BY

FREDERICK WILLIAM FABER, D.D.

PRIEST OF THE ORATORY OF ST. PHILIP NERI.

" Defunctus adhuc loquitur."—*Heb.* xi. 4.

VOL. II.

THE FAITH AND THE SPIRITUAL LIFE.

THIRD EDITION.

LONDON: BURNS & OATES, LIMITED.
NEW YORK: CATHOLIC PUBLICATION SOCIETY CO.

PREFACE.

THE notes on New Beginnings (p. 121), the Management of our Grace (p. 131), the Fear of God (p. 152), and Life (p. 315), were written for a second volume of Spiritual Conferences, which it was the intention of the Author to have published.

The Memoir of the Author, which it was proposed to include in the present volume, is in preparation, and will be published shortly.

J. E. B.

THE ORATORY, LONDON,
Feast of St. Hugh,
1866.

CONTENTS.

—+—

Part II.

THE FAITH.

SECTION I.

THE CHURCH.

CONTENTS.

SECTION II.

THE SACRAMENTS.

SECTION III.

CONTROVERSY.

Part V.

THE SPIRITUAL LIFE.

Part II.

MISCELLANEOUS.

SECTION I.

OLD TESTAMENT HISTORY.

SECTION II.

SPECIAL OCCASIONS.

SECTION III.

LIFE.

Part VII.

THE LAST THINGS.

SECTION I.

THE FOUR LAST THINGS.

SECTION II.

PURGATORY.

Part Fourth.

THE FAITH.

SECTION I.

THE CHURCH.

EPIPHANY LECTURES.

I.

THE HISTORY OF THE CHURCH.

I. The idea of the Church and its kingdom in the mind of Christ.

1. Its royalty—the Man Christ Jesus King—above nationalities—subject to no other power in spirituals — represented in prophecy as the enemy of empires—highest and most mysterious of allegiances—quite a fearful vision to see it starting on its journey across the world.

2. Its exclusiveness in government—in doctrine—in tone and temper.

3. Its supernaturalness—image of Christ—subject to the same misrepresentations and accusations —to the same treatment—yet eluding all with Christ-like vitality.

4. Its sufferings, mingled with its majesty, like His — within and without — opposites unite in hating it.

5. Its triumph, at unexpected moments—in the long run, it gains its end, and survives its enemies. Hence Catholics are not proud when they compare Christ and the Church.

II. The Chronicle of His kingdom briefly sketched.

1. His preaching: little work was done but the novitiate of the apostles.

2. The work of the apostles—in the great towns —seed scattered along the side of the Roman roads.

3. Melting away of the Roman Empire—thus its first victory was over a state.

4. Age of heresies and of patronage—heresy leans towards the civil power; it is in effect a protest against the royalty of Christ.

5. The vision of the papacy—the royalty of Christ coming out still more—peace to men of good will, to others war.

6. Feudal system, and temporalities of Popes—to secure freedom from states, and freedom to teach.

7. Age of the Council of Trent—saints—spirituality—missionary life—laws of the Church.

8. Age of saints of modern life—their characteristics, (1) love, (2) simplicity, (3) love of derision, (4) devotion to Mary, (5) love of Holy See, (6) upon the whole not being learned, (7) full of visions.

9. Progress and civilisation of to-day, in which the Church keeps her ground.

III. Marvels of that Chronicle.

1. Unity of faith, in spite of heresy, controversy, free opinion, or increase of science.

2. Succession of Popes, so long, so holy, so clear on the whole, righting itself after troubles.

3. Preservation of one city, in spite of exiles sieges, &c., &c.

4. Dying out of heresies—the Church simply out-living them.

5. Similarity and reproduction of saints.

6. Two homages to the Church in all ages, intellect and fear—*i.e.*, the faith of devils.

7. That it should be still a living, energising power, frightening grave men out of their proprieties, even at the present day. The late commotion may be thus accounted for—the reappearance of the royalty of the Church, which always frightens men—we were obscure before. Will England reject Christ? *Ecce Homo*, a King crowned but with *thorns*.

2.

THE VICISSITUDES OF THE CHURCH.

I. Why the Church, being what she is, should have vicissitudes.

1. To be like her King, and to represent His royalty.

2. For the perfection of her children.

3. Because it is a conflict between good and evil, and man is free—Michael's war in heaven.

4. Because God is glorified by them.

5. Because faith and loyalty are tested by them.

6. Because God punishes the world by them.

7. Because her children are not true to her high exclusive principles.

II. Kinds of vicissitudes.

1. Vicissitudes in conflicts for doctrine, *e.g*, near triumph of Arianism.
2. Vicissitudes of missionary success, *e.g.*, Japan and Paraguay.
3. Vicissitudes of toleration, *e.g.*, Russia and England.
4. Vicissitudes of temporal power, *e.g.*, in the Middle Ages, and now—according as God provides work for her.
5. Vicissitudes of saints—(1) in times—(2) in places—Ireland and England have had none canonised for three hundred years.

III. Examples of vicissitudes.

1. Momentary triumph of Arianism, illustrating royal patronage, the supernaturalness of truth, and the necessity of a celibate body of unworldly heroes to checkmate evil powers.
2. Lives of immoral Popes—even this lesson might be wanted to show the royalty of the Church as distinct from her grace, yet it is a pious belief that no Pope is lost, on account of St. Peter's prayers for them.
3. The Greek schism—court intrigues—incest of Bardas—pride of Photius—heroism of Ignatius —absence of human respect in the Holy See— providence in the legate's treachery and sin— all how like Henry VIII., save that we had no Ignatius.
4. The Reformation—immense evil, of course, and frightful loss of souls—yet how it has brought out the vitality of the Church, and is now re- futing itself by death or fresh division.
5. Recent vicissitudes of the papacy—like Pius

VI. and Pius VII.—as if a drama of history, which we had come to regard as almost poetical, were acted over again before our eyes.

IV. Lessons learned from these vicissitudes.

1. Supernaturalness of the Church: no need of arm of flesh: English Catholics should lay this to heart.

2. Detestation of compromise—boldness, openness, yet prudent concession to any limit when no principle is compromised: *e.g.* in concordats: yet for this the Church is called double-dealing.

3. Increased intensity of loyal love—what can we fear, when all imaginable vicissitudes but those of Antichrist are exhausted? no new thing can befall us, but his coming.

4. Not to be in a hurry: *we* can afford to sacrifice to-day for the sake of to-morrow, which the world cannot afford to do; picture of the God-like patience and providence-like policy of the Holy See.

The world's fear at the resurrections of the Church. Whilst England is busy building glass palaces, quays, and custom houses filled with the earth's productions, planning to fit the city to receive earth's foreigners, out comes the risen Church, with her defunct hierarchy, and England is filled with rage, fear, convulsions, self-contradictions, fighting, like a possessed demoniac.

3.

THE EMPIRE OF THE CHURCH.

The Church was to be a kingdom in Christ's intention : whosoever should fall on it should be broken,
and on whomsoever it should fall, it should grind him
to powder.

I. The difficulties it had to encounter.

    1. Sin and selfishness—its power was to be in self-
denial and unworldliness.

    2. Prejudices and traditions—it introduced an en-
tire set of new associations—celibacy—vocation—the royalty of the Church attained by its
militia of religious orders.

    3. It had to persuade supernatural doctrines, which
shocked men on two opposites counts, (1) either
by being without analogy, or (2) too analogous
to bygone superstitions.

    4. To overwhelm nationalities : this is the essence
of the Gospel.

    5. To ignore castes—making the laity as subservient
as the clergy.

    6. To stand independent of civil power—and where
half belonged to the Church to claim the whole,
because the temporal half cedes to the spiritual.

    7. Yet it had to compel civil governments, not to
ignore it, but to notice and provide for it : *e.g.*
in England.

II. Wherein its empire consists.

    1. The voluntary homage of the understanding ·

how the world frets at this in men of intellect who are Catholics.

2. Homage of the conscience—occasional romance of this in civil history, but nothing equal to it as a characteristic of the empire of the Church.

3. Love of it superior to patriotism or love of country.

4. Zeal to do or suffer, without any discouraging doubt of ultimate victory.

5. Arbitrary regulation of private life which men will not allow to civil government: *e g.* marriage, fasts, &c.

6. Recognition of its right to meddle with third persons, as in the case of occasions of sin, excommunicated persons, &c.

7. Submission to spiritual punishments.

Thus its empire rests on what men call blindness, *i.e.* on the *cultus* of a mysterious region of the soul, which the sanctions and prohibitions of the Church alone can reach: *i.e.* faith.

III. The character of this empire.

1. It cannot be touched—it eludes the world— it gives way to pressure, and yet loses no volume.

2. It invites persecution as being a kind of persecution itself.

3. Its apparent insincerity, simply because it eludes grasp; it seems like a huge conspiracy against the temporal welfare of mankind.

4. Its appearance and disappearance on the surface of society—it frightens and wearies men— hunted in one city, it flies into another.

5. Its arrogance and historical pretension, with

little or no outward dignity: it seems to be
always proving too much about itself, and no
two men see it in the same light.

6. It is catching, and proselytises without caring
   much to do so, and by putting forward its weak
   points; *e.g.* a lecture on the helplessness of the
   Church is more converting than one on its
   historical glories.

7. Suffering and constraint consolidate it; it com-
   pels its enemies to the savagery of physical
   force; irritable humiliation of this, *e.g.* newspapers lately.

Look at this empire!   What can men do but curse
it, or submit?

4.

THE CHURCH AT WAR WITH THE WORLD.

We have seen that the Church is a kingdom, and
what manner of kingdom it is: now look at the
Church and world alongside of each other.

I. What the world thinks of itself.

1. That it is going to last for ever: so it plants and
   builds and projects and dreams, overvaluing its
   dreams, and, poor blindfold thing, not seeing
   that they are dreams, realising not that it is a
   victim condemned to be burnt, with its sentence
   uncertainly delayed.

2. That there are no other interests but its own;
   ignoring the personality of God.

3. That there is nothing like itself anywhere; yet

the devil could contrive many equal manifestations of his ability.

4. That religion was made for its convenience, to
   satisfy an appetite, and must not forget itself.

5. That there cannot be two opinions about its own
   value; its case is self-evident.

6. That of all vulgar things spirituality is specially
   vulgar, cowardly, and little.

7. It sees no disgrace in eating its own words, when
   convenient—unlike the infallibility claimed by
   the Church. Leading articles of modern newspapers an instance of the hold the world has
   on men without their knowing it, and irrespective of sin.

II. What the Church thinks of the world.

1. No middle course—she judges it enmity with
   God—calls it a devil—the Holy Ghost bids
   her do so. Here war to the knife is proclaimed
   at once.

2. Foolishness of temporal affairs; and how the
   Church contrives to take all interest out of
   them: the world retaliates—builds glass houses
   —shows what it can do without the faith—as
   at the Tower of Babel.

3. The literary character—the Church enforces
   moral element—purity needed for divine
   science.

4. The mercantile character—woe to it—danger of
   it—severe dealing with it *in foro conscientiæ*—
   usury, &c.

5. The political character—the Church frustrates
   it—ensnares it—plays it false without deceit—
   despises it.

6. The domestic character—truth not peace—vocations—confessional—precept of almsgiving.

7. Her quiet faith in her contempt for the world; she assumes it, hardly taking the trouble to reason it out.

III. State of the case with the two kingdoms.

   1. Both claim to be exclusive, and infallible, and imperial, and hereditary.

   2. The Church will not admit the state to co-reign with it:

   3. While the world, because of its weakness, is ready to admit the Church to share its empire, and is maddened because the Church will have all or none.

   4. The mystery of the Church's obedience to the powers of the world is beyond all else, and the ease wherewith she can shift from favour to suffering—one of her most graceful movements.

   5. By the longsuffering of her obedience she attains her end in the course of years.

   6. Hence implacable hatred—the world paying the Church the dread homage of its anger, its hatred, and its fear.

A Franciscan monk amid the Apennines shown the leaders in the *Times*—he quietly philosophises on them. My son! this is but noise, empty noise: these are words of to-day, not of yesterday, nor of to-morrow; God's words effect what they say, so do in her degree the Church's words—this will soon be forgotten like the babbling of a nightmare, humorous even in its horror.

5.

THE CONVERSION OF ENGLAND.

I. What do we mean by the conversion of England ?
  1. Anything sudden ?
  2. Large masses ?
  3. Government or nobles ?
  4. Science or universities ?
  5. The poor in an influx ?
II. Is there any appearance of this ?
  1. None whatever.
  2. Neither is it God's usual way—save in cases of simple-minded nations.
  3. Neither does the looking out for it produce a good habit of mind, but
    (1) Eagerness about conversions and gossip: while the Pope and our principles are at stake.
    (2) Forgetfulness of asceticism, which is our only strength.
    (3) Neglect of the little ones of Christ.
    (4) It is contrary to the tranquillity necessary for high graces.
  4. Neither is it likely in England, because of—(1) Money: (2) National pride: (3) Political power: (4) Adherence to traditions. The servility of Anglicanism is convenient.
  5 We can only look for great successes through sufferings which humility ought to shrink from

encountering lest it should fail: *e.g.* it may be that the reign of Antichrist must come first.

III. The actual work of conversion in England—the gradual incoming of souls.

  1. Most prosperous in all classes.

  2. From increasing divisions elsewhere we may grow to be a huge body, in comparative compactness, and so outweigh others.

  3. Effects of the late tumult.

    (1) Increased inquiry: controversy against us always brings converts.

    (2) Effects of reaction, especially on the animal generosity of Englishmen.

    (3) Comfort of the homage of national pride to the power of Church and Holy See—this is better than controversy.

IV. Have we hopes of more than ordinary success? Yes.

  1. From what has actually happened in the way of conversions.

  2. From the manner in which it has happened—independently of Catholics.

  3. From the increasing loss of all faith outside the pale.

  4. From prophecies and visions of the saints.

  5. From the instinct of intercession for England all through the Church.

V. If we may look for supernatural help, what spirit should this breed in us?

  1. Internal union.

  2. Increased strictness, and unworldliness, and more abundant alms.

  3. Manly assertion of high principle, and fulness of

doctrine: God will be ashamed of us, if we are ashamed of Him, and so will not show the world that we are *His.*

English Catholics do not look like a body whom God would go out of His way to help beyond the common measure; we are more likely to be holding God back!

———

6.

THE LAST AGE OF THE CHURCH, AND REIGN OF ANTICHRIST.

From the first, all the troubles of the Church were regarded as types of Antichrist, as Christ had His types; so we naturally conclude with this. It is not an idle speculation; Scripture puts it before us.

I. The person of Antichrist.

1. A single person. "The man of sin, the son of perdition, that wicked one." * "This is Antichrist, who denieth the Father and the Son." † v. Apoc. xix.

2. Many believed in a demoniacal incarnation— this will not be so—but he will be a man utterly possessed. (Card. Berulle.)

3. Not come yet—Mahomet was not he—the signs are not fulfilled.

4. He is to be a king—his kingdom in visible antagonism to the kingdom of Christ—so all civil oppositions have been precursors of Antichrist.

———

* 2 Thess. ii. 3.   † 1 John ii. 22.

5. Certainly a Jew—uncertain if of tribe of Dan—origin probably obscure.

6. With zeal for the temple, gives himself out as the Messias.

7. With immense talents, awfully assisted by the devil—immense wealth, Dan. xi.—immoral, Dan. vii.; and xi. unparalleled in deceit—deceiving even the elect.

8. His doctrine an apparent contradiction of no religion, yet a new religion. Comparison with French Revolution. (1) He denies the divinity of Christ. (2) Asserts that he is the Messias. (3) Worship of devils. (4) He is an atheist, (5) but begins by affecting respect for the law of Moses. (6) Lying miracles, false resurrection, mock ascension. (7) He has an attendant pontiff, so separating regal and prophetic office.

II. His kingdom.

1. Not hereditary—got by degrees, by fraud, talent, and iniquitous diplomacy.

2. It will begin at Babylon.*

3. It will extend in influence over the whole civilised world.

4. Jerusalem will be the metropolis.

5. When his empire is at its full, it will last only three years and a half.

III. His persecution.

1. Unparalleled horror of it.†

2. In spiritual things—(1) there will be *hardly* any mass, (2) but the worship of his image and the wearing his mark; (3) majority of Chris-

* Zach. v. 11.   † Apoc. xx.

tians will apostatise, (4) but the Church will not be destroyed.

3. Saints will be greater than ever—martyrs greater, as the first fought against men, the latter will fight against devils,* our Lady's Saints, *vide* Grignon de Montfort.

4. Enoch and Elias,† now confirmed in grace, and waiting—they will preach in sackcloth—for as long a time as Christ, *i.e.* three years and a half less nineteen days — their martyrdom — they will lie unburied.

5. Jesus kills him, and comes to the doom forty-five days after; some say that St. Michael will kill him on Mount Olivet.

IV. Protestantism an anticipation of Antichrist.

(1) Its attitude towards the Blessed Virgin Mary, (2) the Mass, (3) the sign of the Cross. (4) All its sects unite against the Church. (5) Its carelessness about Baptism; sixth angel drying up Euphrates. (6) It blasphemes Saints.

V. The Five-and-Forty Days.

(1) Space for repentance. (2) Full of signs. (3) The Lord comes and the weary world is judged and burnt.

Lessons.

1. The reign of Antichrist is to be the last temporal reign: so the Church's last enemy is to be a kingdom, the consummation of the wickedness of all kingdoms; how significant!

2. What part should we take in this persecution? Let us measure it by the boldness of our profession now—by our strictness with ourselves

---

* Suarez in Part. III. Disp. liv. Sect. 6.   † Ecclus. xlviii.

—by our self-denial in charity for others—by
our perseverance in the practices of penance—
by the fervour and the frequency of our prayers
—by the rigorousness of the examinations of our
conscience. It is always to each of us the
five-and-forty days; Christ will come—He will
not tarry—let us have our loins girded and our
lamps burning, that when the midnight cry is
raised, and the Bridegroom cometh, we may go
forward with holy awe to meet our Saviour and
our Judge.

II.

THE HOLINESS OF THE CHURCH.

Various true senses in which the Church is holy;
select the one which, while it is the most spoken
against, puts in the clearest light the difference between
the Catholic and the Protestant religion, viz., the
peculiarities of the Catholic saints.

1. The end of the Christian religion is not to be an
engine of government, a purification of literature, a
civiliser; not to give a standard of morals, but to train
men for Heaven, to form characters whose proper
sphere is not this world at all, who are awkward in it,
and mostly unsuccessful in its ways; it makes men
moral by the way, and in consequence of something
else, but it does not aim at that as an end. Considering the shortness of life and the length of eternity, it
would be almost blasphemy to suppose it could be
otherwise.

2. Now look at the New Testament to see *what sort* of character this was to be :—examples—(1) The Baptist, simply man ; (2) Jesus, God and Man.

  I. The example of the Baptist.

    1. Likeness of John to Jesus, yet discrepancy.

    2. Sketch of St. John—penance in innocence.

    3. Fulfilment of the type in the Catholic religious life.

      (1) Hiddenness.

      (2) Carelessness of reputation.

      (3) Unnecessary suffering.

      (4) Seeking humiliations.

      (5) Rejoicing in persecutions.

      (6) Proportion of prayer to work.

      (7) Contempt of riches.

      (8) Lifelong renouncement of self-will.

      (9) Joy in the world's hatred.

II. Our Blessed Lord.

    1. He is our pattern.

    2. Sketch of His life, and spirit of His maxims.

    3. Supernatural and unworldly characteristics.

    4. Parallel in the Catholic spiritual life.

    5. Now look at Protestantism—it makes good husbands, fathers, citizens, *on tombstones*—let us grant it for once—still it has

    1. No supernatural marks.

    2. No provision for evangelical counsels, as in the Church.

    3. Its perfection is the very reverse of enmity with the world; yet this enmity is of the essence of scriptural holiness.

You would not at all think that the New Testament was the book on which Protestants were formed. If

Catholics would well consider this whole subject, how many difficulties they would find answered! The strength of our religion is in its supernaturalism.

The prayer of Jesus to His Father—how often we should read it and meditate on it verse by verse—I have given them Thy word, and the world hath hated them, because they are not of the world.*

III.

THE LIVING CHURCH.
THANKSGIVING FOR THE DEFINITION
OF THE IMMACULATE CONCEPTION.

They that are in a home, or live amid beautiful scenery, do not realise it: so is it with us in the Church, with all the blessings of her maternal love around us. Thanksgiving for being in the Church: how the Definition brings it home to us

I. The Church is one of God's most wonderful
    works in
 1. Its constitution.
 2. Its destinies and history.
 3. Its supernatural powers.
 4. Its doctrine and teaching.
 5. Its genius and spirit.
II. The essence of the Church is that it is living.
 1. It is not a literature or a philosophy.
 2. Nor a merely authoritative interpreter of God's
    word and will: the swing it allows to mind.

* St. John xvii. 14.

3. Nor is it simply a government.
4. But it is a living participation of the life, the liberty, and the repose of God.
5. Thus it is never an ideal; but an eminently practical power and unity.

III. The Definition is a disclosure of this life.
   1. We have seen a step taken which will be an historical grandeur.
   2. The life and movement of the science of theology and its schools.
   3. The pressure of the living devotion of the people.
   4. The illustration of the Divine Monarchy of the Papacy.
      (1) Its width—world wide.
      (2) Never so naturally expressed.
      (3) Its all-sufficiency.
   5. The whole Church receives the Definition by acclamation.
   6. The total and regardless passing over of the world in this matter.
   7. It concerns Mary, who has always been so deep and strong a portion of the life of the Church.

IV. Lessons.
   1. Greater loyalty to the Church.
   2. Greater devotion to our Blessed Lady.
   3. Greater holiness, because God has spoken in our day.
   4. Perpetual thanksgiving that we are in the Church, whether as old Catholics or converts.

V. The beauty of the heavenly Jerusalem.

———

IV.

PEACE THE LIFE OF THE CHURCH.*

"Pacem relinquo vobis, pacem meam do vobis."—St. John xiv. 27.

I. Peace the legacy of Jesus to His Church.
  1. Naturalness of this.
     (1) Because He is the Word who has lain in the Bosom of the Father from all eternity.
     (2) Because He is the Prince of Peace: peace was His mission.
  2. Strangeness of it.
     (1) Because of what He said of sending a sword.
     (2) Because of what we see around us. When He said it, He knew all that was to come —the world, heresy, coldness. Yet the peace of the Church is not only in spite of her warfare, but almost because of it: the troubles of the world are the materials of her peace.
  3. The nature of this supernatural peace—like that of God.
     (1) Active, without being anxious or diplomatic.
     (2) Affectionate, not the mere privilege of being unmoved.
     (3) Equable, not subject to tides, not precipitate, not intermittent.
II. Why it is that peace is the life of the Church.
  1 Because she is the image of the Most Holy Trinity.
     (1) Her motherhood is the extension of the Paternity of God.

* Preached at the Synod of Oscott, 1855.

(2) She is the mystical Body of the Eternal Son;

(3) And the Spouse of the Holy Ghost who·
animates her.

2. Because she is instinct with the spirit of the
Sacred Heart;

(1) Uniting gentleness with zeal.

(2) Love of God with love of souls.

(3) Detachment from all things, but the glory
of God.

3. Because of the nature of her work.

(1) All work for God is complete, successful,
and so full of rest and peace.

(2) The knowledge and love of God is the centre
of the Church.

(3) This peace is not compatible with mourning
for sinners: *e.g.* Jesus and Mary: *in pace
amaritudo mea amarissima.*

III. This life of peace exemplified in our present
circumstances, and especially in the work of
the Synod.

1 Quiet, pliant energy, elastic, ready for all times
and places. The Church passes gracefully, like
the moon in the heavens, from phase to phase;
or, like the great pontiff of the world, vests and
unvests herself in majesty before the people for
her successive functions, without compromising
the majesty of her unchangeableness.

2. The strong spirit of the ancient traditions controls, and while it controls, intensifies her love
of souls.

3. The peacefulness of her operations. Peace is
her progress, her locomotive power. She is slow,
gradual, supernatural, to superficial eyes timid

and uncertain in her step. Whatever is revolutionary lacks every characteristic of a Divine Work. It is as if she was ever before the Beatific Vision, contemplating Him who is eternal peace.

IV. If peace is the life of the Church, it must be our life

   1. As children of the Church: but

   2. Still more as ministers of the Church. Peace is the perfection of the priesthood; the ecclesiastical spirit is a spirit of peace, for zeal is peace: how calm the Angels are. The Holy Spirit is peace, yet very fire.

     (1) Peace in our work, when we work disinterestedly for God, and leave the issue to Him.

     (2) Peace in our weariness, when we have worked for God.

     (3) Peace is our power as priests, as apostolic men.

       1. In prayer and personal holiness: and the outward order of the Church protects the holiness of each one of her children.

         (1) Mystical life flourishes most where canonical order reigns, rather than in missionary countries.

         (2) The Church is most fertile when most complete.

         (3) The supernatural requires the strict curbing hand of authority, reform, and discipline: and they who are touched by it need hiding in the deep places of the Church.

       2. In the clearness of a calm mind.

3. In the supernatural force peace gives us.
4. In our patience and faith in the action of the Church.
5. In our love of each other, as shown in this Synod. I speak not to you, my Fathers, but to my Brethren in the priesthood. How much does every meeting increase our mutual love, our respect and admiration of each other. I have never been with my Brethren, but a strong sense of being edified has kindled my heart within me. Even charitable rivalries in good works, even blameless jealousies in our diversity of gifts, fade away before the quiet charm of personal communication.

O my reverend Brethren, let us edify each other in the fervour of our peace. It is not the spirit of the age; it is not the wisdom of the world. It is not in this that the successful efficiency of our national vigour, or the developments of our gigantic prosperity consist. It is not man's standard of work or of success. But it is the beating of the Sacred Heart of Jesus in our hearts. It is the indwelling of the Holy Ghost, which, always with us though less perceptible, we have almost beheld and handled in the peace and order and beautiful concord of this ecclesiastical congress. It is the spirit of Jesus, Peace I leave with you, my peace I give unto you : not as the world giveth, do I give unto you. Let not your heart be troubled, nor let it be afraid.

O my Fathers and Brethren, happy, thrice happy they, who sanctifying themselves and others in this heavenly tranquillity, learn to love Jesus and to make

Him loved, more and more, as the years go by; and
so press onward, weary yet cheerful, toiling yet at
rest, smitten yet hopeful, persecuted yet ever unpro-
voked, disappearing, one after another, from the eyes
of their brethren, into the bosom of Eternal and Uncreated Peace!

––––––––

V.

THANKFULNESS THAT WE ARE CATHOLICS.

I. We all pine for liberty—in mountain valleys—in
   fogs—on the wide sea.   The pain of blindness,
   deafness, lameness—all is want of liberty.   It
   is our soul which disquiets our body, yet has
   no true liberty but in loving God.   And in
   love there is no feeling which fills the soul
   more than having received a benefit from God.

   1. Because of His infinite perfections.
   2. Because of what we are.
   3. Because of the difference between that gift and
      all earthly things.

II. The gift of faith the gate to all graces here and
    all glory hereafter; the unutterable joy that
    we are Catholics.

    1. The infallible certainty and absence of all doubt.
    2. The quantity of knowledge about God and grace.
    3. The supernaturalness of the system; the strange-
       ness of the faith which could only prevail by
       heavenly assistance.
    4. The joyous wonder of the unity of various
       nations.

5. The lineage of the old saints.

III. Even persecutions deepen our sense of this great
gift from the feeling

 1. That suffering is power.

 2. That God is with us.

 3. That hatred of the world is a token of the true
  Church.

 4. That ours is really quite a different religion from
  what we see about us.

 5. That God is attacked in us. Whosoever shall
  touch you, touches *Me*, in the apple of My eye.*

IV. How we should thank God for this gift of faith.

 1. Loving thankful humility and acknowledgment
  that all is of God and grace.

 2. More frequent and fervent prayer.

 3. More abundant use of Sacraments.

 4. Aiming at a higher perfection.

 5. Gentle compassion for those who are astray.

St. Jane Frances of Chantal took two days over the
meditation of the faith. St. Teresa, when dying, often
repeated these words—After all, Lord, I am a daughter
of the Church.

VI.

ON THE TREATMENT OF TEMPTATIONS AGAINST FAITH.

Temptations against faith are either a mystical trial
or an intellectual *littleness*. Unbelief comes from two
wants—want of power of mind, or want of purity of

* Zach. ii. 8.

heart. The most obstinate unbelief is that which rises from the union of the two: and as most unbelief rises from such a union most unbelief is obstinate; and what is obstinate is for the most part uninterest-ing. Certainly of all things unbelief is the most uninteresting. My experience is that all *obstinate* temptations against faith come either

1. From unconscientiousness in not acting up to what light of faith we have.

2. From want of devotion to the Sacred Humanity: trying to know God *without* Jesus, who is the *way.*

Is is not true in conversation as a general rule that the cleverest man is the man who makes fewest objections. How many objections against the faith would never be heard, if it were not thought clever to make them.

I. Analogy between faith and purity.

   1. As essentially lifting us above our own nature.

   2. Extreme sensitiveness of both.

   3. Capacity of growth in both of them.

   4. Instinctive character, or something like it.

   5. Universal influence upon our whole character.

II. Characteristics of temptations against faith.

   1. Their unseasonableness—as at sacraments and prayer.

   2. Their importunity.

   3. Their vividness.

   4. The cloud they bring along with them, like temptations against purity.

   5. The atmosphere of earthliness with which they surround us.

   6. The intense pain they cause.

   7. Their swiftness of conquest if we once give way.

III. Treatment.
1. Not direct repulsion.
2. But distraction.
3. Distinguish between faith, and sensation of faith —we may have one and not the other.
4. Not abstaining from Sacraments in consequence.
5. Examen of conscience; this is the chief treatment. Self-knowledge is often the only way to knowledge of God: at least this is the case with many. There is a secret occult connection between faith and conscience: conscience is the reflection within us of the existence of God.

IV. Director's treatment.
1. Very gentle with persons who have them, if they are trying to be good.
2. Very severe if they are not trying to be good.
3. Never make light of them.
4. Sometimes, not always, let them explain.
5. Cultivate sense of *sin* above all things.
6. Christ is the *way*: now many temptations against faith come from want of devotions to the Sacred Humanity, not making Jesus the way, but trying to understand God without Him. St. Catherine of Siena says, Don't dispute with the devil. Now God perhaps does not remove the temptations because of our want of generosity with Him in not taking Him on faith, but disputing with the devil.

VII.

MARY AND THE MODERN CHURCH.

OR,

THE PRACTICAL WORKING OF DEVOTION TO OUR LADY IN THE CATHOLIC SYSTEM.

I.

MARY'S PLACE IN THE MODERN CHURCH.

I. Views of devotion to our Blessed Lady taken by those outside the Church, who yet generally sympathise with Catholic doctrine.

   1. That it belongs rather to the *extent* of doctrine and devotion than to their essence.

   2. That at most a certain amount of waste brightness runs over from our Lord and falls on her; *i.e.*, that she has no divinely intended distinctive place of her own.

   3. That, if allowable up to a certain point, yet it should be jealously looked to as something which *may* lower our views of our Blessed Lord.

   4. That it is an ornament of Catholic worship, and suited in its fulness only to a peculiar class of minds, and that not the most masculine or saintly.

II. These persons find on a nearer view

   1. That Catholics make it of the essence of devotion.

2. That she has her place everywhere and in everything, just as her throne is part of the actual scene in Heaven; Catholics seem to bring her in at awkward and unexpected times.

3. That, so far from being afraid lest Mary should obscure Jesus, they regard devotion to her quite as a condition of a true love of Him.

4. That all this seems to come out more and more startlingly in the lives of the more recent saints, and gets more and more adopted, formalised, and indulgenced by the Church.

III. What may be said on the face of things for the Catholic view.

1. The mere consistency of the view is an argument in its favour so far.

2. The view is so serious as to show that it is a grave practical question, not a mere prettiness; otherwise such a body as the Church would never have committed itself to the extent it has done—*e.g.*, in the *Nihil censura dignum* to the works of the author of the Glories of Mary.

3. The fact that modern saints *seem* to have so developed the devotion is a call to thought, and very serious thought; as by the saints God keeps the world right, and wakes up new life in the Church, or diverts her vigour into new channels, as needed from time to time.

4. It is obviously a question involving a great deal of theology, and the fact that once at least, in the Council of Ephesus, the Catholic doctrine of the Son required a decree of the Mother's honour, should make men slow to judge.

5. What is to be said of the language of preachers,

exaggerations in devotional books, and the like?
They speak, or write, to Catholics. How likely
men are to misapprehend language which comes
from a state of mind with which they are out of
sympathy. Besides, contradiction provokes real
exaggeration. Also, men speak beyond their
growth, just as they venture to pray beyond
their growth.

6. Yet it is bad policy to keep the matter in the
background: three things are against this, the
loss of God's blessing on truth—of Mary's
help—and want of tact in dealing with human,
specially English, nature.

7. Run over what God really did to Mary—predestination—maternity—place in Scripture—
exaltation—actual estimation in the Church.

IV. The object of these lectures is to show the place
of devotion to our Lady in the Catholic Church,
as a genuine integral part of the system, not as
an ornamental or sentimental excrescence, or
mere devotional luxury.

———

2.

THE CHURCH IN INTERCESSION.

Affection is an alarmist; the Church in all ages has
seemed in a peculiar peril, and truly so; saints, even
contemplatives and women, take a strange and unexpected interest in the external fortunes of the Church,
especially the vicissitudes of the Holy See. What a
lesson is this!

I. The duty of intercessory prayer.

  1. It is a Catholic peculiarity, because Catholics alone recognise the unity of the living Church.

  2. Yet the comparative neglect of it.

  3. The reason why it may be neglected is the jejune way of making it.

  4. Two plans may be proposed, but those who have already a plan cannot do better than keep to it.

    (1) Each day to have—1, a saint; 2, an object; and 3, to make an act of virtue, at least interior.

    (2) Intercessory meditation on the state of the Church.

  5. Immense consolation of this practice.

  6. Rapid growth of spirituality fostered by it.

    (1) Spirit of penance.

    (2) Forgetfulness of self, and postponement of self's interest.

    (3) Loss of jealousy—childlike joy at all good.

    (4) Unworldly, nay, anti-worldly habit of mind.

    (5) Warm espousal of the sole interests of Jesus.

II. Connection of devotion to our Blessed Lady with this matter.

  1. Her place in it.

    (1) Our Lord's intercession, of wounds, not of prayer.

    (2) Mary the head of intercessory prayer now, since the Ascension.

  2. Catholic ways of using her.

    (1) Offering the Precious Blood to the Most Holy Trinity by her, as practised by St. Mary Magdalen of Pazzi.

    (2) Reminding Jesus of her dolours and satis-

factions, as taught in His own revelation to B. Veronica of Binasco, and our Lady's to St. Bridget.

(3) Direct prayer to her to intercede.

(4) The fact of her intercession a stay and comfort, as well as a spur to us. She is not a subjective luxury, but an objective life and power.

(5) Praying to Jesus by His love to her.

(6) Her being connected with all the interests of the Church and souls by some one or other of her titles and offices, *e.g.* Regina Angelorum, Apostolorum, Consolatrix afflictorum, &c., &c.

(7) The belief that God has set her over the Church in a peculiar way. What Grignon de Montfort says of the new saints in the days of Antichrist.

We should unite ourselves to her in this matter. Temper of mind produced by habitual intercession; how it sucks us deeper and deeper into a supernatural life, as in the case of Suor Minima di Gesù Nazareno at the time of the French invasion of Italy, and the destruction of the religious houses.*

* Vita. Roma, 1833.

3.

THE CHURCH IN THANKSGIVING.

I. Comparison of Catholic and Protestant notions of worship.

  1. The love of benevolence and the love of desire.

  2. Protestant view, an inferior begging of and paying tribute to a superior: Catholic view, the creature's glad worship of his good Creator.

  3. The Catholic doctrine of spoken or interior acts.

  4. Objectivity and subjectivity, and the tempers of mind they respectively produce.

  5. The personality and *character* of God so realised in Catholic worship.

  6. The three branches of love's worship—(1) Acts of faith. (2) Acts of praise. (3) Acts of thanksgiving.

  7. Heaven is thanks and praise, not petition, at least when intercession is over after doomsday.

  8. Angelic worship. Suor Minima offered the love of all the Seraphim.

  9. The mind of the saints, and the genius of indulgenced devotions.

  10. The Eucharist the culminating point of worship.

II. A glance at ourselves practically.

  1. Neglect of thanksgiving; so forfeiting further blessings. How we importune God for converts: but what proportion of thanks do we give afterwards? So we come to look at the Church as a party, making God's glory and their precious souls but secondary to our *esprit de corps.*

2. Sanctifying effects of thanksgiving.

3. It is the natural result of the thought of God growing into us.

III. Our Lady; what the Church intimates by having a feast of her Presentation, so using her as an oblation of praise.

   1. The Blessed Virgin Mary the trophy of God's love.

   2. The only sinless creature.

   3. The worth of her doings, sufferings, worship, and acts of love.

   4. God's predestination of her; see some of the novenas in the Raccolta.

   5. Her exaltation praises God.

   6. Modern Indulgences connect her with devotion to the Most Holy Trinity: and in fact she stands in a peculiar relation to the Three Divine Persons.

   7. Attributes, creation, redemption, meet in her; the Sacred Humanity is the tie-beam of creation.

   8. Mary's being is itself a perpetual praise to God, as men say that earth, and sea, and sky, with all their beauties and their wonder, are.

   9. The Song of the Three Children; they call in elements, we call in Mary.

4.

THE CHURCH AT WAR WITH HERESY.

I. The Church nowadays is mingled up with heretics ; there are no purely Catholic countries; this is quite a feature of the times.

  1. There is no civil power to coerce heresy: for good or evil the Church has lost this ally.

  2. The world's scorn at the parental ways of the Church in prohibiting books, freemasonry, &c.

  3. Peculiar facilities of heresy—printing, facility of intercourse, domestic life, scientific associations.

  4. Temporal prosperity at present apparently with heretical countries.

  5. The dangers in which the faithful stand.

  6. Difficulties of theological study from the parochial and educational needs of the huge multitude of the baptized.

II. Now the Church mentions as a fact, *Gaude Maria Virgo, cunctas hæreses interemisti in universo mundo.* How she does this.

  1. Historical connection of the fortunes of the Church with movements in favour of Mary's exaltation.

    (1) Christian art—Mary the softening element in the Middle Ages.

    (2) Tridentine definition about venial sin—devotion to her has protected the doctrine of the Sacred Humanity ever since.

    (3) Battle of Lepanto—her new feast of the Rosary.

(4) Immaculate Conception in present needs, and against the torrent of modern impurity, and low views of sin and its stain.

(5) Growth of her feasts, and cultus generally.

    1. In 496 Gelasius I. instituted the feast of her purification to destroy the Lupercalia.

    2. In 847 Leo IV. added an Octave to the Assumption, because of a wild beast infesting Rome.

    3. In 1096, Urban II. ordered the daily recital of her office against the Turks.

    4. In 1243, Innocent IV. added an Octave to the Nativity, because of his conflict with the imperial power.

    5. Gregory IX., combating with the Emperor Frederick, instituted the Angelus three times a day.

    6. Boniface IX., after fifty years of schism, instituted the feast of the Visitation.

    7. Paul II., in the troubles of 1464, the feast of the Presentation.

    8. Pius V. and Pius VII. that of Auxilium Christianorum.

    9. Pius IX. made the Visitation a greater double.

2. By the growth of doctrine about herself. (1) Council of Ephesus. (2) St. Augustine and the Pelagians.

3. Her doctrine the touchstone of heresy: almost the only doctrine unborrowed by one or other of the modern heretics, which can hardly be said of the primacy, even in a qualified and mimic way; we need not be surprised therefore

at its being a rock of offence to seekers outside the fold. Analysis of heresies—woeful drama of Satan's warfare against the Church—all resolve themselves into a destruction of the Divine Maternity of Mary.

(1) Cerinthus and Ebion, by denying the reality of Christ's Sacred Humanity.

(2) Arius attacked the consubstantiality of the Son; so that Mary's dignity became nothing.

(3) Nestorius made Mary Mother of an Human Person.

(4) Eutyches taught that the human nature is absorbed in the Incarnation by contact with the Divine Word; and so that Mary is Mother *neither* of God nor man.

(5) Pelagius had no need of Mary, his naturalism making the Incarnation an effect without a cause, by denying original sin.

(6) Mahomet denied the Divinity of Christ, and so her Divine Maternity.

(7) Protestantism attacks *all* the consequences of the Incarnation; hence its special rage against Mary.

(8) Jansenism has had an innate antipathy to the *cultus* of Mary; this comes of its doctrine of the invincible tendencies of concupiscence or grace.

(9) Rationalism revives in the doctrine of myth the old Humanitarian heresies; and so makes all communications of Deity with humanity a mere prejudice.

(10) Pantheism looks at Christ as an individual personification of humanity; and according

to the Pantheist theory, every man is radically consubstantial with God; the individual is a humanised portion of the substance of God, so Mary is nothing.

4. By intercession, as the Mother of the Incarnate Truth and Wisdom.

5. By raising up saints, *e.g.* St. Dominic and the Rosary.

6. Devotion to her preserves men from infection. The evils of living among heretics are

   (1) A controversial tone of mind.

   (2) That we are ashamed of distinctive doctrines.

   (3) That we explain away to smooth prejudices.

   (4) Loss of enlightened and keen faith.

     Now, this devotion keeps up a supernatural tone, and is a running protest against low and unsound views. Thus she destroys heresy by limiting its infection.

7. Medals, scapulars, rosaries, &c.—such interpositions happen by them, as though God in Mary were confounding the strong things of the world by the things that are weak, and making things of which it might almost be said that they are not, as it were contemptuously bring to nought the things that are.

5.

THE CHURCH AT WAR WITH SIN.

I. God gave to the Church the exterior of the world for awhile in the Middle Ages.

1. The outward framework of society was Christian.

2. The civil magistrates used coercive power for the Church and her ends.

3. Estimation of the religious life.

4. Language framed upon Christianity, even down to the names of wild flowers.

5. Earth covered with material emblems and poetical admonitions of the faith.

6. Semi-ecclesiastical character of civil solemnities and military enterprises.

7. The great current of ideas went along with the Church.

Result of all this: it was a protection to the timid: human respect and all imperfect motives were on the side of religion.

II. Contrast of modern times.

1. Divorce between the Church and civil powers: Concordats as between enemies, or at least rivals.

2. Education and intellect taking a separate, often an antagonistic line.

3. Low esteem of the religious life, and notions of priestcraft.

4. Fewness of the clergy to grapple with the new feature of large towns.

5. Growth of pauperism, and consequent growth of crime.

6. Different idea of religion, as though it had no right to concern itself with temporal things.

7. Ideas, language, prejudices, all run counter to the Church.

Result of all this : we are more in the condition of the early Christians under the Roman Empire, with uncertain patronage and a fluctuating public opinion at best.

III. Thus the Church has now to war with sin in other ways, and to be more persuasive and less magisterial. Where that warfare lies.

1. In the depths of pauperism, or the pride of science, or the world-worship of wealth.

2. With secret thoughts and refined modes of sin.

3. With commercial, political, and working-hours arrangements right against her.

4. In the confessional, the schoolroom, and at the deathbed.

5. By a series of awakenings and excitements.

6. A hidden uncheered work, a martyrdom of patient weariness.

7. Seemingly a losing and certainly an undignified battle, losing here, gaining there, in dust and smoke, with results uncertain, confusion, misunderstanding of good people, and cross purposes. How little the instinct for souls is appreciated even by Catholics.

IV. Our Lady's help in the warfare with sin.

1. The fact that devotions to our Blessed Lady spring up and are fostered and systematised *chiefly* among those who have to work for souls.

2. The fact of her share in the foundation of orders and congregations for this end, *e.g.*—

   (1) The Jesuits. Life of St. Ignatius, Orat. Series, vol. ii. pp. 98, 99. Da Ponte, Orat. Series, p. 149. The Blessed Alphonso Rodriguez said that one great end of the Society was to spread devotion to the Immaculate Conception.

   (2) The Passionists.—She revealed their habit to B. Paul of the Cross. Life, Orat. Series, vol. ii. p. 201.

   (3) The Redemptorists. St. Alphonso said that she in the early days of the Congregation *mi consigliava per tutte le cose della Congregazione.* With them the rank of her feasts is raised, and they keep many which are not common to the universal Church.

   (4) Sulpicians. She designed their Church, &c. Olier's Life, ii. 243.

   (5) Conceptionists, obviously.

   (6) Oratorians. St. Philip said that he should not have thought of founding the Congregation of the Oratory, but that the Madonna was its Foundress and Mother.

3. Third fact:—that parishes and cities most devoted to her are spiritually the most flourishing, in them the Sacraments are best frequented, &c., which shows that devotion to her is a converting power, and not only so, but also a special aid to perseverance.

V. Other miscellaneous ways in which she helps in this warfare with sin.

   1. Missions. What St. Alphonso said of the sermon

on the Madonna.*   See also the life of the
Blessed Leonard of Port Maurice.

2. Devotions to her and indulgences.

3. Her feasts; and singularly this month of Mary,
   which seems to interfere with Church feasts, is
   encouraged by the Church to war against sin
   and to repair the laxities of ill-kept Easters by
   which men lose their Lenten gains.

4. Medals, scapulars, and rosaries.

5. Confraternities—how much experienced mission-
   aries have always encouraged them.

6. Education of the young and orphans.

7. Works of mercy to recover the fallen, and suc-
   cour those in occasions of sin.

How completely she has grown into the missionary
and converting system of the Church! You might as
well endeavour to get a man's veins neatly out of his
body, and yet leave him pretty much the same living
and healthy being as before, as try to extricate devotion to Mary out of the animated and vigorous system
of the Catholic Church.

---

* The innovators proclaim that devotion towards the Holy Virgin is
injurious to God; they combat her power and the efficacy of her intercession: it is our part to show how powerful and how advantageous a
thing it is to lean on this Divine Mother, and how much God is pleased
and honoured by our doing so.—*Life, Orat. Series*, vol. ii. p. 155.

6.

THE CHURCH MAKING SAINTS.

I. The Church works by flesh and blood, by living
men, not by rules, arrangements, systems,
organisations and material helps; she lives and
works, and advances by saints.
  1. Saints are raised up as heroes for special works,
e.g., Athanasius, Bernard, Dominic, Francis,
Charles, Alphonso; martyrs also and doctors;
St. Pius V. very specially.
  2. The saints are the most supernatural and Christ-
like part of the Church's work.
II. Mary's share, and the share of devotion to her in
the training of the saints. How curious we
ought to be to know what had been a distinctive peculiarity of *all* the very various saints.
  1. The fact that all the mediæval and modern saints
have been noted devotees of Mary.
  2. Their lives show that devotion to her was inseparable from all their growth and career; so
that it was not an accident, but a property of
their holiness.
  3. This comes out the most in the most interior
and mystical of the saints.
  4. Her external share in training the saints, by
visions, revelations, colloquies, and inspirations.
  5. Thus the most supernatural of the Church's
work is in a special sense Mary's work.
III. The congruity of this.

1. She was the actual guardian of the Sacred Humanity, of the Saint of saints; also she had a share in training St. Joseph, and St. John Baptist.

2. She was the queen and mistress of the apostles, specially St. Peter and St. John.

3. She was herself the highest created *person* in holiness, queen of all angels and of all saints.

4. The saints become transformed into Jesus, grow into His tastes and likings, so they perforce imbibe His perfect and intense love of His predestinated Mother.

5. Devotion to the Most Holy Trinity is the highest point of unitive contemplation; the saints grow into the dispositions of the Three Divine Persons; and so into the dispositions of their election of Mary, and their complacence in her, as Daughter, Mother, Spouse.

IV. As a matter of fact the saints make this devotion; it grows in their hands; each one leaves something more behind him, which, as the invention of saintly men, the Church takes up and authorises and grants indulgences. The science of Mary has always been the science of the saints before it became the science of the schools.

V. Conclusions to be drawn from all this.

1. That this devotion is not a mere ornament.

2. That it does not lead *from* God, as love of God is essence of sanctity, and what was a peculiarity of the saints must lead *to* God, nay, be a short road to union with Him.

3. That it cannot obscure Jesus, for to say that they

are copies of Jesus is the very definition of the saints.

4. That there is no need to be jealous of this devotion, for the saints are safe men and sure guides.

5. Nor any need to keep it in the background among Protestants, as God has been pleased to inspire the post-reformation saints the most strongly with it.

6. That ours is a false devotion, if increased love and strictness do not keep pace with it; for it was to the saints a principle of growth.

———

7.

MARY MAGNIFYING GOD.

I. The object of all these lectures has been not so much to explain the controversial and theological difficulties or beauties of devotion to Mary, as to show the practical working of it in the system of the Catholic Church. I have endeavoured to trace this in various functions of the Church; it now remains to trace the same effect in the mind of a convert to the Church.

1. Most converts have felt it as a difficulty, either before or after their conversion.

2. In the beginning it has been with them rather an act of faith in the Church than a devotion.

3. If it has been a matter of growth, the result has been to deepen the thought of God; so much

so that on looking back a few years, a convert
will probably confess that Mary has been to
him a new and marvellous teacher of God, His
Attributes, and the mystery of the Most Holy
Trinity. This is simply a fact of experience,
an induction of many cases, and it should have
its weight with those who are not yet in a
condition to make such a retrospect.

II. How she magnifies God.

    1. Her predestination, Immaculate Conception, and
queenship in heaven, illustrate His gracious
ways as Creator; and against many modern
heresies her whole doctrine wonderfully explains
the relation between creature and Creator.

    2. Her doctrine mitigates the difficulty of there
being so much permitted evil.

    3. She illustrates His character as Redeemer, herself
having been redeemed in the highest sense, and
co-operating with the work.

    4. Thus she prevents low views of Jesus, forcing up
our conceptions of Him, as it were, by her own
height; without her we should hardly have
realised His Sacred Humanity at all.

    5. She magnifies God by teaching high views of
grace, and of possible attainment of sanctity.

    6. She throws a distinctive light on the Three Divine
Persons; try to think how much of our devo-
tional realising of the doctrine of the Most Holy
Trinity is from the Catholic doctrine about her.

    7. She interprets the Attributes of God to us; see
how they reposed joyously in Mary's soul, and
gave light out from it.

III. This is not a theory, but what has actually been

the process in many minds; the thought of God has grown as devotion to Mary grew; the estimate of His ever blessed Majesty has by her means attained a height which once seemed unrealisable. This will be true to all, if their devotion to her be true; and to be true it must be

1. Closely allied to practice and to advance in strictness.

2. It must *grow*——so do not be unreal, precipitate and insincere, or force things. She *takes root*, says Scripture in the office of the Church, in the elect, and roots, remember, spread (1) slowly, and (2) by means of storms.

3. Be loving, but be sober too; and do not affect novelties unsanctioned and unindulgenced by the Church.

And now may the Mother of the Creator forgive whatever has been here said of her amiss, or in ignorance, and remember her promise in the Office of the Church, *Qui me elucidant, vitam æternam habebunt;* they who *explain* me shall have eternal life.

Part Fourth.

THE FAITH.

SECTION II.

THE SACRAMENTS.

I.

THE SACRAMENTS A FOUNTAIN OF HAPPINESS.

YOUNG men are sometimes melancholy in spite of their youth: but no good comes of it, as it does to the old; it is the business of youth to be happy.

I. Happiness belongs to youth.

    1. It is natural to the beginning of life, when life is a grand and cheering prospect.

    2. Happiness is what youth gives out, from its strong body, fresh mind, new powers and affections.

    3. Young men mostly do best when happiest.

    4. Religion must be your chief happiness.

    5. Sin should be your only real unhappiness.

II. The Sacraments the grandest fountain of happiness.

    1. Their supernatural and miraculous character.

    2. They make us happy because they make us strong against temptations, &c.

    3. Because they make our tastes unearthly, and heavenly.

    4. Because of the keen sense of a state of grace.

    5. Because they make perseverance comparatively easy.

    6. Because they make us feel God so near.

    7. Because they simplify religion, and pack our duties up into a convenient compass.

8. The peculiar joyousness which the sacraments
    give :—
      (1) The joy of confession—as sons with a father.
      (2) The joy of communion—as friends with a
         friend.

Thus the Sacraments give a happy life—prepare a
happy death—make even judgment happy—and then
hand us on to eternal happiness with God.

II.

THE CONVERSION OF A SOUL FROM SIN.

I. Creation and Conversion.

    Creation—(1) In a moment; (2) With a word.
      (3) With no semblance of effort. (4) Or of
      contrivance. (5) And God rested when it
      was done.

    Conversion—(1) Long. (2) By many means.
      (3) With look of effort. (4) And of contriv-
      ance; and (5) There is no sabbath to that work.

II. In the fortunes of empires than in conversions

    1. The arrangement is less.

    2. The hourly interest taken is less.

    3. The consequences are less.

    4. The degree and manner of divine interference is
       less.

III. Machinery of conversion : picture a man in mortal
    sin : there wants

    1. The power of the Father to be exerted on his
      behalf : the wisdom of the Son and the love of

the Holy Spirit all bought by the Precious Blood.

2. Prayers and dolours of the Blessed Virgin Mary —for the sake of the Precious Blood.

3. Angelic aid—earned by the Precious Blood.

4. Knowledge of the Gospel—the doctrine of the Precious Blood.

5. Merit of works—through the Precious Blood.

6. Moment of contrition—foreseen from eternity and disposed for the honour of the Precious Blood.

7. Sacraments—application of the Precious Blood.

8. Joy of God, Mary, Angels, Saints and Holy Souls—because of the Precious Blood.

9. Revival of merit, and reward—vitality of merits being through the Precious Blood.

All through this process how marvellously hidden is the affront to the majesty of God—because of the Precious Blood!

III.

HOW TO CONFESS WELL.

I. Before confession.

1. To have set times.

2. Frequent.

3. Careful examination of conscience.

4. See if all uncharitable thoughts are cleared out.

5. Good act of contrition, and prayer for contrition, before approaching the sacrament.

II. Faults in confession.
1. Excusing oneself.
2. Mentioning the faults of others.
3. Or the names of those who have wronged us.
4. Introducing irrelevant matter, and even worldly topics.
5. Telling your own good works and pious practices. Goodness of short confessions.

III. After confession.
1. Thank Jesus for His Precious Blood and the easiness of pardon.
2. Do your penance as soon as you can.
3. Renew your purposes of amendment to Almighty God.
4. Do not reflect on the sins you have confessed.
5. Never mention to others what you have confessed, or your penance, or the priest's advice to you, or your own resolutions.

IV. What passes in the soul at a good confession.
1. The cancelling of sins.
2. The pardon of eternal punishment.
3. The entry of grace.
4. The recovery of lost merits.
5. The conferring of new grace. From this theologians draw the conclusion, that the soul of the penitent is richer after the confession, than it was before the sin.

Eternity is too short to thank Jesus for all that is done in our souls in *one* confession.

IV.

HATRED OF SIN.

I. The knowledge on which it is based.
1. Of the Divine character.
2. Of the corruption of our own nature.
3. Of our own most peculiar forms of evil.
4. Of the punishments due to sin.
5. Of the immense system necessary to its remission.

II. The affections which feed it.
1. Love of God, to make reparation.
2. Desire of heaven, and eternal salvation.
3. Fear and distrust of self.
4. Devotion to the Passion.
5. Contrition, which stands to it in the relation both of cause and effect.

III. Its results.
1. Worthy thoughts of God.
2. Corroboration of our faith.
3. Enlightened discernment.
4. Excessive delicacy, without scrupulosity of conscience.
5. It makes the harder parts of the spiritual life easy.

IV. Its nature.
1. Specially Godlike.
2. Interior disposition of Jesus.
3. Habitual state of saints.
4. Not natural to us, but wholly supernatural.
5. It continues to grow, till as it were by growth

it brings us into the presence of God's purity, there to be happy for ever.

It is a great robust grace that can almost do all the sanctification of our souls by itself.

V.

PURPOSE OF AMENDMENT IN CONFESSION.

What is confession? Is it not then most strange, and as frightful as it is strange, that there is so little improvement in the world? Let us look into ourselves, and perhaps we may find reason there for most serious alarm. Confession is not of the lips only, but with the heart. A great missionary says, that crowds of Catholics are damned, not so much because they have no opportunity of confessing on their deathbed, or from want of examination of conscience, or from want of full and minute accusation, but from want of real purpose of amendment. Of two soldiers on the field, one may die confessed without purpose, and be lost, the other unconfessed with contrition and purpose, and be saved. This purpose must be

I. Firm, from hatred of sin; look now at past falls; we cannot change so rapidly.

II. Universal,—no reserve, no infirmity kept back— no use thanking God you are free from such and such sins; the question is, are you resolved to commit no more the one you are given to?

III. Efficacious—explain what it is to have a right

good will. If a full grown man leans on a switch and falls, whose fault is it? The propension of his body? no, his own choice of a switch. The marks of not having an efficacious purpose are

1. Falling immediately, and almost without effort, into the same sin.

2. Thinking, Oh, I will mention it in confession: whereas confession is not a tax which God takes on sin, but a remedy to prevent it in future, and heal it in the past.

3. Necessity. Saying I'm so poor—I cannot sell my things—they will laugh at me.

4. Habits of sin, producing
   (1) Facility to fall.
   2) Difficulty to rise.
   History of the habit—horror at first of sin— God has still the same horror.

5. Not putting into execution the means suggested by our confessor.

Cheer those who are making a fight: Oh the price God sets on a right good will!

VI.

THE OBLIGATION OF RESTITUTION.

How consoling are the extensive powers of the keys of the Church. What a comfort that we can bring our sins under them. One thing is beyond their power, *i.e.*, to annul the obligation of restitution, or to make us safe while we neglect it; importance therefore of getting a clear idea of this obligation.

I. The nature of it:

1. Who incurs it? Thieves, cheats, retainers of stolen goods, accomplices, those who use unfair weights and measures, ask unjust prices, tell lies about nature of article, &c., &c.

2. All the alms, fasts, pilgrimages in the world, won't do instead of it.

3. From all vows, censures, excommunications, the Church can free you, not from this.

4. To die without the sacraments is a great evil, but to die without restitution is a greater.

5. "*I cannot*,"—necessity of rigid interpretation of this.

6. Broken promises—(1) renew and multiply sins (2) make confessions sacrilegious.

II. The manner of it:

1. Masses, alms, &c., will not do instead; the words of Zacheus.*

2. For *insensible* robberies, restitution may be made to the poor, &c., but not for other robbery.

3. You must incur whatever expense is necessary— expense does not do away with the obligation.

4. Infamy resulting from it is no excuse, because you can avoid it.

III. The time of it:

1. The instant you can—life is uncertain—heirs untrustworthy.

2. Before confession, if possible; great grace is gained by this.

* Luke xix. 5.

3. As much as you can, if not all; and what you can, at once.
4. Dreadful delusion of putting off till death.
   (1) Because of uncertainty of opportunity.
   (2) Because you have no right to reckon upon grace.
   (3) Because of sins multiplying meanwhile.
4. Because the real sacrifice is gone from it: although the obligation is discharged, yet it is in the meanest way possible.

Curse of ill-gotten things in a house, like possession of devils; it works for generations—in weak health—madness—bad deaths—horrid accidents.

VII.

SCANDAL.*

I.

THE NATURE OF SCANDAL.

I. We know who the devils are, and what their office is; we cannot think of it without shuddering. Suppose we heard that there was a secret club among our fellow-men, who had met the devils by midnight, and had made a league with them against us, what would our view of these men be? With what horror we should avoid them! Suppose further that they took so much of the

* Preached at St. Wilfrid's, near Cheadle, 1849.

devil's work upon them, that the devils re-
mained almost idle in hell, or wandered about
the earth looking on contentedly with no need
to interfere.   This is scandal.

II. Why I am going to occupy the next three or four
Sunday evenings in treating of scandal.   State
of the mission.—(1) Grace of conversion.   (2)
Succeeding time of temptation.   (3) Giddiness
of young women.   (4) Shamelessness of young
men.   (5) Indifference of parents about their
families.   (6) Carelessness about setting good
example.

The chief guilt lies on young men, and on their
parents.   The account I have to give—hence my duty
and real love of plain speaking.   My determination to
take every step to destroy scandals.   Wish not to be
forced to refuse the Sacraments : beg all to come on Sunday evenings, and lay to heart this important subject.

III. Definition of scandal—examples of it are

I. Setting bad example.   (2) Light conduct on the
part of young women.   (3) Wicked language
among young men.   (4) Neglect of exercising
parental   authority.   (5) Protestant   schools.
(6) Admitting   immoral   company   into   the
house : what such a house becomes—a part of
hell—the opposite of what a Catholic Church
is—a factory of the devil ; the angels regard it
with horror—the deathbeds of its inmates.

IV. Characteristics of scandal.

1. The ease of it, and its irretrievableness; pray
that the overflowing of all your scandals may
be stopped.

2. The swiftness of its spread.

3. The power of one scandalous person : *e.g.* Henry
   VIII. depriving a whole nation for hundreds of
   years of Sacraments, and the Blood of Jesus.
4. The difficulty of reparation.

V. Sins of youth : difficulty of keeping young persons
   religious. Obligations of parents—what it is
   to communicate in other men's sins—parents
   before the judgment seat.

Horror if we knew that one was now in hell, whose
damnation we had caused—how his groans would
fight against us with God—day and night, summer
and winter, Sunday and weekday—the opposite of the
intercession of saints.

———

2.

THE INJURY IT DOES TO GOD.

Where is God ? Far off ? No ! above us, and
beneath us, and around us, and by our side ! His ear
is at our lips, His eye looks into ours. How wonderful
is God, and how wonderful His Presence in every
secret nook of land, and sea, and sky ! Yet when by
scandal we league with the devils against Him, they
would fain persuade us that He is far away, and that
the terrors of His justice will perhaps never come nigh
us. The horror of speaking and acting against one
whom we believe absent, but who is secretly close to
us. If when we take His name in vain, the little
finger of His power were to touch us, we should fall
to the ground a heap of smoking ashes. The great
lesson His omnipresence teaches is, that His like and

dislike form the only reasonable or safe rule of action.
His dislike of scandal, and the injury it does to Him.

I. His hatred of it, shewn by our Lord's calling St.
Peter Satan, and by our Blessed Lady's being
espoused to St. Joseph, and by what St. Paul
says of eating flesh.

II. It robs God of souls, the only thing He values.
Look at Jesus on the Cross! Ah, who would
rob Him of souls which it cost Him so much
to buy?

III. It is greater than the sin of the Jews who
crucified Jesus, as He values a soul above all
His Precious Blood.

IV. The sin, quite strictly speaking, is acting the
part of a devil. The awfulness of the devil's
personality, carrying his hell about with him,
even now in church. If you had seen St.
Michael in the act of ejecting those lost spirits,
and seen on the other hand the surpassing
loveliness of God, would you deliberately have
thrown in your lot with theirs?

V. It is worse than the devil's sin, because of the
sheep's clothing. It helps the devil to do
what he cannot do himself, because of his
hideousness if he let himself be seen.

VI. Additional horror of sin in God's sight, when the
sinner gets nothing by it but the devilish
pleasure of seeing Him offended, and souls
lost.

VII. We cannot understand how people can come to
hate God eternally, as they do in hell; yet
scandal gives us a glimpse of it.

Address hardened sinners. Have you made up

your minds to offend God still? Well, life seems
your time, and earth your place; but God has His
time and His place. Oh no word can tell, no thought
conceive, the heat of the fires which are there, nor the
intolerableness of the anger which kindles them, nor
the weary, weary, hopeless cruel length of that eternity
through which they burn!

Address others. Think of yourselves in your
mother's arms, just after baptism—who would have
thought you would league with devils against God?
Have you done so, have you robbed Him of souls?
&c. Alas! alas! yet there is hope in His Precious
Blood. O blessed confessional, O sweet healing sacrament of peannce! O joyous, joyous flowing of the
Precious Blood of Jesus! how it flows on and on;
summer heats dry it not, and winter winds freeze it
not; it needs not a Church, nor a holy place, all times
and all places are its own; wheresoever there is a
true priest, there it flows; it darts out at his
whispered absolution, as plenteously as it darted from
the side of Jesus when the spear pierced it, it leaps
out as hot as the sweet and loving life of the Sacred
Heart, from which it comes. O blessed confessional!
O sweet and healing sacrament of penance! O joyous,
joyous flowing of my Saviour's Precious Blood! Come
to it, my Brethren, come and wash yourselves in its
bright red baptism, which shall wash away all spot
of sin, and make you clean, and white, and innocent
as when you lay just redeemed on your mother's arm,
and the dear angels of our God looked on you, and
loved you, and smiled, and prophesied good things
about you!

3.

THE INJURY IT DOES TO THE SOULS OF OTHERS.

The value of a soul—what it is—its destiny—the anxiety of God, the angels, the saints, and men on earth about its welfare—sacraments and the like—it has to leave its body—to gain it again—wonderful prospect, ten thousand times more than to be king of all the world.

The injury scandal does to the souls of others.

I. It robs souls of God: what this is, and what it implies: it so far puts the soul into the condition of a damned spirit: loss of God is the worst torture of hell.

II. The sin lives, and breeds after death, while we are in hell: instances of this—bad books—seduction—corruption of play-fellows—children not corrected by parents, and not having parents' example of frequentation of the sacraments.

III. Scandal shows that we value self, and the gratification of our lusts above the law of God, and the souls of others. It is hatred of our neighbours carried to a hellish excess. Can you fancy having up before you one of your neighbours, who has done you no harm, looking at all his features, scanning them over, then for your own gratification condemning him, if you could be God for five minutes, to eternal fire?

IV. Extreme and brutal cruelty of all this; what would you think of a young man who preferred to holydays and merry-makings the torture of poor animals, who loved to hear their cries, and see their poor limbs twist and writhe; what would you think if he went on to mangle and torture your little babies? with what horror would you regard him! he gluts himself with their sobs and blood! How much more all this with souls!

V. What pleasure can you have in damning others? do you not know that the crowd is one of hell's most terrific tortures, as expressed in our Lord's revelation to the *Sœur de la Nativité.*

VI. Picture of souls complaining for vengeance before the judgment seat of God against you: a son pleading for his father's damnation, a daughter for her mother's; two young men that parted in early youth, and the wide world came between them, meet there, accuse each other, and cause each other's everlasting ruin.

Oh, how different things will look when eternity begins! How hard consciences, and blind eyes, and careless hearts, how they will be visited with the light of another world! and what men laugh at now they will weep for, aye, weep tears of agonising fire for ever and ever!

4.

ON THE INJURY IT DOES TO OURSELVES.

Who our guardian angel is—how he loves us—how sweet and tender his ministry is—his feelings, when we commit the sin of scandal. Astonishment of the

holy angels in general at seeing men urging each other
into the mouths of hell, and laughing while they do it.

Injury scandal does to ourselves and to our own
souls.

I. The way in which it hardens our consciences, and
takes away all our shame; the horror of running
up an account with God without thinking of it,
and almost without knowing it.

II. It sets the guardian angels and patron saints of
those we scandalise against us, and also our
Blessed Lady. Misery of losing any help in this
battle of life and death which we are fighting.

III. Difficulty of repentance, because of the hardness
of reparation.

IV. Forgotten scandals of early youth, all noted in
God's book—accuse yourself of these in your
next confession.

V. Deathbed, with no means of reparation. Deathbed
of Berengarius. The horrors of an affrighted
deathbed.

VI. Augmentation of the pains of hell, as the sin goes
on spreading wider and wider.

VII. No mention of pardon for it in Scripture, but it
is spoken of as making it better for the offender
to be cast into the sea.

Best reparation is frequentation of Sacraments, and
good examples, pious pictures in the house, &c., &c.

God's creation of a beautiful soul—its baptism—all
Christ does for it—the splendour and sweetness of its
innocence. How beautiful will be its crown and
throne in heaven!—a boy or girl steps in—teaches it sin
—seduces it—God is beaten—Jesus worsted—angels
made to weep—our Lady robbed—the soul damned.

Oh, is there one here present who has taught a boy or girl to sin? a most awful position is yours. I will not say you are not forgiven, but I am sure that if you are, it has been hardly done; and lest you should not be, oh bewail it in confession now! and then let years roll on, and daily before God say, I perhaps have lost a soul; some one perhaps will hate God for ever in the fires of hell, and scream most dreadfully in his tortures, and it is I who have sent him there! Now, my dear Brethren, my sad task is done, and when I 'ook back on the picture of scandal which I have drawn, when I ponder its injury to God, to souls, to ourselves, when I think of the value of a soul, the Blood of Jesus, and the love of God, I shrink into myself with horror. How many of you have been the cause of souls being lost! how many of you will be lost, because of the scandals you have given, given even since Christmas last? Come to a young man's death-bed—see what it is like, look at him unable to make a confession—think of the journey his impure soul is just about to take—what a prospect before him! Oh hell is bright and red, and the thunder of its fires, and the acclamations of its cries and groans intolerable; and yet although there be no rest, no hope, no God, it seems but a light punishment for such a sin as scandal. My Brethren, may your Saviour Jesus Christ, your tender Mother Mary, and your own patron St. Wilfrid, be with you, and teach you so to lay to heart what you have heard, that you may carry the memory of it, and the blessing of it, up to the very minute when your soul shall sit upon your white lips, and then take its long dark flight into eternity.

VIII.

GOD'S VIEW OF OUR PAST SINS.

Our sins are quite the most important things which have happened to us in our lives, because they have to do with our eternity, and are now irrevocable.

I. What we think of them in the retrospect.

1. We are amazed at their number, malice, endurance, and circumstances.
2. We see now, when the fit is not on us, how completely all was our own fault.
3. We are astonished at the multitude of neglected graces.
4. We can hardly believe the patience of God, considering the outrage.
5. We can see nothing in ourselves meriting the grace of conversion.

II. But the question is, what is God's view of them?

1. He remembers them, but, lo! they are gone from His book.
2. He has no anger whatsoever, and they cannot influence His judgment.
3. He has crowns ready even for poor struggles which actually ended in falls.
4. He even prizes us as conquests of the Blood of His dear Son.
5. He is more indulgent to present imperfections because of past sins.
6. Like the saints, it seems as if He blessed us all the more for having injured Him.

7. He acts as if we had laid Him under an obligation in letting ourselves be converted.

III. What must be our present state, to have a right to believe all this of ourselves.

1. We must be truly contrite, and all that is implied in that.

2. We must be trying to love and serve Him for His own sake.

3. We must delight in humbling ourselves under His hand.

4. We must not let His mercies make us forget our sins.

5. We must rejoice, because He loves to see us rejoice.

Melancholy in a creature is a kind of injurious reflection on the Creator.

Oh happy we! for what does it all come to? That now if we be only truly penitent, our past sins are motives for God to love us more; and for us they are the fuel with which love lights her happy cheerful fire. How beautiful is the merciful Gospel! I do not say we are to be without fear of being judged. But fear may be a happy fear, like a child's fear, and the greater I feel the weight of my passions, the more utterly and confidentially must I lean on Jesus my Saviour.

My dear Brethren, I can hardly understand what it is not to believe. I see no difficulty in the Most Holy Trinity. I exult in it. As to the Incarnation, I walk up and down in it, as a spacious garden of beautiful trees and golden sunshine, with the fragrance of flowers and song of birds. The Blessed Sacrament looks to me as plain as a clear cloudless sky in June. If I could be an infidel. it would be when I had looked over the

vast boundless ocean of the patient tenderness of God;
what I find it more hard to believe, is, that being the
beast and devil which I know myself to be, I should
see my God at all hours, with a smile of love and a
readiness of mercy, unspeakably, unchangeably a Father,
a Friend, a Brother, oh more! almost a Servant, whose
delight in my worthless soul I can neither exhaust nor
understand.

IX.

FRUITS OF A GOOD COMMUNION.

Jesus loved us to the end, not only to the end of
His three-and thirty years, but, as it were, even to the
end, the limit, of wisdom, power, and love. He left
us not relics of Himself, garments and the like, but His
own Flesh to eat. Oh how awful and sublime must
the Catholic religion be, when it is actually founded
upon this stupendous truth, this Real Presence of Jesus.

What an important act must a good communion be!
What are its fruits?

I. Foremost—the increase of sanctifying grace.

II. Remission of venial sins, through the acts of love
which it excites.

III. Preservation from mortal sins.

   1. By special sacramental grace.

   2. By raising devotion.

   3. By giving power against temptations.

   4. By putting devils to flight.

   5. Perhaps God keeps devout communicants out of
     occasions of sin.

IV. Remission of temporal pain due. Thus, indirectly every good fervent communion lessens purgatory.

V. Spiritual sweetness, which infallibly comes if we do not hinder it; it consists in a readiness and cheerfulness of the will in religious duties.

VI. Special union with Christ, the value of which we shall never fully know on this side the grave.

VII. The obtaining of glory hereafter, and life eternal.

VIII. Effects upon the body.

 1. It diminishes the heat of concupiscence.

 2. Excites good imaginations.

 3. Secures the resurrection.

 4. Consecrates our bodily limbs, as churches are consecrated.

All our Lady's communions at St. John's Mass those fifteen years. Unite yours with hers.

X.

HARDENING OF HEART FROM SLOVENLY COMMUNIONS.

We ought to get better as we get older, and perhaps in some respects we do. But in others we do not. I want to point out an ugly feature in our growing older.

I. It is that our hearts get harder.

 1. Oh how much, all through life, have we put down to grace, which after all was only nature.

2. We get used to devotions, and feel less sensible sweetness.

3. We get used to eternal truths, and so are less frightened by them.

4. We get used to our own little sins, and so put up with them more contentedly.

5. So altogether we get a sort of dead, dull, professional feeling about the spiritual life, which is exceedingly mischievous.

II. Effects of this hardness of heart.

1. Our devotional habits sink into formalities.

2. What was once a holy hopeful despair about our ever attaining to perfection, has become a wisdom, a discretion, almost a consolation.

3. Bodily mortifications are dropped, and hours of prayer abridged.

4. A mitigated form of worldliness returns, but it will not be mitigated long; we may trust worldliness for that; where it comes, it comes to reign, and it will reign at last.

5. The result is that we look on first fervours, not as things which common sense tells us ought to have increased, but as vehemences which were never meant to last.

III. Now I will name the cause of this hardening of the heart—slovenly communions.

1. What a communion is, and what makes it slovenly.

2. Very few people should have very frequent communion.

3. Requisites for daily communion.

(1) Living out of the world.

(2) Or a life of singular mortification.

(3) Or a pressure of sorrows.

(4) Or a very self-denying almsgiving.

(5) Or a great gift of the fear of God and of profound reverence: it was the practice of saints to intermit communions, in penance or to get reverence.

IV. Danger of communion too frequent for the life we are living—it often makes all life one long broken promise.

V. Living beyond our grace is often the loss of souls.

Is it best to lessen our communions or to lift our lives? Of course to lift our lives. Well, are you prepared to try to do so? and that very notably and very bravely. If not, then I am afraid that your safety requires a less frequent communion.

XI.

ON THE INFLUENCE OF CATHOLIC PRIESTS OVER THEIR CONGREGATIONS.

"Called by God a high priest according to the order of Melchisedech. of whom we have much to say, and hard to be intelligibly uttered: because you are become weak to hear."—Heb. v. 10, 11.

This is certainly a very wonderful thing: because, (1) it has always been so; (2) and in all countries; (3) when it has been departed from, punishment and curse have mostly followed; and (4) there seems no human reason ready at hand to account for it. Protestants throw it in the faces of us Catholics that our priests have so much power over us: yet surely it can be no reproach, but on the contrary it is a most wonderful thing, a kind of perpetual miracle, showing men which is the true Church, and attracting them into that true Church in a most heavenly way. St. Philip seeing the character of a priest. Character remains through eternity.

Let us inquire the causes of this influence.

I. From their being unmarried: awful solemn aspect of celibacy.

II. From their special devotion towards the poor: priests and poor are remarkably singled out by our Lord, as the materials of His Church, and the sight of this attracts the rich as well as the poor.

III. From the confessional:—lawfulness of this influence, comfort of it to penitents themselves, affectionate character of it, and its disinterested unselfish temper shown by experience and actual results: a confessor is father, teacher, physician, judge, yet judge of mercy.

IV. Supernatural. From our Lord's imparting to His priests a portion of that mysterious attractiveness of Himself mentioned in St. John x. There is something so irrespective of talent, or wealth, or power, as to be very plainly supernatural in this.

V. Supernatural.—From the powers of the priest to consecrate—to absolve—to bless—to cast out and drive away evil spirits. This power is not their own, because bad priests have it as well as good ones.

No need to prove the lawfulness of this influence, because the very causes of it show its lawfulness, and the salutary results as well: awfulness of people striving with priest. How proud then, say Protestants, must priests be. Ah! how little they know: let a priest hold up his right hand, and remember the morrow's consecration: how he will sink down, and fear God, and tremble at the shadow or the name of sin, and weep like a little child at the sad thought of his own unworthiness.

XII.

EXTREME UNCTION.

I. Life is a vale of tears and frequent miseries, which the Church is beautifully occupied in soothing. There is no corner of darkness into which she does not penetrate : no hiding place of the evil one, short of hell, whither she does not follow him to hinder or to heal his mischief.

II. God's Providence lovingly provides for all our trials with an affectionate minuteness : hence common sense would argue for a special sacrament in sickness.

III. Scripture argument: reality of the sacrament: outward form—promise of grace—institution of Christ.

IV. Effects of it.

    1. Increase of sanctifying grace: right to special aid in temptations.

    2. Remission of sins. (1) Venial. (2) Mortal indirectly.

    3. Destruction of relics of sin.

(1) Torpor of mind.
(2) Horror of death.
(3) Fear as to salvation.
(4) Low Spirits.
(5) Proneness to sin.
4. Relief of the body.
    (1) Sometimes cure.
    (2) Sometimes alleviation.
Neither of these to be infallibly looked for.

V. Duty of frequent prayer for a good death, and especially that we may have the last sacraments of the Church. Ah! politics lighten not individual woes; that is the divine office of the Church: thanksgiving to God that we are Catholics.

Part Fourth.

THE FAITH.

SECTION III

CONTROVERSY.

I.

THE REASONABLENESS OF THE CATHOLIC RELIGION.

I.

INTRODUCTION.

Importance of Catholics in this country knowing the principles of their religion. I speak to Catholics chiefly. Controversy, for the most part, disfigures the question it seeks to elucidate. It is the duty of the Church to *teach*, and her privilege that her teaching is divine *truth*.

I. The reasonableness of the Catholic religion.

1. If there is one God, then there is one truth; contraries cannot be true together; hence those who call us antichrist are really the most logical of our enemies.

2. All sects profess to be Christian, yet Christian doctrine must be *one*.

3. All profess to be Catholic, but whether they are or not is surely a visible fact.

4. Reasonableness does *not* mean that reason can measure faith, or limit it, or do instead of it.

5. Reason is *the* gift of man; all else changes in his history, that does not; hence a thing to be

reasonable must, (1) be so in relation to history —(2) to Scripture—(3) to the nature and wants of man—and (4) to what we know of the character and perfections of God.

II. Catholicism in relation to history.
  1. The Church ought to have an outward and world-wide history, because
    (1) If true, it is the greatest institution in the world.
    (2) A divine one, embracing all the interests of humanity.
  2. Its beginning traceable only to the apostles.
    (1) Cannot be fixed elsewhere, even on hypothesis of this or that doctrine having a date ;—extreme absurdity of that hypothesis.
    (2) The theory of corruption begs the question of divine origin ;—impiety of it.
    (3) St. Austin's opposite theory of apostolical tradition.
  3. It is, *at least*, and undeniably, the oldest form of Christianity. What is implied in this?
    (1) That it suits all times and climes.
    (2) The dangers it has dealt with.
    (3) The epochs it has constructed.
  4. It is at present the widest spread form calling itself Christian; this is a visible historical fact.
  5. Its amazing unity of spirit in all ages and lands. Enemies point to the uniform genius of popery
  6. The work it has done for the world.
    (1) Kept the faith through the ten persecutions.
    (2) Broken up the Roman empire.
    (3) Converted the barbarians.
    (4) Nursed infant civilisation.

(5) Fostered law, philosophy, art, and literature.

(6) Been the great peacemaker on earth.

(7) The mother of the oppressed and poor.

7. All other so-called forms of Christianity are off-shoots from it.

   (1) At an assignable date.

   (2) For a reason in which even other heretics did not concur.

   (3) On principles often abandoned by themselves afterwards.

   (4) With more or less of acknowledged sin attending the separation.

   (5) And splitting within themselves afterwards

8. All heresies together make up in their totality the doctrine of the Church. Thus—

   (1) She is distinguished from all simply by her claim to the Church.

   (2) And whenever her claim has been denied, it has led to division.

9. The beginnings of Protestantism simply looked at as actual facts.

   (1) In Germany.

   (2) In Switzerland.

   (3) In England.

First fruits in all these were (*a*) divorce, (*b*) polygamy, (*c*) political troubles, (*d*) intolerance, (*e*) quarrellings.

Contrast of all this with God bringing good out of evil, which is ever through suffering, through patience, through love, through sweet speech, through silence, through calmness and trust.

2

IN ITS RELATION TO SCRIPTURE.

If it be a fact that there is somewhere in the world a book which comes from God, which is divine, not human, it is plain that it very much concerns the Church, nay, that it must simply belong to the Church. Let us now consider the relation of the Catholic Church to the Bible.

I. She was the keeper and guardian of it.
  1. Showing the utmost care and solicitude about it.
  2. In spite of the special edicts of the Dioclesian persecution.*
  3. Attempts of heretics to corrupt it.
  4. Particular See of Rome deciding differences about the canon, *e.g.* Decree of Gelasius.
  5. Multiplying copies in the dark ages.

II. Her view of the Bible stated.
  1. Its inspiration, and all its teaching *de fide*.
  2. As a document of proof, she being the living court.
  3. As a collection of revealed principles on which theology is based.

III. Her treatment of the Bible.
  1. Manuscripts, printing, and numberless translations.
  2. Reverence of the principle of interpretation by authority.

---

* Neander. Hist. of the Christian Religion. Torrey's trans. vol. i. p. 201.

3. Her carefulness in the matter of allowing the
perusal of it to her children.

IV. Her doctrinal harmony with it, *e.g.* as regards—

    1. Baptism.   2. The Eucharist.   3. Confession.
    4. St. Peter.   5. Extreme Unction.

V. Harmony of form, discipline and ritual, *e.g.* wash-
ing of feet, rubrics of mass, excommunication, &c.

VI. Indirect harmony of the Church with the Bible.

   1. Our Lord was God, and so foresaw all the inter-
    pretations of the Bible.

   2. Protestants would not have spoken as the Bible
    does of the Blessed Virgin Mary, Eucharist,
    absolution, St. Peter, or almsgiving.

Now, do not look only at each separate branch of
the argument, but at the whole together; does it not
show that the relation in which the Church, simply as
a fact, stands to the Bible is the one in which she would
stand to it, supposing her to be what she claims to be?

VII. Then compare with this the Protestant treatment
of the Bible.

   1. Their turning into apocrypha what militates
    against them.

   2. Their absurd view of the Bible as a book con-
    verting nations, itself unscriptural.

   3. Yet their practical irreverence, as the people of
    Thibet to their llama, and their god.

   4. Luther calling the Epistle of St. James an epistle
    of straw.

   5. Calvin on our Lord's language about baptismal
    regeneration.

   6. The Epistles often preferred to Gospels.

   7. Their principles of interpretation, *e.g.* about St.
    Peter, the H. Eucharist, &c.

8. "Without note or comment," abdication of reason, as if under magic; yet loud wrangling about meaning.
9. The destruction of our Lord's example.
10. Cold disregard of precept of fasting. Extreme Unction, and Confession.
11. The way in which texts are simply regarded numerically.
12. The practically Jewish way in which mere external reading of the Bible is regarded as a meritorious work, and how it stands in the stead of an interior turning of the heart to God.

Again look at all this put together, and do not Protestants evidently regard themselves as the masters of the Bible? Protestantism is an eminently unbiblical religion.

3.

IN ITS RELATION TO THE NATURE AND WANTS OF MEN.

The force and necessity of this branch of the argument: it suits, yet corrects and elevates.

I. The Catholic religion eminently professes to forgive sins.
   1. This is the great need of men.
   2. What Christ did for us, what He does in us.
   3. Protestantism only announces the fact.
   4. Misery of uncertainty—laxity of self-absolution.
   5. Fitness of some external declaration, and that of divine institution, *i.e.*, absolution.

II. It is a religion of authority, and claims and exercises a dispensing power.

    1. If the Church is a society, there must be a living body to govern, and it must be divine.

    2. Authority is a question of fact: the doubt is what authority men will follow.

    3. Protestantism is a perfect slavery to the yoke of unauthorised traditions.

    4. Looking at human actions, there must be a dispensing power.

    5. Self-dispensation makes everybody his own pope, and leads to license.

III. Difference between precept and counsel. (1) Fitness of this. (2) Protestant disregard of it.

IV. Adaptability of Catholicism to all governments, as a kingdom not of this world—political character of Protestantism, both as to troubles, to connection, and to missionary enterprise.

V. Naturalness of the whole system of spiritual direction.

VI. Intercourse with the dead and the spiritual world.

    1. Strange confining of itself on the part of Protestantism to material things.

    2. The want of this intercourse a proof against the divineness of any system.

    3. Unity and harmony of the Catholic system.

VII. The marvellous tempering of external observances with an interior spirit.

    1. This moderation one of the most admirable things in Catholicism.

    2. Precepts of the Church: duty of witnessing to the faith.

3. Protestantism—vocal prayer—no interior acts— mere belief, dead faith—done anyhow.

VIII. Religion made by the Catholic system the great business of life.

   1. Protestantism tends to formalism, and so prac- tically is against weekday religion.

   2. Catholic classification of sins : examen and con- fession.

   3. We live under a system of minute laws in daily operation : Protestants acknowledge this, and even call it a *yoke :* it would be if saving our soul were not *unum necessarium.*

   4. Sacraments at every turn of life.

   5. Obligation of restitution, of avoiding occasions, and the like.

IX. It has been in all ages the religion of

   1. The poor,

   2. The sorrowing,

   3. The sick, and

   4. The dying.

X. It has always and everywhere joined political liberty with obedience to law, introduced purity of morals, defended the divine institu- tion of marriage, and abolished slavery, simply by its spirit, not by any political rights or power.

XI. Its adaptation to our nature, as well as startling likeness to its founder, shown in its tenderness to sinners.

   1. Prisoners.

   2. Murderers.

   3. Giving up no one.

   4. It can afford to trust to professions of repentance.

All this to such an extent that Protestants scorn the Church, as the Jews scorned Jesus, for eating with publicans and sinners.

4.

IN ITS RELATION TO THE CHARACTER OF GOD.

For a religion to be reasonable it is not enough that it should fit in with the history of the world, harmonise with the revealed Word of God, and suit our nature; it must also be a fitting manifestation of Him who is the Author of reason, and this in two ways; it must suit what we know of His character, and it must be of a piece with what we know of His past dealings with His creatures.

I. Catholicism suits what we know of the character of God.

  1. The justice of God is magnified by it, not only in the Atonement, but

    (1) In the doctrine of penance and mortification.

    (2) In the practice of indulgences for forgiven sins.

    (3) In the doctrine of good works, which exalts His sanctity.

      Impiety of the Protestant system of imputation of the merits of Christ.

  2. His mercy.

    (1) In the doctrine of grace.

    (2) In the ease of pardon and iteration of certain sacraments.

(3) In the stress laid on corporal and spiritual works of mercy.

3. His truth.

(1) In the strictness about orthodox doctrine—compare Protestant sects, and worst of all, Anglicanism, with it in this respect.

(2) In its exclusiveness—one God, one only truth.

(3) For its positive character, compared with the idle negations of heresy.

4. His communication of Himself—in its eminently missionary character—*Propaganda* is a word of reproach among Protestants, who compare us with Pharisees for proselytising.

5. Its universality is an image of the omnipresence of God.

6. The way it swamps temporal in eternal interests.

7. Its indestructibility by persecution : on Protestant showing Protestantism has been put down in Italy and Spain—not so Catholicism here, even by horrors worse than the inquisition.

II. Catholicism of a piece with what we know of God's past dealings with His creatures.

1. Its consistency with

(1) The patriarchal dispensation in sacrifices, visions, and voices.

(2) With the Jewish dispensation in priesthood, external pomp, spiritual government, &c.

(3) Also with the latter in its change to kingly magnificence.

(4) With both the old dispensations in its miraculous character—gift of miracles promised in the Gospel.

(5) Also with the Jewish in the mysterious Presence of God, only the Blessed Sacrament outdoes theirs.

2. Its being hated by the world as the world hated God made man.

   (1) Intellectually, in politics, science, &c., as Jesus was called mad.

   (2) Morally, as being stern, or firm, or enthusiastic, as Jesus was buffeted in His Passion.

3. The Divineness of its supernatural character.

   (1) Value of the Precious Blood.

   (2) Hiddenness of the Divine Manifestations to Saints.

   (3) Power of the Sacraments.

   (4) Rome and Peter's Chair, all boldly chanced on this—man *dared* not do so.

Conclusion (1) The Creator has a visible Church on earth.—(2) It is the creature's duty to find it out and to submit to it.—(3) Case of those who come close and come no nearer; *we* need not condemn them; of their own body, the major part, the senior part, the governing part does so; they are split among themselves, and the cause of the split is their different degrees of nearness to Rome. Nay, we condemn not— God is slow—grace is undermining habits of pride and sin—many are honest who seem not so—we may love them as known to God, admire what is good, speak plainly for truth's sake, and their souls' sake, and help them on by prayer.

II.

ENGLISH CATHOLICISM.

I.

ACTUAL POSITION OF CATHOLICS IN ENGLAND.

I. The Jews in their captivity a type of Catholics
in England; the children of those who were
masters of the world now oppressed, almost
smothered by heresy; the processes they went
through.

  1. Hatred with fear.—(1) Hot persecution—(2)
Penal laws enforced.—(3) Concealment.

  2. Hatred with spite.—(1) Civil disabilities.—(2)
Tone of literature and public feeling.—(3)
Persecution in private life.

  3. Hatred with contempt.—(1) Latter years of
penal laws. — (2) Progress of repeal.—(3)
Irish policy.

  4. Contemptuous liberality.—(1) Ministerial craft.
—(2) Carelessness about religion altogether
brought in kindness to Catholics; it was credit-
able to be kind, and *now* safe.

  5. Reviving fear.—(1) From growing power.—(2)
Attractiveness to men of intellect shown.—(3)
Disproportion of means to ends actually effected.
(4) Suspicion of possible truth of supernaturalism.—(5) Disappointment at happiness
and steadiness of converts.—(6) Surprise at

the Church's awakening, like our Lord's resurrection.

II. Past position of English Catholics.

    1. Concealment of chapels — mass—ecclesiastical
dress—sign of the Cross—all the externals
which impress men : success of this compulsory
concealment, as a species of persecution, so long
as the persecutors contrive to keep it undignified.

    2. Suspiciousness of those who offered themselves
as converts—difficulty of instructing them—
likelihood of their falling away—few means of
grace to help them—this led insensibly to their
keeping to their own, *i.e.* to parochial rather
than missionary functions.

    3. Civil disabilities acting on morals.—(1) Concealment superinduced timidity.—(2) At best
esprit de corps was substituted for religion.

    4. Civil disabilities acting upon patriotism.—(1)
Forcing foreign education.—(2) Absence from
court.—(3) Bigotry of Protestant society.—
(4) Shaping of national character on heresy,
formation of language, connection of national
glory with it; so the land has to be converted
over again.

III. Present position of English Catholics.

    1. Publicity—disabilities removed—influx of converts, rapid growth—patronage of the Liberals
—revenges of time on heresy, specially of a
literary kind—exposure of Protestantism, and
men's weariness with it.

    2. Unlucky brands of the past apparently burned
into us.—(1) Unenlightened love of the old
state of things, and reluctance to see that its

time is passed.—(2) Desire to seem English, yet hitting the wrong nail on the head, *eg.* keeping back doctrine, valuing as favours what are rights, talking liberal, &c.—(3) Fear and half-shame of our own doctrines.—(4) Low view of externals, shallow jeering at them; *esprit de corps* did instead of them; so men fell after 1829.—(5) Unmissionary character, so as even to use the word in a wrong sense : *e.g.* mission for parish.—(6) Fraternising with vulgarity and wickedness if against an enemy. —(7) Aptitude to be dazzled by state favour and literary or scientific compliments, and so to barter truth.—(8) Timidity become chronic and unreasoning, as if it were the normal state of English Catholics.

The necessity of realising that the Church is an aggressive and conquering thing; it is the Church of Jesus Risen; awful is the miracle of her resurrection, so unlooked for that it almost seems to drive her own children to the verge of unbelief.

———

2.

WHAT PROTESTANTS WOULD EXPECT ENGLISH CATHOLICS TO BE LIKE.

I. Suppose a man whose study and prayer the grace of God has blessed so as to fill him with doubts about his own religion, and with admiration of the Church; what are his data ?

1. He reads Catholic books.—(1) Dogmatic.—(2) Devotional. They are for the most part necessarily foreign.

2. He reviews what Catholics have done, and have been in history.

3. He reasons on his reading, and draws conclusions, and pictures things.

4. He goes abroad and sees Catholicism in the Italian, Spanish, and German cities.

5. He applies all this to England, adding what he thinks due

   (1) To the purifying influences of persecution.
   (2) To the healthy action of moderate poverty.
   (3) To what he thinks the superior sense and logic of the English mind.

So he looks with deep interest not unmingled with awe on his persecuted fellow-countrymen. They keep very much to themselves, or hide when out— they are a kind of sanctuary to his eye—he wonders what is behind the veil; he is predisposed to take the highest view.

II. What kind of thing he expects.

1. The marvellous results of union among them, going far beyond mere matters of faith.—(1) Pious opinion, (2) taste, (3) co-operation, (4) mutual sympathy, (5) subordination, (6) perfectly organised intercourse with each other.

2. The Catholic temper mingling with, enlightening, and ennobling their patriotism.—(1) Love of foreign Catholics.—(2) *Covetous* love of their usages—(3) Ardent love of Rome.

3. The supernatural character formed by their religion; he thinks of—(1) the Pope, (2) the

Blessed Sacrament, (3) our Lady, (4) purgatory, (5) indulgences, (6) doctrine of grace, all unforgotten in their minds.

4. The principles and tests of success upon which the children of the saints naturally go.—(1) Absence of human respect.—(2) Unquerulous confidence in God.—(3) Unflagging cheerfulness. —(4) Love of humiliations and contradictions. —(5) Jealousy of human help or political allies.

5. Outward demeanour and piety.—(1) Government of tongue.—(2) Modesty and recollection of manner.—(3) Devotion to Blessed Sacrament. —(4) Predominance of love over sense of duty.—(5) Spirit of giving to the limit of their means.—(6) Humility.—(7) Awestricken view of heresy.—(8) Especial love of reviled doctrines.—(9) Unworldly aspect of a suffering Church.

6. He thinks how all this would be deepened by the peculiar circumstances of English Catholics. —(1) The contempt in which they lie.—(2) The absence of temporal preferment.—(3) The knowledge of the sympathy of the Catholic world.—(4) The solemnising memory of the martyrs.—(5) Persecution and suffering, if they do not enslave, vulgarise, and degrade, add dignity and supernatural health to a Church.

III. He sums it all up: his perplexity: there has been no canonised saint since the Reformation, not even in Ireland: oh! perhaps it is the want of convenience for forming the processes, or expense, or what not: he will advance, lift the veil, and find

1. Extensive asceticism.
2. Ecstatic nuns and supernatural convents.
3. Rumours of constant miracles.
4. It will be another world to him; the world of grace blooming and bearing fruit.

Shall we disappoint him? Let us be humble and see.

3.

THE REAL ASPECT OF ENGLISH CATHOLICISM TO THE EYE OF THE INQUIRER.

I. We must now suppose our inquirer to make Catholic acquaintances, get introductions, &c. —he sees for himself—puts things together— and comes to a conclusion. We must premise

1. That he is likely to make mistakes, for want of deeper knowledge of our religion.
2. That the disappointment of his ideal expectations renders him likely to exaggerate.
3. That he views things from without, as not yet a convert.
4. That the picture therefore may not be the true one; but, which is of immense importance, it is one which seems true to inquirers, and so helps or hinders conversion.

All this must be borne in mind to qualify the apparent unkindliness of the picture.

II. He proceeds to his inspection of things: his very object is to criticise and be censorious; the

result is a matter of life and death with him :
it is unreasonable to be angry with him, on the
contrary, we may learn from him.   What strikes
him among us ?

1. Jealousy of foreign usages, *e.g.* Rome—of devotions, yet they succeed when tried—historical
bias to nationalism.

2. Light view of heresy : want of eye to detect,
want of heart to weep over it.

3. Fear of our own doctrines, specially the controverted ones.

4. Finding no difficulties in the objections of adver-
saries—disheartening as showing narrowness.

5. Want of union, and spirit of locality in charities
and large plans.

6. Chiefly poor: this strikes him as a mark of
intellectual failure.

7. Neglect of externals.—(1) Want of asceticism
in this—(2) Ignorance of human nature.

8. Reluctance to admit the supernatural : this makes
him doubt our faith, not prize our prudence.

9. Eagerness to limit ourselves to what is of faith :
a badge of sectarianism.

10. A certain un-English tone of thought—(1)
reserve, (2) want of proselytism, (3) pomp of
agreeing with heretics who see through it.

11. Literature which might be written by non-
Catholics,—a scandal because of the way in
which true Catholicism savours all things, and
makes itself felt everywhere diffusively.

12. Moving in society for years without being
known to be Catholics—horror at this—poor
Jesus Christ, as St. Alphonso said.

13. Want of love of reading, and keeping pace with knowledge.

14. Constant origination of plans, and as constant failure from want of steadiness and concentration on an object—this so odd among Catholics.

15. Overweening desire for esteem and respect of Protestants ; being content with destroying their prejudices without gaining their souls—they see through the selfishness of this.

16. Amazing human respect—towards wealth, power, title ; essential vulgarity of this, and hatefulness of it to Englishmen.

17. Narrowness and want of sympathy with other men's plans ; each has his own, and thinks it not the best only, but the sole one.

18. Dread of enthusiasm and worship of human prudence ; no failures unteach this ; absence of the heroic element.

Is any part of this true ? it may be overdrawn, exaggerated ; still it is a fact that inquirers, and earnest ones, take this view, and draw back, thinking the Catholic body in England imbecile as an instrument of conversion, and unable to inspire itself with vigour and dignity.

Oh, the fearfulness of the corroding atmosphere of heresy ! we have been no land of Gessen in the midst of plague-stricken England.

4.

THE WAY IN WHICH WE ACT UPON PROTESTANTS.

I. Having now learned what we can from the view a
thoughtful inquirer takes of us, we may gain
a farther knowledge of ourselves from looking
at the way on which we act on others.

1. One of the best tests of a body like the English
Catholics is efficiency in acting upon others for
their conversion. We cannot ignore Protestants, we cannot sit at ease, and take care of
ourselves, we betray Jesus if we do: to be sensible of our missionary obligation is the condition of our blessings; we must realise at every
turn that this is not a Catholic country, and
that every one of us has a mission.

2. Hence it is that we must legislate for conversion;
we must look to Protestants and infidels, to
what will tell upon them, influence, attract,
shock, perplex them; we must avoid repelling
them without harming our brethren; we cannot
enjoy our religion in peace.

3. Means of conversion—(1) Controversy—(2)
Ceremonial—(3) Preaching; this last the best
—1. In itself as most divine—2. As meeting
Protestant ways better—3. As English.

II. Manner of preaching is the test of high principle.
One way is fear of our peculiar doctrines, and
partial exhibition of them in order to avoid
offence, *e.g.* Blessed Virgin Mary, persecution, &c.

1. Because of charity, you may backen inquirers.—
   It is the duty of charity to lead on our own
   people, to put the whole truth before others, not
   to entrap them ; half truth is always more odious
   than whole truth.

2. Because of what the Apostle says of milk for
   babes : and primitive reserve.—This applies to
   evangelical counsels, and to gradual instruction
   —primitive reserve not parallel, books, printing,
   open churches, &c.

3. Because of the common laws of persuasion.
   Openness is the most persuasive earthly thing
   —revealed truth the most persuasive supernatural thing.

4. Because of the difficulty of making yourself understood.—Not if you preached fully on system.

5. Because such preachers are popular with Protestants.—Yes, Protestants give up their prejudices
   to you, but do not surrender their poor souls.

6. Because moral preaching meets a popular objec-
   tion.—But it does not save souls, and it sacrifices the Catholic audience ; dogma for the
   pulpit, morals for the confessional, though of
   course not exclusively.

7. Because otherwise you are engaged in perpetual
   controversy.—No ! statement is the persuasive
   thing to an English mind, logic, consistency ;
   the excellence of dogmatic preaching is in
   statement put and left without controversy.

III. This manner of preaching, *when it succeeds,* converts men to one religion by teaching them
   another ; odiousness of this ; trace an imaginary
   history of it—an inquirer—difficulties made

light of, images, Blessed Virgin Mary, indulgences, persecution, pope, shown how slight the
differences are—wants absolution—converted
—excitement goes down—startled at things—
chill of surprise—makes reflex acts—withdraws
from Blessed Virgin Mary—finds odd things in
history about persecution—(1) Settles down into
a bad Catholic—has no director—becomes an
apostle of mischief—judges for himself—makes
bad confessions—is lost—(2) Is indignant—
apostatises—gives scandal—loses his immortal
soul.   This is the natural tendency of reserve
worked out.

5.

FEAR OF OUR OWN DOCTRINES.

I. Method of teaching opposed to reserve; full
   exhibition of our doctrines, more especially those
   which are maligned and controverted.
  1. What our doctrines are.
    (1) Revelations from God.
    (2) Wonderfully beautiful in themselves, and so
       persuasive.
    (3) Convincingness of their consistency, and full
       exhibition needed to bring out that con-
       sistency, *e.g.*, Blessed Virgin Mary not only
       a great saint, but Regina Sanctorum.
    (4) Lose their charm by reserve.
    (5) Special blessing on boldness about blas-
       phemed truths.

(6) God the Revealer also the Converter of souls, not we; He loves His own work in His shape of it.

2. Upon whom our doctrines are to tell.

(1) Catholics, instruction, perfection, love.

(2) Converts, perseverance, reward, thanksgiving.

3. Externs, necessity of openness, that they may have every chance God gives, and so His full truth in its persuasiveness: we have to deal with them as souls, not merely to smooth their prejudices.

II. Mistake of reserve as a matter of *principle.*

1. Because truth is God's, not our own—we have no right to meddle with it.

2. Because of its intrinsic beauty; we ought to trust it; *e.g.,* warmth of converts to Blessed Virgin Mary.

3. Because of the loss of supernatural help, *e g,* if we preach not Blessed Virgin Mary and saints.

4. Because it as a system of doctrine, not as a system of morals, that the Gospel was to be preached; *e.g.,* humility and other virtues because of the Incarnation; love of Jesus the motive.

5. Because reserve tends to keep our own people down and so to weaken their power to convert, as well as to stunt their growth in holiness, and so to sacrifice them to heretics.

6. Because Christian prudence is against it: prudence does not consist in not aiming at an end because too hard and too high, but in choice of *means.*

7. Because it withdraws a chief help to perseverance from converts: what with their sacrifices and the sad state of England, doctrine seems their sole inheritance, just as grace is their sole recompense.

III. Mistake of reserve as a matter of *policy.*

1. Because the high line succeeds best in everything. Oh, how we need to realise this!
2. Because the devil attacks most the doctrines he fears most: so he teaches us *what* to preach.
3. Because the English hate half the truth; they are irritated by it: suspicion keeps men back, not anger.
4. Because we have already, justly or not, a bad character for mental reservation.
5. Because fear of our own doctrines makes men (1) dislike *them,* and (2) doubt *our* sincerity.
6. Because we preach a different religion, and so take people in, and they are disappointed: primitive reserve was lest men should take the doctrines to be what they are not—ours lest they take them to be what they really *are.*
7. Because we don't realise how much Protestants know: distinguish *kinds* of Protestant ignorance.

IV. Actual failure of this line so far.

1. Ill name Catholic controversy has.
2. Movement outside the Church, unhelped but by *foreign* Catholics and travel.
3. Paucity of conversions.
4. Success of the opposite method of conversion.
5. Want of growth and depth among ourselves from want of dogmatic teaching and meditation.

6. As a matter of fact we do not attract our fellow-
countrymen.

Rome and Roman ways, these are the attractions;
God has put a spell into them.

6.

THE INFLUENCE OF THE PRESENCE OF PROTESTANTISM ON THE ORDINARY CHARACTER OF CATHOLICS.

I. Having seen how the presence of Protestantism
may seem to an inquirer to influence our way
of acting upon others, it remains to consider how
the same presence may seem to tell upon ourselves. We must bear in mind throughout—

   1. That the view put forward is the one taken of us
by those external to our body.

   2. That there is an opposite side of the question.

   3. That what lowers a man more than anything
else in England is the want of correspondence
between his profession and his action.

   4. That also when a man is supposed to be afraid,
all respect for him is gone in England.

   5. That we have to deal with Englishmen, and must
do it in an English way.

II. Ways in which the presence of Protestantism
might influence ordinary Catholics.

   1. Effect of continued ridicule—to make us ashamed
of our distinctive doctrines, and so of the very
doctrines which are of value, as the *points de*

départ between the two religions; our strength is in them, as Samson's in his hair—

2. Effect of continued controversy—to look more at what is easy to prove than what is—(1) true, (2) deep, (3) most honourable to God, (4) most persuasive to the earnest heart, as opposed simply to the head: we work without hope, except on the earnest heart.

3. Effect of continued intercourse, unless jealously watched—to superinduce a spurious charity which is real uncharitableness: difficulty of realising the soul; the prospect of eternity for those we daily meet takes us by surprise if we are not given to meditation.

4. Effect of continued attempts to please—to make us value overweeningly their good opinion and respect, so as (1) to sacrifice God's honour, and (2) be cold and remiss about conversion: danger of resting in the mere removal of prejudice as an end.

5. Effect of continued political agitation—(1) to make us careless about our choice of friends and allies—(2) to make us recoil into over little jealousy of political patronage—(3) to put out of sight altogether the St. Thomas of Canterbury view of things.

III. The results of these things, supposing them to be worked out.

1. The process doctrine goes through: (1) timidity through fear of ridicule; (2) paring down to make it controversially presentable; (3) measuring truth by the views its enemies take of it; (4) anger at the supposed imprudence of

those who put out unveiled truth; (5) attachment to our own abridged doctrine; (6) forgetfulness of what the real full doctrine is like; (7) surprise at coming across it unawares; (8) repugnance to it; (9) disloyalty to Rome and implicit heresy.

2. The bringing out of our religion something different from real Catholicism: a new religion without the blessing, without the promises: harm to ourselves, robbing of the poor and simple, utter imbecility in conversion.

3. To cease to look at it, and to think it absurd and unmannerly to look at our Protestant fellow countrymen as *souls* in danger of damnation; power of this view as a means of persuasion, and awful home-striking reality of it.

4. To make us obtuse about heresy, and careless when we see it—what heresy is—how Saints feel—charity begins with God and Jesus: realise martyrdom for doctrine: martyrs of Gorcum.

5. *God* lost sight of—something else put instead of Him, just as by Protestants, only with different developments.

I do not mean to say these are always developed— I have been putting forward the view of an extern— how, if it be true, would such Catholics have acted under Diocletian or Elizabeth?

7.

THE INFLUENCE OF PROTESTANTISM ON THE DEVOUT CHARACTER IN CATHOLICS.

I. Saintliness is the converting power: neither England nor Ireland have had a Saint since the Reformation.

   1. To the world saintliness comes out as gentleness wedded to high principle. It always seems to come off second best at first, and triumphs in the end.

   2. Distinction between Saints and common Catholics —counsels and precepts—love and duty.

   3. A middle class between Saints and common Catholics—devout and high-minded people— importance of this class—what St. Teresa says of the value Jesus sets on such souls—necessity of cultivating them—the way in which English Catholicism acts in manufacturing such people is a fair test of it.

II. How Protestantism affects such people :—

   1. By narrowing the largeness of Catholic truth.

   2. By cultivation of human respect.

   3. By its atmosphere.

   4. By the essentially unsupernatural character of the controversial temper.

   5. By our not being a Catholic country, which is an *à fortiori* argument for avoiding all uncatholic evils which we can avoid, instead of being more uncatholic than we need.

III. Particular instances to exemplify this.

    1. The imperfect putting forward of purgatory: its connection with devotion, the place it occupies in the *via purgativa*, and even in the *via illuminativa*.

    2. The imperfect putting forward of our dear Lady: her connection with holy living, and calls to perfection: ascetical influence of devotion to her.

    3. The fear of claims to miracles and of Saints' lives: subtle Protestantism of this: connection of Saints' lives with sanctity: distinction between imitable and admirable; men would have them purely the latter.

    4. Infrequent use of indulgenced devotions: quote the life of St. Bridget, raised up in great measure to teach holy souls the value of indulgences.

    5. Imperfect realisation of the grace which goes along with images, pictures, beads, medals, and other blessed objects: the power of simplicity which is in faith in such things.

    6. Views of vocation and virginity: how these are influenced by what is around us.

    7. Want of freedom and variety in recommending penance, caused by the seen evils of puritanism before us: the rule for the million won't do for God's chosen souls.

    8. Inordinate fear of delusion in the spiritual life caused by fear of our own weapons for meeting it: so we quietly take a low ground because it is safe: in all this there is a want of real awe of the most Blessed Spirit who works in these souls.

9. Infrequency of painful self-sacrifice in the way of almsgiving—how this produces a standard of practice most prejudicial to the devout character.

10. English character opposed to meditation: our bustle passes into our religion.

IV. The grand want of England is a school of spiritual directors.

    1. This is nobody's fault, but our misfortune, and a necessity, owing to missionary circumstances.

    2. What God vouchsafed to do for France in the great religious movement of the 17th century.

    3. Let us without neglecting externals put them below this, and make this a subject of special prayer to God.

Wonderful amount of grace abroad, not only calling men into the fold, but, as priests in their hidden life well know, calling souls in the fold to perfection—this last far the greatest work—(1) for its own sake—(2) for the sake of its reaction on the former.

III.

THE RISE AND PRESENT CONDITION OF PROTESTANTISM.

I. Protestantism an object of interest to Catholics.

    1. Because it is a widespread and successful heresy.

    2. Because so many whom we love as fellow-countrymen, &c., live in it.

3. Because three hundred years' experience gives us a distinct view of it.
4. Because it is such a wonderful confirmation of Catholic doctrines.
    (1) Because nearly every Catholic doctrine is held by some sect.
    (2) Because their only unity is hatred of us.
    (3) Because it has so signally failed in missionary work.
    (4) Because of what it has worked itself out into.

II. Its rise contrasted with the rise of Christianity, in its causes of success.
    1. The personal character of its first preachers and founders.
    2. In what it promised to do for men in the way of independence of thought, and license of action.
    3. In the countenance of power, which fostered it: it did not, like the Church, begin with the poor.
    4. In the appetite for mixing itself up with politics: *e.g.* in France.
    5. In its being an armed body, persecuting as well as persecuted.

III. Its present condition throughout the world.
    1. In heathen lands, merely like an army in occupation.
    2. In Germany, France, Geneva, Italy, Scotland, England.
    3. In its strife with Tractarianism, its domestic enemy and traitor.
    4. Its failure in grappling with the question of pauperism.

5. The progress of historical research, even in the hands of Protestants, is favourable to the Church, and against old prejudices.

6. The growing disposition in England to return to the faith of our fathers.

7. The increasingly negative character of Protestant teaching.

The instinctive fear, which it is at present exhibiting, of the true Church of God. No national predisposing causes of success are to be found for the present energetic movement towards the Church: let us be humble, and pray, work hard, and wait for God: grace will do what we desire. Quietness, happy quietness, is the sign of Catholics.

————

IV.

PROTESTANT NOTIONS OF OUR BLESSED LORD.

The name of Jesus the watchword of His people—the love of Jesus their mark—the worship of Jesus their religion.

I. Samples of professed heresy about the Person of our Lord among Protestants.

  1. Socinians (and Quakers) go on "the Bible only" principle, and so are Protestants: yet they deny His Divinity.

  2. Luther held

    (1) That the Divine attributes were communi-

cated to the flesh of Christ, and so that His flesh was ubiquitous.

(2) The disgusting dogma of impanation.

3. Calvin held

(1) That the flesh was conceived separate from the Word.

(2) That our Lord did not die for all.

4. Almost all deny

(1) The union of the Godhead with the Body in the tomb.

(2) The title of the Mother of God : what comes of this.

5. Anglicans quarrel about the Real Presence ; but all agree (art. xxviii.) that, whether it be there or not, there is to be no worship of the Sacrament.

II. The practical way in which Protestants realise the Person of our Lord.

1. Meditation is a kind of prayer almost unknown to them.

2. They clip His atonement by denying the ease of reconciliation in the Sacrament of Penance; and His example, by scouting the Evangelical Counsels.

3. They shrink from minute details of His Passion.

4. They think of Him as one who lived eighteen hundred years ago, rather than as living Man to-day; this comes of having no B. Sacrament and no Madonna.

5. They are as distant with Him as if He had never been Incarnate.

III. All Catholic things gather round our Lord.

1. All doctrines radiating out from Blessed Sacrament.

2. All rites and ceremonies.

3. All feasts and seasons.

Our life and strength is the love of Jesus. Protestantism is Satan's copy of Christianity. It is fast waning: heat and life are oozing out of it: history is against it: experience is against it: reason is against it, and faith not in it, and earnestness against it too: our life, I say, is the love of Jesus—and by that love, hot, loyal, self-sacrificing love, we shall live down and master with hardly an effort the counterfeit Gospel of three hundred years ago

---

V.

LECTURE ON CONVERSION.

I. Present movement *—its universality—absence of human means to account for it—what is grace, and the grace of conversion—what it costs a man to become a Catholic—the awfulness of living in the midst of a visible interposition of Providence, and the consolation of it.

1. Three hundred years experience of Protestantism; its immoral and irreligious tendency.

2. Coldness and illnature of the Establishment towards the poor.

3. Marriage of the clergy.

4. Want of confession and Extreme Unction.

5. Astonishment to find the Catholic doctrines so different from what they had been represented.

* 1848.

II. Behaviour of Protestants to converts—their inability to understand grace—always looking out for interested motives—their strange fear of the Catholic Church—they tolerate immorality sooner than Catholicism.

  1. Behaviour of relations—fulfilment of our Lord's prophecy.

  2. Behaviour of Protestant ministers.

  3. Behaviour of masters, employers, customers, and the like.

  4. Inconsistency of all this with the English Protestant principle of liberty of conscience.

  5. Contrast of behaviour of Catholics to converts, and their disinterested kindness to them.

III. Behaviour of converts—immense importance of this—how it ought to preach Christ and His truth—even in the case of quite young people.

  1. Gentleness, sweetness, meekness under rebuke.

  2. Greater obedience and obligingness to parents and masters.

  3. Boldness in confessing the faith—Church-going—Friday's abstinence—sign of the Cross—bowing at the Name of Jesus.

  4. Abstaining from argument, and putting forward love of God as the business of a Catholic.

  5. Diligence in reading and making themselves good scholars : the Church only desires increase of light.

Continual prayers to the Blessed Virgin Mary for the conversion of England.

VI.

ON JOURNALISM.

Everything in the country which presents itself as an antagonist influence to the Church, must be an object of special interest to the Brothers of the Little Oratory—so newspapers. The influence they exercise is immense, and they pretend to exercise it as organs of public opinion.

I. What, then, is public opinion?

1. The opinion with which circumstances enable the few to inoculate the many. Men go by authority—this is a fact, say what we will of it.

2. Power of it shown by the history of popular delusions.

3. Morality of it—corruption of man's nature —what St. John says of friendship with the world.

4. How far we may appeal to public opinion, or use it to our own purposes.

II. History of public opinion.

1. Early traditions, poems, and ballads.

2. Professions and philosophies.

3. Politics; sides in peace and war and civil war.

4. Government proclamations.

5. Debates—unreported, reported.

6. Responsible press.

7. Journalism.

III. Journalism a type of ungodliness: it represents the section of human intellect which, when in good humour, thought our Lord mad, in indifference was Pontius Pilate, and in bad humour gnashed its teeth upon Him. Journalism has, in fact, all the characteristics of a bad despotism.

1. Irresponsible.
2. Secret.
3. No principle but success.
4. No limit but failure, and so no justice.
5. Mercenary or pecuniary element—necessary self-interest, not as with despots, for the good of others is their good too.
6. Truth overwhelmed by force—brute force—of circulation, pre-occupation of ground, influence, not meeting nor needing to meet a question fairly.
7. It has all the evils of being hereditary—it is a mere accident who turns up to start or put down a view—low class of mind wanted, no beauty or grace, no election; it is a *chance* despotism.

IV. The position of Journalism.

1. The world's side of the question.
2. Growth of individual judgment not at all proportionate with it, nor spread of intelligence.
3. It comes against the Church just when physically tyranny is obliged to cease.
4. It probably will enter deeply into antichrist's system—Julian's education schemes.

5. We cannot use it with equal effect—so it is to be looked on as an inconvertible evil.

6. It may destroy itself, as all human powers do.

Conclusion—Journalism is a powerful, tyrannical, and triumphant scoundrelism.

Part Fifth.

THE SPIRITUAL LIFE.

I.

NEW BEGINNINGS.

I.

WHAT HAS BECOME OF OUR OLD BEGINNINGS.

CASSANDRA in the streets of Troy, obliged to prophecy, although she knew nobody would believe her, a type of preachers and writers of spiritual books. This is especially the case about beginning over again.

I. New beginnings.

   1. The authority of the saints, even of recluses like St. Anthony.

   2. The simple necessity of the case—for what else is to be done?

   3. It was an absurdity not to expect it beforehand.

   4. Souls are never lost because their beginnings break down, but because they won't make new beginnings.

   5. Why don't we believe this? Because our old beginnings have disheartened us.

II. Well, then, what has become of our old beginnings?

   1. We think them so many mistakes, shames, failures, and cowardices.

   2. But they are in reality gone to heaven as merits.

3. We should have been much worse now, if we had not made them.

4. They are capital foundations for new beginnings.

5. We are distinctly so much dearer to God because of them, and therefore distinctly so much more likely to succeed in our fresh beginnings.

6. We have gained many graces by failure, which we should never have gained by success.

7. It is often a remarkable mercy for a new beginning to break down, because it was in a wrong groove, and would have come to grief at last.

8. In truth, the disappointments of our past spiritual life, its heaps of rubbish, as I may call them, are incredibly full of choicest revelations of the tenderness of God.

III. Therefore, I say, begin again—Lent is the time for new beginnings—but how to begin?

1. Begin generously, not with much, only without any definite limit or reserve.

2. Break distinctly at once with some one thing which is not for God—we will pray for each other that God may show us some such thing within our souls.

3. Do not think whether it will be a failure or not—what matter? it is the battle, not the victory, which is the real success in divine things.

4. Found it more deeply in prayer than your other beginnings were.

5. Whatever the beginning is, accompany it with a greater effort after humility.

I believe many heroic and saintly lives will be

found at last to be simply an entanglement of generous beginnings.

2.

LITTLE ENCOURAGEMENTS.

A journey uphill all the way—crossing the sea where it is always rough—running for life with a wild beast pursuing us—having to do something very accurately, yet having to do it in the dark—having to pick our way speedily over slippery rocks with the tide rising round us faster than we can advance; all these are figures of the Christian life, of the hot, arduous, doubtful, nervous race for the salvation of our souls.

I. Reflections suited to our present state.
 1. The thought of hell is intolerable, and yet multitudes go there daily.
 2. The avoiding of sin is not so easy.
 3. Many think they will be saved, and are not.
 4. Many begin well, go on a long time, and end badly.
 5. We hate trouble, and yet we must take considerable trouble to be saved. Now all this looks amiss—have we any encouragements?
II. Shadows of predestination—their value, and substantial comfort.
 1. Sweetnesses in devotion—they don't often come to the worldly—they are *little* shadows, but still shadows.

2. Temptations—do we resist—do we overcome—
   do we lessen them ? anyhow, do we fight ?

3. Pleasure in Church services and devotions—
   this shows a *taste* which may be a root of
   heaven.

4. Frequenting the sacraments; this is not a
   certainty, but near to it, a *bright* shadow.

5. Improvement of temper—we are slower to anger
   —anger lasts less time—we are more sorry
   afterwards.

6. Feeling humble, *i.e.*, thinking less well of ourselves than we did last year—a *grand* shadow.

7. Getting kinder—more thought for others—a
   gentler tongue—more charitable judgments—
   more generosity—more forgetfulness of self—
   this is the shadow of Jesus Himself.

III. How we may safely use all these as encouragements.

1. If we refer them all to God and His goodness.

2. If they increase our faith, quicken our hope,
   heat our love.

3. If we do not rest contented in them, but
   press on.

Encouragement is a grand help to holiness.   I know
that from one point of view we are all of us much
worse than we believe ourselves to be ; but I believe
also, that from another point of view we are all of us
better than we think.   Our dearest Lord contrives to
be pleased with many things about us, which we shall
never know till we are dead, and judged and saved.

———

3.

LITTLE DISCOURAGEMENTS.

I. How matters stand now.

1. God.loves us more daily, and the Blesed Virgin Mary, and the angels, and saints—joy of being loved, and so loved.
2. Yet we feel discouraged, and are quite eloquent on the gloomy side.
3. Well, this too is an encouragement; for it shows we have the matter at heart.
4. Besides, we do feel a peace and pleasantness really in our hearts.
5. Moreover, every day is a piece of final perseverance—only be true and unaffected.

II. Now let us discuss the discouragements.

1. We do not reach our mark.
   Of course not, but this shows we aimed generously.
2. We are intermitting in our efforts.
   Did we not expect to be so? Else would it not be a miracle?
3. Our temptations are more vehement.
   Capital sign—the devil has had to put out more power; besides, so long as the temptations displease us, they are as good as beaten. Sometimes we ourselves make them more vehement by arguing with them, or being too frightened of them.
4. New kinds of temptation assail us, and new kinds of faults are disclosed.

Best sign of growth—more light—and more
light makes room for love.

5. We fall most when and where we try most.
   This shows we have hit the right when and
   where;—(1) God, (2) the devil, (3) nature
   explain these falls.   God lets us fall for
   humility, the devil causes falls by extra assaults,
   nature through weariness and petulance.

6. The things we took on ourselves have grown
   miraculously heavy and are too much for us.
   Then change them and take something less:
   change is a relief: gentleness is not always
   cowardice, or if it is, then cowardice is sometimes wise: all I wish for you is a goodnatured director, and then I like your feeling
   these things heavy.   Oh, if priests were more
   goodnatured, how many more souls would be
   saved !

7. Weariness grows upon us, and also grows less
   bearable.
   Well! this shows that nature is suffering, and
   so that you are really mortifying yourselves:
   every pious person has the fidgets occasionally,
   —and like a successful vaccination, it shows
   that grace has taken.   .

8. The exercise of charity is more difficult.
   Invariable sign of first progresses, like the
   irritabilities of convalescence, our fresh light,
   our very increased love of God make us less
   charitable.

9. Prayers and spiritual exercises seem more dull,
   and have to be done with effort.
   God would not let this be, if He did not think

you had got on : take it as your mortification, and your *only* one, and never mind other mortifications just now : the effort is just the violence which our Lord says takes the kingdom of heaven by force : ask God for sweetness and complain to Him of His having taken it away.

III. I am afraid you will think me most provokingly and perversely cheerful. But the fact is, I have no eye for darkness. I can never see anything but light anywhere. It puts me quite in spirits arguing with these discouragements : you are getting on famously; there is a fine quiet work going on in your soul, as all these things tell me.

1. If you fret, be more generous with God, and then you will get it more quickly over ; generosity makes short work with difficulties, but it was a very sharp operation.

2. But sometimes it is safer to be longer : vehemence does not suit brittle things.

3. But will this state of things last long ? Certainly not, *if* you keep your spirits up.

4. What shall I do, what is best for me just now ? Increase in devotion to the *Saints !* I lay great stress on this.

5. But what if I die as I am now ? Well ! you will be saved !

4.

THE GOD WE HAVE TO DEAL WITH.

In the spiritual life there are two people at work—
God and ourselves: and who works most? God;
who can doubt it?

I. Spiritual life is an estimating things at their true
    price, weighing them by their true weights,
    measuring them in just measures, and number-
    ing them in right order.

    1. But price, weight, measure, and order are the
        character of God, that is, depend on it and
        Him. Hence the indispensable necessity of a
        right view of God.

    2. One of the devil's chief arts is to give us wrong
        thoughts, hard thoughts, or too easy thoughts
        of God.

    3. God requires to be revealed separately to each
        soul.

    4. Our idea of God almost involves our future life,
        and even the success of our eternity.

    5. Intense reverence for God is the best augury for
        our new beginnings.

II. Now let me see how God deals with us in our
    beginnings.

    1. Content with very little, if it is from the heart.
        Dear St. Francis of Sales said one day, in that
        nice way in which he used to say things: God
        is content with little; for He knows we have
        not much to give.

2. Ready to wait our time—in prayer, penances, and resolutions.

3. Rewards minutely—on the whole makes more of little things than we do.

4. Revives merits, and·does not revive demerits.

5. Makes immense allowances: using His inexhaustible wisdom: all through the Bible God is on the side of laxity, man on the side of strictness—example of the woman taken in adultery.

6. Is more anxious for our salvation than we are ourselves: *suck* that wonderful truth.

7. Sees good where we cannot see it—*e g.* faults of beginners which piety itself engenders: just as strengthening medicines give headaches, bring out rashes on the skin, or otherwise derange us.

8. Sets His value on *efforts* as the real things which are personal to Himself: efforts are easier than accomplishments, and are always successes.

9. As Creator He is drawn to our weakness and attracted by it.

10. Inexplicable leniency of all His judgments—were He not God, and so holy a God, it could not be.

11. Follows our lead, and goes our road with us. What a sight the angels see—God following His creatures all the world over, like a lacquey, following the lead even of school-boys or of school-girls—and respecting the free will of children in the nursery.

12. Yearns to be familiar with us, and hence is sometimes pleased even with our petulancy,

which shows *trust*, and wounded feeling, which shows *love*.

13. His understanding of our nature, and so of the sinlessness of first motions—which we can hardly realise, as in temptations, distractions, and first thoughts.

14. The immense value He sets on faith is an immense consolation to us: for faith is a gift: we are almost passive; it is a grace which we can increase without penance.

15. He will do anything for us, and vary it for our own private selves and peculiar souls, if only we are—(1) very reverent, (2) full of thought —and (3) desire Him. Blosius says that the desire of contrition or of devotion to the Passion is often dearer to Him than the reality. There is something beautifully piteous to Him in the sight of our desiring good things too high for us: this is in itself a revelation of God.

III. What follows from all this? That we must have—

1. An immense esteem of grace: this runs like concrete under all the foundations of the spiritual life.

2. A filial confidence in our Heavenly Father.

3. An abiding gentle sorrow for sin.

4. The contentment of humility with little things, and with our own outward slowness.

5. The vigour of encouragement, and the elasticity of inveterate cheerfulness.

St. Francis of Sales says that the best and most successful beggars are those who are the most deformed, and have the most frightful sores; they attract alms: so is it with us when we lie before the door of God's compassion: so that our very wretchedness is our treasure to trade with in the things of God. Our misery seems positively to widen the immensity of His mercy.

II.

ON THE MANAGEMENT OF OUR GRACE.

Questa è la maggiore perfezione di tutte le virtù, e grazie, mante nere umilmente i doni ricevuti.—BEATO EGIDIO.

I.

THE ABUNDANCE OF GRACE.

The management of our grace is our one work, the occupation of time, and the securing of eternity—the sole occupation by which eternity is secured.

I. Our position in the world.
   1. Its beauty and magnificence in a physical point of view.
   2. The grandeur of our intellectual gifts.
   3. The power and diversity of our moral endowments.
   4. The manifold glory of civilisation.
   5. The magnificence of the world in a social point of view.
   6. The gorgeous destiny of humanity considered as one—the progress and good of the race.
   7. Yet all this is merely subordinate to the end for which we were created.

8. Which is, to become likened to God, and to see Him eternally face to face.

9. To this end all our natural gifts, and all conceivable natural gifts conceivably multiplied, avail nothing; not even a little, but, standing by themselves, absolutely nothing.

II. The necessity of Grace.

   1. We need some supernatural gift in order to attain our end.

   2. This gift must be a created thing, working within, gratuitous, for an eternal end.

   3. It is either a certain communication of the Divine Nature, or an impulse of the Divine will.

   4. It surrounds us in both these shapes in indescribable variety, and incredible abundance.

   5. It weds itself to all our natural gifts and endowments, but as sovereign to them.

   6. We are therefore on the earth as the old astrologers imagined themselves to be, surrounded with strange powers, and instruments and potent spells, and heavenly witchcraft.

   7. Holding sweet substantial communion with the invisible God, such as no legends ever dared to depict; no matter if rich or poor, scholar or simple.

   8. This is our real life, using all the grandeurs of mind, morals, civilisation, and physical things, as mere means to our end.

   9. Our spiritual life, therefore, is the wise or unwise management and administration of our grace: and this is our present subject—a very grave one,—to the careless, full of such shadowy fears—to the earnest, full of brave

encouragement. Pelagianism is the strength of all that seems most delusively fresh in the aspect of the times, and especially wears the look of a false healthiness.

III. The abundance of grace.
  1. In kind.
    (1) Actual grace, of which there are many subordinate kinds.
    (2) Sanctifying grace.
  2. In quantity.
    (1) Never beneath, *i.e.*, falling short of the amount of temptation.
    (2) Often quite irrespective of any temptation.
    (3) A sort of supernatural inundation of our natural life.
  3. In number.
    (1) Yet though an inundation, it is not indistinguishable or uniform.
    (2) Several of them are given to each of our deliberate actions, words, thoughts, and endurances.
    (3) Graces for past, present, and future, are in us in some sense all at once.
  4. In weight.
    (1) Greater than that of the temptation, taken by itself *without* our *totality* of corruption.
    (2) Pressing just where our character would desire the weight should press.
    (3) Yet never so as to violate the freedom of our will; not even by the efficacious suavity of victorious grace.
  5. In seasonableness.
    (1) Prophetically preparing us for what is coming.

- (2) Concentrating itself on opportune conjunc-
  tures of time.
- (3) Suiting the peculiarities of our characters,
  which requires grace to time itself very differently, as, for instance, with a slow man
  or a swift one.

6. In superabundance.
   - (1) Almost embarrassing and distracting; graces
     seem all round, not so much coming as
     already come, and we only have to put
     ourselves in connection with them, just as
     the earth and air are always charged with
     electricity.
   - (2) At least this is the case, provided we are
     earnestly striving to love God.
   - (3) Each of us probably has more grace than the
     highest saint has ever corresponded to. Yet
     some *seem* to have it only by drops; per-
     haps some really have it only so—there is
     great inequality, as in Tyre and Sidon,
     Bethsaida and Corozain.

7. In unintermittingness.
   - (1) Sanctifying grace is an unintermitting state,
     only forfeited by deliberate sin.
   - (2) Actual graces are most likely unintermitting.
     Council of Sens, also of Trent,* *Christus
     jugiter influit virtutem.* *Nieremberg* says †
     that now under the Christian dispensation
     there are probably more saints in a few
     years than there would have been in
     thousands of years in a state of innocence.

---

* Sess vi. cap. xvi.
† Prezzo della Divina Grazia, lib. iii. cap. 12.

(3) Suspended only when we sleep—our understanding always being illuminated—also one
grace involves another, and so makes life
an enchainment of graces.

To me there is at first sight something almost depressing in these thoughts, because our responsibilities
are proportioned to the abundance of our grace, and
our lives are so mean and scanty. We seem to be
floating evermore in the sea of God's magnificence,
catching His sunlight on us, and yet, alas! we are
what we are. It is not only the Xaviers who have
need to say to God, Forbear! forbear! But what a
deeply sobering, hushing thought it is, that we shall
be judged not only according to our works, but according to our grace!

————

2.

THE VARIETIES OF GRACE.

They are more various than the flowers and per-
fumes of the earth; they are almost as various as the
individualities on earth—at least in their combina-
tions.

I. What regulates these varieties.

1. Our needs, which are changing almost hourly.
2. Our position, with its own dangers and therefore
   its own requirements.
3. Our time of life, with which our temptations vary.
4. The age in which we live, whose dominant spirit
   affects every one of us, up to the degree of
   almost seeming to control our liberty.

5. Our own characters, with which that spirit of the age combines.

6. The country which we inhabit—both because of its circumstances and its national character.

7. The particular prayers of our Blessed Lady, the Angels, and Saints, who see God's particular design upon us.

8. Those with whom we associate, or who lie around us, seemingly passively even, in life.

9. What the good of the Church may require from us.

10. Our vocations and interior attractions.

11. The character of our favourite devotions.

12. Also the various perfections of God: graces often *seem* to come from some one attribute of God, and then from some other: also they sometimes *seem* as if they come more appropriately from One Divine Person rather than from Another.

II. The common *forms*, under which these various graces come to us.

   1. Warnings.

     (1) Sometimes in prayer.

     (2) Sometimes in apparent chances.

     (3) Sometimes in the unintentional words of others.

   2. Depressions.

     (1) Shadows, apparently causeless, cast over our spirits.

     (2) An inward melancholy in the midst of sunshine.

     (3) Inexplicable presentiment of evil, drawing us back to God, and so hindering its fulfilment.

3. Touches.
    (1) As if the finger of God rested on some part of self hitherto unknown to us.
    (2) Causing sharp pain, with peace, and no warning beforehand.
    (3) Very sudden and brief, so that we can hardly recal them; they come even out of times of prayer, though oftenest then.

4. Sweetnesses.
    (1) Sometimes sudden and unexpected.
    (2) Sometimes slowly oozing up from beneath.
    (3) Seeming to change our whole man, and make us forget the past.

5. Chances.
    (1) Outward accidents and apparent judgments.
    (2) Curious conjuncture of outward occurrences with some inward change of grace *just before:* probably the arrangement of our Guardian Angel.
    (3) Books, sermons, meetings, and conversations.

6. Lights.
    (1) After earnest prayer in difficulties.
    (2) Or quite sudden and unsought for, and before the difficulty comes.
    (3) Flashes, or steady lights, or a mere thinning of the darkness.

7. Sacraments.
    (1) Which seem to vary their operations as we need.
    (2) Also other graces are commonest while under their operation.
    (3) So many of our graces are hiddenly dependent on their frequency.

III. The graces of individuals.

 1. Each man has his grace, in kind and in degree, not to be passed.

 2. Few even of the saints fulfil this intention of God upon them.

 3. Distinctly, all men have not the grace given to be technically saints.

 4. Many failures in the spiritual world, because of shooting ahead of our grace.

 5. Some are called to perfection, who will not even be saved short of it. Judas possibly an instance of this.

Again, holy fear comes over us; grace makes us afraid. What we want in this world of delicate operations is clear spiritual discernment; and discernment comes of three things—(1) slowness—a contented slowness based on a knowledge of our misery—(2) recollectedness—(3) the practice of the Presence of God.

3.

THE JEALOUSY OF GRACE.

There is hardly a single subject connected with our salvation, which is of more importance than this, *the frivolity of all of us.* There is a certain flightiness and flippancy, a certain deep-laid frivolity in the soul of man, which is to me the most inexplicable of its phenomena, by far the most painful of its problems.

 I. The practical acknowledgment of the sovereignty of God is the basis of the spiritual life.

1. All dealings with God are necessarily full of grace.
2. The very vicinity of the Creator to the creature is full of risk and nervousness.
3. Above all is it so in supernatural matters.
4. His will is our law, and the one form of our sanctification.
5. We often do not understand Him and His ways.
6. Yet He is absolutely beyond our criticism— criticism is irreverence.
7. We cannot prophecy what He will do with us, we can only trust.
8. Thus in the spiritual life we are as it were environed with huge, intricate, seemingly capricious, and swift machinery.
9. All we can do is to fear greatly, and to fear lovingly, and to shrink as far as we can from worldliness.

II. The jealousy of God.
1. This is His own revelation of Himself; He complains like an injured lover; awfully seems to give way to wails of wounded feeling. God is like a wounded eagle in the echoing mountain vales, or as a sorrow-stricken poet on the forlorn heights of song.
2. He will have the whole heart, not half; His love must be exclusive, and sovereign, and absorbent.
3. His dealings with the Jewish people exemplify this.
4. The way He withdrew from those who did not trust him, as from King Joas,* and from the young man in the Gospel, who cared more for his gold and silver and precious stones, for his

* IV. Kings xiii.

orchards and vineyards, and corn-lands, and sheep-walks, and pastoral wells.

5. His turning to the Gentiles, as if jealousy were His road to them, a *passionate* feeling.

6. So with nations in Christian history, He withdraws, as from the Gerasenes.

7. So with the rise and fall of religious orders, sometimes such swift decadence.

8: So even with His saints, when they hesitate.

9. So in the peculiar grace of vocation to individuals.

III. The extreme jealousy of grace.

  1. Its changeable demeanour.

    (1) Sometimes importunate, knocking long, for years, at our hearts; sometimes asking only once.

    (2) Sometimes slow—we see the grace long before it comes—sometimes very swift; the only thing is to sit watching with door open in the heavenward side of our hearts, and the other side shut close enough.

    (3) Sometimes it knocks loudly, sometimes inaudibly low.

  2. The higher the graces the more jealous they are.

    (1) Because of their rarity.

    (2) Because we are to be passive, and so with detached hearts.

    (3) Because such graces calculate on our sensitiveness to divine things.

  3. The delicacy of its touch.

    (1) Hardly felt in the crowd and hurry of life.

    (2) Often seems an imagination only, not a real spiritual touch.

    (3) An effusion of talk or a loud laugh is enough to make us insensible to it. A long talk, however innocent, is uncongenial to the Holy Ghost; a loud laugh frightens Him away like a startled antelope flying to its coverts.

4. It is easily oppressed, as if its life was frail and invalid-like.

    (1) Missing our prayers and other spiritual exercises can suffocate grace.

    (2) Soon overlaid by love of bodily comforts, nice eating, clean arrangements, punctual service, recreation, fresh air, solicitude about health, a little inconsiderateness to servants, &c.

    (3) It is almost instantly obscured and paralyzed by worldliness.

5. Withdrawal of grace; frequent, unexpected, seemingly wayward.

    (1) Because of our not corresponding to it.

    (2) Because we have presumed upon it.

    (3) Because we have been discouraged by the sacrifices it entails.

6. Withdrawn graces seldom come again.

    (1) We see this in the matter of rejected vocations.

    (2) Also when our answers to God have been ungraciously delayed.

    (3) Also certain kinds of prayer and other gifts, when forfeited, seem forfeited finally: we may have others, we shall not have those again.

7. Any loss of grace is irreparable.

(1) 'A lower degree of glory for ever.

(2) Fewer graces henceforth in life, and those
fewer probably of a lower kind: no conversions are so rare as those from an
ungenerous subsidence in the spiritual
life.

(3) Each loss is a weakening of the assurance of
final perseverance.

Of what use frightening us with all this, unless you
point out how we are to meet our difficulties? Why
even if I did not do that, it would be of great use.
Mere frightening is of great use, so long as there is a
chance of being lost: for being frightened is a chance
less of being lost: so that in truth being frightened is
itself a grace, and a very jealous one. We are not
often frightened—and we might make much of it if
we chose. But I *am* going to tell you the *means,* &c.

IV. By what means we must meet this jealousy of
grace.

1. By swiftness, so as to keep pace with the rapid
magnificence of God.

2. By slowness, so as not to overlook Him as He
hides by the way.

3. By vigilance, so as to see Him in the dark, and
where He is burying His graces.

4. By prepared attitude, ready to seize the grace as
it flashes past us.

5. By generosity, to avoid the ungraciousness of
delay, when God purposes anything suddenly.

6. By self-oblivion, so as to have an undistracted
instinct for God.

7. By holy covetousness of grace, so as to win grace

to us, for it is equally covetous to possess our hearts.

8. Sometimes taking the initiative, because such reverent venturesomeness is dear to God.

9. By growing in love, because love simplifies all things, and by one process accomplishes the other eight.

Is the spiritual life, then, a walk of terror? Indeed it has its times of terror, panics which love knows how to seize upon, and use. It is not a walk of terror but a walk of fear—and it is fear which makes sensible the sweetness of love. And what are love and fear together but a happy timid trustfulness?

"This is not a pleasant view of the spiritual life." But will you have pleasantness instead of truth: do you require comfort rather than salvation? Let me remind you of the two Apostles Peter and Paul. St. Peter—sojourning here in fear. St. Paul—he that thinketh himself to stand, let him take heed lest he fall. No! comforting sermons do not make comfortable ways of salvation—nor do hard sermons make them harder than they really are. God made them, and there they are. You cannot make another God: you must take Him as you find Him. I can but draw one conclusion from this study of the jealousy of grace —that it is an extremely serious thing to have to do with God.

4.

THE KNOWLEDGE OF OUR GRACE.

The knowledge of our grace is very necessary to the right management of it.

I. The Pelagianism of worldliness.

1. Worldliness stops all our senses and instincts against God.

2. It makes us indifferent and callous to our eternal interests.

3. It is the spirit of a region in which we settle everything for ourselves.

4. A certain amount of unbelief always goes along with it.

5. It is unable so much as to apprehend the true idea of grace; for worldliness is chiefly the inordinate and supreme satisfaction of natural propensities which are not in themselves sinful: utter delusiveness of all spirituality which is not accompanied by some amount of bodily discomfort.

II. The knowledge of our grace.

1. Most men have it not.

2. Waste of grace from the ignorance of it.

3. We should have at least a general idea of what God is doing with us.

4. We miss inspirations from not discerning them; and God's work in our souls is a continuous whole, seriously marred by breaks—so we should avoid them.

5. The knowledge of our grace is no interference

with humility; on the contrary, it rather deepens it.

6. It also breeds reverence rather than familiarity.

7. Yet it must not lead to excessive self-introversion.

III. How to acquire the knowledge of our grace.

  1. By doing always God's present will. *Se fate il bene che conoscete, arriverete a quello che non conoscete.* (A saying of Blessed Egidio.)

    (1) For this is the best exercise of simplicity.

    (2) And simplicity is light.

    (3) God is only availably present in the present: past and future are in the spiritual life only forms of self.

  2. By a life of prayer.

    (1) Prayer also is an atmosphere of light: in it we see far, we see clearly, we see truly.

    (2) It is also an atmosphere of sensitiveness to supernatural things.

    (3) We must, like St. Austin, make special prayer for self-knowledge.

  3. By taking great pains to be recollected.

    (1) Recollection is the absolute condition on which many graces are held.

    (2) It has power to detain God.

    (3) It is an almost infallible amulet against delusion.

  4. By assiduous ransacking of our conscience.

    (1) In the practice of both general and particular examen: especially this last, which in the purgative way is almost the highest kind of prayer.

    (2) It must be continued for a long time; for it only tells in the long run.

(3) The mere absence of it is the tangled growth of abundant faults.

5. By spiritual direction.

(1) We must be honest in it: *i.e.* seek only God and improvement.

(2) We must distrust our own self-love, and above all, our own untruthfulness: people true with every one else are often untrue with their directors.

(3) We must act by it: there are few things in which obedience is of more value than the matter of our actions.

6. By abiding sorrow for sin.

(1) No better or more successful stock to graft graces on.

(2) It enables us as it were to feel the weight of each separate grace.

(3) It allures fresh grace to us by the grateful wonder in which it keeps us at the grace we already have.

7. But still we shall not know all our grace; for such is God's will.

(1) For the sake of humility: we shall be allowed to gain as much knowledge as is adequate and practical.

(2) More knowledge might hinder God's further purposes upon us: He is always a hidden God, especially in His sanctifying operations.

(3) We never see ourselves quite truly until we see Him; and in the vision of Him we shall find ourselves out for the first time.

IV. Unknown graces.

1. These are probably more than those we know of.

2. Good people, earnestly good people, are always better and deeper than they think themselves.

3. The most important graces generally work underground for a long time.

4. In all graces the being fitted for some unknown post in eternity may be more considered by God, than mere fitness for our post on earth.

5. Unknown graces, or the thought of them, a source of fear and wariness.

6. But also a source of most happy confidence.

7. The practice of thanksgiving for them a wise and acceptable devotion.

Observe—that the knowledge of our grace is less dangerous, because less likely to lead to scruple and faint-heartedness, than the knowledge of our faults. For in the case of knowing our graces, our knowledge of God is increasing out of proportion with our knowledge of ourselves; whereas in knowing our faults, although the knowledge of God increases with our knowledge of self, it does not increase proportionately, and so becomes exaggerated and falsified.

————

5.

CORRESPONDENCE TO OUR GRACE.

Whole sanctities may follow from corresponding to one single inspiration. Look at the avenue of graces from the Immaculate Conception! It almost tries our faith, and yet correspondence is the adequate account of it all, so far as Mary was concerned.

I. What correspondence is and implies.
 1. It implies an habitual attitude of waiting for grace.
 2. A quick discernment and intelligent perception of it.
 3. Prayer for grace to use grace rightly.
 4. Immediate deliberation.
 5. Renewal of our intention for the glory of God.
 6. Quietly beginning to act on the grace.
 7. Obstinacy and heroism in difficulties.
 8. A constant lifting up of our hearts to God.
 9. Our Lady is the trophy of perfect correspondence to grace.
 10. All others, even saints, have failed.
 11. It is an absolutely necessary thing.
 12. Yet in its perfection the rarest of graces.
II. What our correspondence must be like.
 1. It must be prompt.
  (1) No deliberation when we know the movement to be grace.
  (2) Yet no hurry or bustle: which is always a loss of time, and a slackening of speed.
  (3) Generally what our instincts first prompt is best, if we are otherwise habitually recollected.
 2. It must also be brave.
  (1) We must gaily disbelieve in the impossible.
  (2) We must not listen too much to the querulousness of nature.
  (3) Yet we must remember that spiritual bravery is always very self-diffident: it is chiefly encouraged by its distrust of itself, because it realises God more.

III. We must be passively indifferent to all wills of God, which grace may reveal.

  1. Our own will must disappear as far as possible.

  2. We must not stop to see too much how our new grace will fit in with old plans.

  3. We are more often attached to our work than to Him for whom we work, and many graces are lost in this way.

IV. We must reverence our grace and vocation.

  1. God disposes of us reverently. See Wisdom xii. 18, in the *Latin*.

  2. We must reverence our grace, because it is in a measure a revelation from Him.

  3. When we look at our graces simply as comforts or facilities, we are in evil plight, and in the act of sinking to a lower spiritual level.

V. We must increase our fear as our gifts increase.

  1. The gifts of God have their dangers.

  2. They are only means: therefore we must not rest in them.

  3. We must especially be afraid of our power of deluding ourselves by them.

VI. We must be slow.

  1. Slowness is the characteristic of those who have a great presence of God.

  2. We must be slow, even while we are swift. Some men mix up deliberation with action: this won't do: act always swiftly, but be as long as you please deliberating beforehand.

  3. Recollection is the secret of the union of the two things.

VII. Correspondence is our sole work.

  1. Of itself it will do everything: for grace mostly

takes the initiative adequately : we need seldom invent anything ourselves, or make experiments.

2. Without it nothing else will do anything.

3. It was in itself, as we have seen, our Lady's perfection.

VIII. The horror of grace uncorresponded to—wasted grace.

  1. It is a secret reserve of God's wrath.

  2. An important unexpected witness at the judgment.

  3. It holds back graces that want to come to us.

  4. Through it they come to us with their freshness taken off.

  5. It is a disability for many higher graces.

  6. It affords secret nutriment to old habits of sin.

  7. It is a hidden fountain chilling fervour into lukewarmness.

  8. Many efforts of our wills, and powers of forming habits, and precious time are sunk in it as in a frozen sea.

  9. It is another whole life, invisible, alongside of our visible life.

  10. It hardens our hearts, and intercepts the grace of final perseverance, for no grace comes without some effort—if it does not soften it hardens.

IX. Dependence upon grace is the result of our whole inquiry.

  1. It must be utter, and cannot be exaggerated.

  2. But it may become lazy and superstitious.

  3. It reveals to us our own nothingness.

  4. Yet at the same time the power of our generous wills for God.

5. We must remove nature as far as possible, and substitute grace, as a new foundation, as if we were underpinning a house.

6. It must be a dependence in detail, not merely in general.

7. Alas! how very little we do depend upon grace.

8. This the cause of nearly all our past failures.

9. This dependence is the best earnest of final perseverance.

10. And why? Because it is the most copious and stimulating source of prayer.

Correspondence was the devotion of Mary, the shape of her holiness. Our Lord did not correspond, because His grace did not grow; His was another kind of correspondence. It belonged to her as a creature; so let it be our love of her, and our imitation of her, which is our highest devotion to her; so also let it be our love of Jesus, as it was her love of Him; He was to her, as He is to us, the Giver of all graces, great and small.

If you are young, look onward to the opening trials of life; if you desire to find yourself strong in God's grace, and established in holiness, you must be sure of prayer; if you are middle-aged, and not so holy as you feel you should be, and look on to old age and its peculiar difficulties, you must be sure of prayer; if you are old, and look on to death, &c., be sure of prayer. Let us all look into the bright heaven above us; are you to be there? is it to be your everlasting home? be sure of prayer. I have said many things of grace, many hard things, many practical things, but the answer to all questions, the solution of all

difficulties, the inference of all inquiries, the conclusion
of the whole matter, all these lie in one thing, in lives
of prayer!   You have only two things to be frightened
at, your great grace and your little prayer.

III.

THE FEAR OF GOD.

I.

THE UNITY OF GOD.

The strength of the Creator makes His creatures
incredibly strong.   A sudden death gives us a kind of
measure of the strength of a human soul.   We could
hardly have conceived that so delicate a creation could
have borne such an instantaneous transition from this
world to the next, and yet have continued to live.
When long sickness, or the still longer noviciate of
old age, have sequestered us from outward life and
have gradually undermined the connections between the
body and the soul, it is more easy for us to conceive
the soul enduring its great change, simply because it
has been forewarned of the change, and because the
change has been very gradually effected.   But when a
· man, full of hopes and plans and impetuous activities,
drops down dead in the middle of the street, and enters
at once, in the midst of a train of thought or with a
half finished sentence upon his lips, into the unimaginable silences and solitudes of the immaterial world,

we cannot help feeling that there is a wonderful indestructibility in the soul which hinders it from rushing
back into nothingness in the panic of so unutterable
a change. Yet the soul goes through something of
the same kind when it is converted from worldliness
to God.

The ordinary life of the present day seems an almost
impossible life for the salvation of our souls. The
strength of religion is in its simplicity. The strength
of worldliness is in its variety. Each succeeding age
the world appears to acquire a new multiplicity.
Knowledge multiplies it. Education multiplies it. It
is multiplied by whatever makes it more rapid, and
gives it a greater mastery over time. It is multiplied
by whatever renders it more crowded and more diversified. If we know what is required for the salvation
of a soul, even carrying laxity to the very limit of what
is safe, and that itself would not be a very safe thing
to do, we shall be exceedingly frightened if we look
out upon the ordinary life of the present day. The
number of things which there are to do, the rapidity
with which we are to do them, the instantaneous succession of new works and new duties, the coming of
these new duties not singly but in crowds, the serious
and imperative exactions of religion alongside of all
these occupations and objects,—these things really
make life to be nothing but a disheartening fight
against time, distance, numbers, and impossibilities.
The fight is the more oppressive, because it never in-
termits, and the more disheartening because it must
necessarily be unsuccessful. It is impossible to do
what we have to do. It is impossible to do well what
we actually do. It is like trying to make our medita-

tion in the streets. Everything around us is crowd and distraction. Duties contradict duties. One responsibility hampers another. Every business entangles itself with other business. Uncongenial work always arrives at the most inopportune moment, and incompatible things perversely make a point of coming together. Deliberation only precipitates matters; and life, like a river, merely delays in order to get up its speed. We are bewildered, and bewilderingly fascinated, by the look of inextricableness which there is everywhere around us. Modern life rejoices in strong lights; and its lights are too strong to see by. We are dazzled with the glitter; and a dazzled man is worst off than a blind man, because he has all the disadvantages of blindness without its tranquillity. We are deafened by the clamour of impatient intersecting interests; and deafness more than anything else makes a man lose his head, and stand still when he ought to go on. A deaf man is always more likely to be driven over than a blind man. Everything around us is self-important; and the bluster of so many self-importances wearies us like a high wind. Manifold occupations lay siege to us all day long, and they open their batteries against us even in our dreams at night. The whole world is always showing fight; and it cows us like a loud disputant who never convinces us and whom we know it is hopeless to think of convincing. There are so many things to see, so many things to hear, so many things to say, so many things to suffer, and so many things to do, that we become stupefied by trying to be active. What would we give, if the planet and the whole thing might only stop for a few minutes till we had time to take breath, and look about us, and see where we are, and what is the next best thing to do? But it may not be. Wave comes on the top of wave. We shall reach the shore; we may trust the very waves themselves for that; but shall we reach it alive?

Let us change the scene, and make a silence round us. Let us go back some three thousand three hundred years. It is not as a moment to God. It will be but as a moment to us hereafter in our eternity. Thousands of years then will be swifter than moments now. We are amongst the ravines of Sinai. Here we have room. Here we can breathe. The silentness of the desert is full of peace. We are come to Horeb, the mountain of the Law. Its ancient peaks, weather-streaked with red and grey, rise up like monumental pillars in the clear sky. The tents of Israel, dusky tents woven of camels' hair, brown as if the sun had scorched them, are all around. All is unnaturally still. A whole people is listening. If a pebble were to detach itself from the cliffs, and roll down into the ravine, the noise would sound like a profanation. The very outspread wilderness lies listening. The noiseless sunshine rests motionless on the stones, and casts no shadows, as if it feared to make audible footfalls if it moved. Moses, the herald of the Eternal, is making a proclamation to heaven and earth, as well as to the Jewish people, to all ages as well as to the one to which he spoke. In that peculiar impressive scene of oriental barrenness, sequestered from the great nations and the highways of the nations, he is uttering the whole meaning of life, the whole secret of creation. The echoes of the rocks drink in the sound, and do not give it back again. Ages afterwards Mahomet's false

creed echoed it, as if it had become the very genius of
the place, as if the very air of Arabia, its soil, its sand,
its rifted crags, were impregnated with the doctrine of
the Unity of God, as if the voice of Moses had written
it in picture-characters upon the monotonous countenance of the wilderness! "Hear, O Israel, the Lord
thy God is one Lord!" All truth and all wisdom, all
time and all eternity, all counsel and all law, were in
that single proclamation. If the people, clustered
round their tents, were silent that they might hear,
surely, now that they have heard, they are yet more
silent. For a while at least, eternity displaces time, and
creatures hush themselves in unconscious adoration.

"Hear, O Israel, the Lord thy God is one Lord!"
Yes! "One Lord." Yet who would have thought it?
Life does not look like it. Simplicity, unity, oneness
—all things are to be reduced to these. The doctrine
of the Unity of God is not merely an external truth.
It is our rule, our meaning, our own life. There is no
God but God; and the One God is all in all. The
proclamation of Moses is a heavenly revolutionising of
earth. "This was the covenant which the Lord our
God made with us in Horeb."

"Hear, O Israel, the Lord thy God is one Lord."
Let us take this truth to pieces, that we may see how
vast a truth it is. By dwelling in its magnificent
spaces the soul becomes magnificent itself. Our littleness clothes itself with grandeur out of the very
boundlessness of this truth. The sunken stony troughs
of the desert, and the cloistered defiles of its rocks,
melt away from our minds as if they bounded our
thoughts too much. All creation lies before us without
horizon, and its immensity proclaims the Unity of God.

We look outside of ourselves, and all belongs to God, comes from Him, goes to Him, leans upon Him, witnesses of Him. He is in us, and in what we see, and between us and what we see, and far onward where we cannot see, where we shall never see. Within us, all belongs to Him; all came from Him, except sin; and all, sin most of all, is going to Him to be judged. Behind us lies that interminable wilderness of unintelligible beauty, the unbeginning eternity of God, and then the abrupt chronicle of the angels, and then the world's pathetic history, and a planet strewn with generations of the dead. Before us lies some unknown, unexhausted lapse of time, and then the grand, the jealous, the exclusive, the absorbing eternity. Everywhere, always, helplessly, inevitably, inextricably we are clasped in the arms of God. What a fear must this be to him to whom it is not the one joy of life!

The Unity of God! Beautifullest of doctrines! What we see, then, is not true. Things are not as they seem. The look of things is a deception. They are not in reality manifold. They are only one. All things are one because God is one. They are one in their origin, one in their meaning, one in their mission, one in the unity of their conclusion. Time is number, order, and multitude. This is what tries us, tempts us, perfects us. But the singleness of eternity is the unity of multitudinous time. God is one. The one God is our one occupation. We have no right to have any other. Any other is trivial, nay, is even wrong, if it excludes God, or so much as forgets Him. Nothing is to the point except God. One thing is necessary, said our Blessed Lord, compressing the whole gospel into one sentence. The whole of wisdom consists in a clear view of the unnecessariness of all other things. Because God is one, He is everywhere; because He is one, all things belong to Him; because He is one, nothing is worth anything but Himself. All our life that lies away from God is dissatisfying vanity now, and everlasting bitterness hereafter. Are we then leading one life, having one care, busied with one occupation, engrossed with one thought, mastered by one love? Are all things about us one even as God is one, so awfully, so simply, so wonderfully, so adorably, so triumphantly one? It is in the Unity of God that all contradictions agree, and all difficulties disappear, that all little things are made great, and all great things small, that all liberty is controlled and all captivity set free. O weary, loud, secret, monotonous, changeful, self-occupied London! is there not an ear deep down in our hearts, which, clear amidst the shouts and clangours of the modern capital, is for ever hearing that old Hebrew voice from the Arabian solitudes, "Hear, O Israel! the Lord thy God is one Lord?"

The Unity of God? There are many things which look important, many things which have a great deal to say very speciously in behalf of their importance. But faith, like death, silences many voices, and answers many questions very quietly, and makes many important things unimportant without taking the trouble to degrade them. In truth there is nothing important to God. All the questions of life become one question as they revolve round Him. Is there any God? What sort of God is He? What does He want to do with us? What does He expect us to do for Him? What will happen to us if we refuse or neglect to do it? In the answers to these questions, or rather the answer to this one question, lies all practical religion, the entire significance of life, and its sole importance. There is a God. He is a God of unspeakable sanctity. He wants us to copy His holiness, that we may be with Him in open vision to all eternity! and if we do not copy His holiness, whether through rebellion or neglect, He will punish us with a punishment so horrible and so endless that it will not bear being dwelt upon.

All this is almost universally believed: yet look at the lives of men, and see how their practice illustrates their faith! The outline of every town is broken with towers and steeples. The bells ring out on Sundays and feasts. There are crosses at the heads of the grassy graves. The name of God is on our money and in our forms of law. We garnish our conversation with it. Our libraries swarm with books about Him ; and a thousand outward memorials, down even to the very dates of our inscriptions, testify to our belief in His existence and in our own relation to Him. Yet do our lives look as if we were afraid of anything except earthly enemies or earthly loss ? Is there any look of fear about them at all ? Do we act as if we were acting for some one else, as if we might be interrupted at any moment, as if the eye of a superior were always upon us ? The presence of God is a terrific publicity, not only for the tongues and hands, but even for the unspeaking hearts of men. Would men, if they saw us in private, perceive that we felt we were not alone, and that there was no such thing as loneliness for a creature ? Only the Creator can

be lonely.   Is not our attitude that of persons who
are their own masters, and have to give no account to
any one, but are responsible only to their own self-
respect ?   The pursuit of pleasure, the climbing of
ambition, the nervousness of accumulation, do these
things look as if they were done for God ?   Cast your
eye into that green field yonder—those restless horses
looking about them as they feed, those assiduous
nibbling sheep, those quiet incurious cows feeding or
recumbent do not look as if they were worshipping
any unseen king of angels; I doubt if to angels' eyes
there is any greater look of worship about the hordes
of men.

God is unseen.   Perhaps here is the secret of our
indifference.   Yet in His being unseen is the first
reason for His being feared.   If there is a God He
must be worshipped.   If He is a holy God, He must
be worshipped with fear, because otherwise our worship
would not be a holy worship.   If practically God is
not worshipped, it is because practically God is not
feared.   Because God is not seen, we can forget Him,
and so not fear Him ; or we can make false pictures
of Him, and so not fear Him rightly.   But it is of
the very nature of faith that it is a sight, the seeming
of the unseen ; and therefore faith in God must bring
fear of God, and, as God is one, our fear is one, and,
as God is everywhere, our fear is universal, and, as He
is eternal, our fear of Him is incessant.   Is it worth
while to occupy some Conferences with proving that
God is to be feared ?   I think so.   But why have I
begun by dwelling on the Unity of God ?   Why so
especially on His Unity ?   Because experience seems
to tell me that this is the right attribute out of which

alone the right fear comes. Sinners may well fear
God because of His surpassing holiness, and creatures
because of His enormous power, and subjects because
of His irresponsible sovereignty, and children because
of His infinite paternal jealousy, and saints because of
His incomprehensible judgments.   All these are holy
fears.   Let us not be wanting in any one of them.
Nevertheless our fear will not have the efficacy it
ought to have, it will not persuade the heart so forcibly
or rule it with so royal a constraint, unless its first
source is in the glorious and overwhelming faith of
the Unity of God.

There is no other God but God.   Here is the grand
fountain of that fear of God, which does most honour
to His Divine Majesty, and which is most full of the
spirit of adoration.   It is the Unity of God which
especially gives to His service its exclusive rights to
our whole and our unintermitting attention.   It is
His Unity which represents to us His glory as everywhere and as concerned with everything, because
everything exists solely for its sake.   It is the Unity
of God which shows us how exclusive, how absorbing,
how supreme, how altogether single and alone, religion
is in its claims upon us; and it is out of these considerations that a true, wise, and holy fear proceeds.
We must not be content with fearing God in some of
His perfections, and loving Him in others.   As we
must love Him in all, so we must fear Him in all.
We must not simply fear His power or fear His justice,
but we must fear Him, and fear Him because He is
what He is, the infinitely holy and sole God.   The
great fruit of the fear of God is not to make us serve
Him fearingly, but to make us do nothing but serve

Him, serve Him exclusively, only Him, always Him,
and Him in all things. Childishly simple as this
truth appears, it is not always clearly understood.
Fear ought to produce, and does produce, a right and
holy *manner* of serving God; but its proper legitimate
fruit is to make us abandon everything else except
His service: and this latter fear is based upon the
oneness and the soleness of God. Men would have
truer notions of God, if they meditated more often
upon His Unity. If the spirit of adoration is essential
to all holiness, we must remember also that it is a
spirit which is never perfect unless it flows from our
faith in the Unity of God.

Out of God's Unity comes the attribute of His
immensity. His immensity includes all creatures
within itself, and excludes all ends except God Himself. He occupies, and fills to overflowing, all possible
existence. Wherever we look, there are the rights,
the claims, the properties of God. Actions become
duties and involve responsibilities, only because all
things are God's. It is thus that life is a worship,
and furthermore that it is a worship of fear. God's
immensity is His omnipresence, and the echo of His
omnipresent silence in our hearts is the hush of holy
fear. See how He lies inside our life, and round
about it and under it, and blends it, without mixing
it, with His own awful presence. In some local
heaven or other there is the Vision of His open
majesty. In every nook of earth there is the thrilling of His omnipresence. He concurs with every
natural movement, effort, action, or repose. Grace is
the invisible communication of His Divine Nature, or
the vibration of His Divine Will. His sacramental

life in the Church is a practical communication to
His assumed human nature of His Divine ubiquity.
His personal indwelling as Three Persons in the inner-
most shrine of our unexplored souls is the satisfaction
of His creative love, by means of His uncreated
immensity. How can we say any of these things
without feeling that, as creatures so awfully and so
sacredly possessed with God, we must worship Him
with fear? God is not a mere brightness of life.
He is not only a grand love now, to become a grander
enjoyment hereafter. He is a law, a supremacy, a
sanctity, an uncreated law, a sole supremacy, an
irresponsible and exacting sanctity. The love of
Him is itself a law, and it is a law because of His
sovereign holiness. The very fruition of Him in
heaven is a law, and it is His holiness which makes
it law. The answer of the human soul to all this is
fear, a fear which is a love as well, and a joy, and a
brightness, but still an exceeding great fear. It is
fear which makes love a worship, and enjoyment an
adoration. There cannot be worship without fear, and
there cannot be an unworshipped God.

You will wonder I am taking so much pains to
explain what needs no explanation, and to drive into
you what you have always known and always thought.
I grant you have always known it, but I doubt if you
have always *thought* it; and it is to make you *think* it
that I am taking so much pains. A worship must be
a fear. This is what I am saying. Now let us look
at the two opposite poles of God's creation, heaven and
hell, and see what they have to teach us about fear, and
how they teach it us out of God's supreme Unity.

Everywhere God is worshipped. The diversified life

of the animal kingdom is truly a worship of the Creator, though it is not a worship of intelligence. So also the life of the reprobate in hell is a worship of God, though it is not a worship of the will. Hell is the land of everlasting fear. Fear is the only reasonable thing, the only congruous thing, in that appalling life. The incongruity of fear in hell consists simply in its divorce from love. The life of the lost is not one of mere suffering, as if God had done His worst, and there was nothing more to fear because there was nothing more to expect. The desperate immutability of hell dispenses not its victims from fear. Fear is perhaps one of the most exquisite sufferings of that manifold punishment. The very hopelessness of the state is itself an immortality of agonising fear. The excruciating severity of the chastisement is also itself a fear. Its continuance is a terror. The thought of its endlessness onward and onward for ever keeps up an intolerable panic in the soul, from which its clear and undoubting knowledge of its own state allows it no escape, not so much as that escape of mistiness and indefiniteness where sinners upon earth contrive to find some counterfeit of peace. The hatred of God cannot of itself be otherwise than a paroxysm of infuriated fear, while God's hatred of the lost soul must be to it a fear beyond words, beyond our present thoughts, a very undying death of terror. Try to think how infinite love must hate if it hates at all, and you will see how inconceivably dreadful to a reprobate soul must be its sense of the holy hatred of God. Thus hell worships God with an equable, sustained excess of fear, which is the only truth of hell, the sole reasonable profession of its faith. God is one; hence there is no escape, no choice, no alternative. The Unity of God, which inundates the blessed with jubilee, is to the reprobate the very hopelessness of their punishment, the very foundation of their despair.

But the worship of heaven is not less a worship of fear; for fear is the exceeding joyousness of adoring love. All creation, whether in its extremity of bliss, or its extremity of woe, must fear a God who is the sole God, and whose glory absorbs all the possible praise of all possible creations. The fear of heaven is the thrilling of beatific joy, the trembling of an ecstatic adoration. This fear does not tremble because its happiness is insecure, or because there is any cloud between God and itself. It trembles because of the immense majesty which it sees, because of the amazing familiarity to which it is admitted, and because of that vehement intensity of love to which the glorified soul is raised. All through heaven, except within the tranquil infinity of God Himself, this rapturous fear is universal. Nay the higher we ascend in heaven, the more utter and the more self-abasing is the jubilee of fear. I can conceive that the higher nature of angels would fear more than the lower nature of men; and that the highest grace would tremble more than a lower grace, because it sees God more clearly, or more deeply. I can think of Mary's fear as an ocean of purest praise lying ever before the delighted eye of God. But the fear of the Sacred Humanity of Jesus before the uncreated fires of the Holy Trinity seems to me the crowning magnificence of heaven, because it is its crowning sanctity and its crowning love. It is one of the thoughts of which I never weary, and to which I find myself returning again and again without effort and without intention. Clearly God must everywhere be worshipped. Clearly all worship of Him must be fear, because else it would not be love. Clearly fear must reach its greatest height in heaven, because the worship of heaven is the purest and the truest: as clearly, it seems to me, is the blissful Unity of God the primal fountain of all the creature's fear.

Fear then is the lesson which heaven and hell conspire to teach to earth: and fear is earth's great want in divine things. Multitudes of men are wholly indifferent about God. In hell there is no indifference. Indifference is but the want of fear. Multitudes are altogether forgetful of God. They do not advert even to His existence, much less to His law. In hell neither spirit nor soul forgets Him for one moment. Creatures must first have ceased to fear their Creator, before they can forget Him. We on earth take liberties with God. Even piety is perpetually lapsing into a kind of impertinence, and it is an impertinence brought about by weariness, But piety only becomes wearisome when it is wanting in reverence; and the lack of reverence comes from the lack of fear. Nay the best of us are ungenerous with God; and ungenerosity is but a form of the want of fear. In some respects, you see, earth has need to learn from hell. But how much more has it to learn from heaven. Earth is certainly not the home of happiness; but how much less happiness is there upon earth than there easily might be. What there is is only solid, fresh, invigorating, at ease, and finding life sweet, when it is in the hidden hearts of those who fear God. It beams in their eyes with a special light; it gives to their voices a peculiar tone: it makes their hearts beat with a quiet gaiety, which belongs only to those who fear the Lord their God because He alone is God, and there is none other God but He.

———

2.

PUNISHMENTS AND REWARDS.

Retribution is the complement and the consequence of creation. We came from God, and we are going back to Him. Every life, which He has called out of nothingness, is with irresistible inclination returning to Him. This return is inevitable. It belongs to the act of creation that every rational life should be solemnly and formally approved or disapproved by Him. By creating He has put Himself under an obligation to exercise His justice upon every soul of man as upon every spirit of angel. God being what He is, it is impossible to conceive of creation without a day of judgment. It is as impossible morally for creation to exist without a judgment, as it is physically impossible for judgment to exist without creation. Reward and punishment, therefore, are not gratuitous parts of the divine economy under which we are living. They are necessities in the creation of a God who is all-holy. All reasonable life must necessarily be responsible. All human life with inevitable bent and breathless celerity is for ever streaming back to the feet of God. Helpless in its career, helpless in its velocity, its frightened cry continually is, Enter not into judgment with Thy servant, O Lord. But this universal prayer cannot be answered to the letter. It can only be heard as a profession of faith, and as a petition for mercy. God must judge us. He must exercise His censorship upon every single separate life; and His censorship, like all divine things, must be operative and efficacious. It must not only imply, but it must actually be punishment or reward. The end for which we were created involves judgment and retribution. Punishment and reward are the necessary ways in which God will exercise and manifest His perfections to each of us. Each of us will be infolded and gathered into His justice, either for weal or woe. There, inside His justice, as in an impregnable fastness, lies our eternity; there and nowhere else. Blessed for evermore be the immensity, the exactitude, and the unspeakable sanctity of His justice!

But can we say these things without fear? If all creation lies and lives in the expectation of the divine justice, can its life be other than a life of fear? All judgments are nervous things. There is something in our nature which is peculiarly sensitive to all judgments, even to the very fact of being judged at all. What must this be when a divine judgment is in question? What else can it be than a fear, whose reasonable excesses nothing short of an assuring revelation can have any right, as well as any power, to tranquillise? Let us consider this matter more at length. There is nothing to be said which we do not already know, and which we do not take in at a single glance. But consideration will delay us over the matter, and grace will come with the delay. The worship of God is a worship of fear, because of His rewards and punishments. This is the obvious proposition with which

we are going to occupy ourselves, and we will begin
by speaking of punishment, not because it is either
prior in God's intention or more natural to Him, but
simply that we may avoid having to end with a consideration which we should not entertain at all, if it
were not absolutely necessary to the health of our
souls.

We must love God very tenderly to be able to think
of Him in His anger. We could not bear such a
thought, if our faith did not lean upon the immensity
of His love. But in order to understand rightly the
fearfulness of the divine punishments, we must first
get an idea of what anger must be like in the all-holy,
all-perfect God. What would not creatures do in
their anger, if only they had the power? It is simply
the want of power which curbs them. Anger would
break the whole world to pieces, if it could. How
awful is it then that God's anger, which must in itself
be so much more terrible a thing than a creature's
anger, is in possession of infinite power. There is
nothing to restrain it. There is no limit to its energy.
Anger, anger in God, anger omnipotent, it is not easy
to think of these things without sinking on our knees,
and hiding our faces in our hands, and praying a prayer
in our hearts which we should find it difficult to put
into words. But God's anger is not only infinite in
power, it is also infinite in wisdom. There is no blindness in it, no ignorance, no passion, no obscurity. It
is in itself nothing less than boundless, self-collected
wisdom. Neither is it ever sudden or precipitate.
We are amazed at its slowness, at its patience, at its
seeming deliberation, at the way in which it lets itself
accumulate. Yet all this makes it a thousandfold more

terrible when it comes. It gathers itself up before it
springs, as if to make its aim more certain, as if to
acquire velocity and force with which to spring.   But,
while it is slow in its growth, it is also unintermitting.
It is always advancing, always multiplying itself.   Not
inconsistent with this characteristic slowness anger in
God is also marked by an unspeakable vehemence
which is not passionate, because its impetuosity is incomparably beyond the possible energy of any created
passion.   It is as if the whole force of the immense
Divine life were thrown into it, at once expanding and
yet concentrating itself in the glorious outbursts of
His wrath.   Yet is it also unutterable peace.   It lives
in an immensity of calm light.   There is no quickening
of the pulses.   There is not a shadow of change, not a
trace of perturbation.   There is no burning, no ruffling.
God is not agitated, He is not provoked.   Hence He
repents not of His anger, neither is His bliss over-
shadowed by the horror of the darkness or the torture
of the penalties in which His anger has involved His
guilty creatures.   The anger, which blows through
hell like the blasts of an insufferable tempest, is nothing
less than uncreated tranquillity, and the beatitude of
inviolable repose.

How wonderful in God are those two abysses, the
abyss of power, and the abyss of wisdom.   They are
the wells out of which the Divine anger draws its
waters everlastingly.   But there is a third abyss, an
abyss of love ; and, alas ! it is out of that depth that
the anger of God draws most of its intolerable
perfection.   Wounded love, slighted love, despised
compassion, neglected grace, and coldness which refused
to be heated, a hardness which would not be softened in

the furnaces of Divine love, even when their fires had been fed with Gethsemane and Calvary, these are the fountains of the overwhelming wrath of God, the imperturbable provocations of His infinite, insatiable, unsparing justice. His anger is the sister of His love. Behold, then, these three abysses, the abysses of power, of wisdom, and of love. Take them into your soul by reverent meditation. Measure them diligently, measure them repeatedly, were it only to convince yourself how immeasurable they are. Then try to conceive the unfathomable resources of God's vindictiveness. Alas! we can only adore in panic-stricken silence the mere possibilities of the divine anger. Let us hold the painful vision well to our inward eye, that our over-buoyant nature never may forget it. There is salvation in the bare remembrance of it.

But the unfathomable resources of God's vindictive anger do not present themselves to our minds as a mere inexhaustible immensity, a vast store or treasury garnered up in His omnipotence. They are a living unity. They have a shape, a form, a mission. They come in order. They precede and follow, by the action of a majestic law. They are not inert, unwieldy, or unsorted. They are set in array by the Divine perfections. They are the wonderful and worshipful action of unbounded holiness. If they are terrible by their number, their weight, their measure, and by their kinds, kinds to which creation affords no parallel because they have no shadows in created things, they are most terrible by the appalling magnificence of their justice. The justice of God's anger is in reality its unbearable splendour. Justice!

it seems as if justice must be unjust to so miserable and infirm a thing as a creature. Mercy surely, nay rather the laxity of indulgence, were the only appropriate justice to such a helplessness as human fraility. Justice is so royal, so decisive, so inevitable, so intolerably truthful;—how shall creation live under such a rule? Its minuteness looks like cruelty to the necessities of our negligence, its unchangeableness a tyranny to a fickleness and a levity so unavoidable as ours. Is it not, then, hard in Him to make justice the arbiter of our eternity? In all the records of the saints is there an attitude of grace which fills us more full of awe than that of St. Paul, small in stature, and with the dignity of his countenance weakened by his sore eyes, boldly throwing himself on the sheer justice of God, and claiming his " crown of justice " which it has been the business and as it were the duty of the " just Judge " to lay up for him? Surely if it be not foolish to use such words, there would be something less terrible in God's anger, if it were less just. There is something very crushing, very hopeless, in the thought that God is always so completely, so immutably, so unanswerably in the right. Even the right to complain is a right which cannot belong to creatures. It is denied to them by the very fact of their creation, a creation about which they were not consulted, and yet which must have eternal consequences to every one of them.

 This is what anger is like in God. It is nothing monstrous or disproportionate, or passionate, or loud, or tyrannical. It is calm, orderly, equitable, noiseless as omnipotence, tranquil as infinity. Our souls are attracted to the contemplation of it by its succeeding beauty. It unlocks for us the most wonderful theology of God. It illuminates the highest pinnacles of the divine perfections. It, and it alone, enables us to understand the excesses, the disproportions, the extravagances of Divine love. How shall we speak worthily of this exceeding beauty of the Divine anger? To our ideas anger is a thing which comes and goes. Who can conceive of a whole life of anger, of vehement, yet equable and sustained anger? Yet look at the inexplicable adorable permanence of anger in God through all eternity as part of the Creator's blissful life! What must His anger be for Him to rejoice with infinite jubilee therein?

Let us rest awhile, and go over again this account of what anger is like in God. We see how far short of our thoughts our words are: and how far short of the reality are our feeble thoughts! Yet what is the soul obliged to say to itself? This anger of God, this incomprehensible mystery—I have actually incurred it by sin. It has once rested upon me. It once intended eternal punishment for me. Is it resting on me still? Has it withdrawn its terrible intention? I live in God. I live upon God. I cannot do without Him. He is all in all to me. Why then do I ever think of anything, except avoiding His anger and securing His love? God can be angry. God is always angry, always angry with some of His creatures. Is He angry with me? Oh how foolish life looks by the side of the wrath of God! It takes its pastime, parades its liberty, and makes a noise with its silly pleasures; and all the while it is hemmed in by the beautiful, holy, everlasting anger of the Most High! Incredibly silly, unserious life! It is like

a baby clapping its hands and crowing at thunder
and lightning.

If there be an insanity among the sons of men it is
unseriousness.   Do not men see that the unprovoked-
ness of God is one of the glories of His anger ?   He
is silent.   He makes no sign.   He interrupts nothing.
Pleasure, folly, lightness, and self-will run smoothly,
and the mere smoothness is mistaken for a blessing.
The great broad river of mercies flow from His throne
with as full a current as ever ; and the sunshine of
forbearance, almost of complacency, is upon its waters
incessantly.   It is as if saints and preachers were
critical, and God indulgent, because He had some
higher, vaster, and more benignant principles of criticism ; and of a truth omniscience must needs bring
with it an immense benignity.   All life is a pressure of
manifold urgent laws.   But it does not seem so.   God's
love makes Him look as if He did not notice things.
There is nothing which Providence looks less like
than urgency.   We think God more than patient with
our foolishness ; we think Him pleased, just as fathers
are pleased with the exuberant nonsense of their children.
Why will not men see that all this is not only compatible with God's anger, but often a manifestation of
it ?   He must be either unwise or unbelieving, who
does not tremble at the slowness of God to be provoked.   Nay, is not the Divine patience itself part of
the Divine anger ?   In the Andes the winds are
seldom still ; but, when they are still, the Indians hear
the indescribable moaning of the volcanic fire, and they
dread that imprisoned murmur more than the howling
of the angry blast or the crackling of the mountain
thunder.   Heavenly Father ! may we never for an

hour forget the glories of Thine anger, or yet that its greatest glory is that it is the anger of a Father!

The pressure of such an anger must be intolerable, and the ways in which it revenges itself unutterably terrible. Its punishments must be almost incomprehensible from the very extremity of their fearfulness. All things in God are so successful, so complete, so triumphant, so superabundant, that we tremble to think of the amazing severity of His chastisements, especially when we have rejected Him as our King, and disowned Him as our Father. Let us think of the characteristics of the Divine punishments. There is, first of all, their inexorable holiness. They are so just that they leave no ground for complaint, while we are so guilty that we have forfeited all right to complain. The sense of being wronged is a support to the pride of our endurance. It imparts a dignity to suffering and a toughness to the human will, which makes it respectable even amidst the indignities of torture. But there is no such thing in the punishments of God. Our will is unnerved and prostrated by guilt and shame and exceeding fear. The soul in its chastisement cannot collect itself, cannot put itself into an attitude to endure, cannot make out a case for itself, can neither concentrate itself nor yet distract itself. It is all loosened by fear, all abandoned to irresistible panic, all sickened by the faintness of manifold terror. This comes of the holiness of the divine punishments. Moreover holiness is exacting. We see this even in our own intercourse with holy men. There is something exacting about them, something which hinders our being at our ease, something which almost chafes us, as if they were not doing us justice. This is only a shadow of the exigencies of God's sanctity. It demands such a full measure of retribution. It exacts such a minute correspondence of pain to guilt, throwing into the scales its own infinity of requirements besides. It is so insatiable of reparation, and claims such unimaginable restitutions. Who can think of these things without fear? The lost soul has thrown away the Passion of our Blessed ‹Lord, and so has left itself alone with the un'created sanctity and the vindictive justice of God. It has to cope with these amazing perfections of His all-holy majesty, and it has to cope with them by suffering the extremes of their severity. When we add to the terrible unforgettingness of the Divine justice the triumphant jubilee of its successful vengeance, the holiness of God's punishments makes us turn away from the vision of them as something which we are too feeble to endure.

Need we add that the holiness of God's punishments implies a most transcendent severity? Yet we have no figures by which we can even vaguely bring home to ourselves the nature or degree of this severity. Nothing about fallen men has been so inventive as his cruelty; and a very slight acquaintance with history enables us to put down a sum of barbarous infliction, of ingenious torment, of protracted misery, and of diversified agony, which it is intolerable to think of. But the severity of the divine punishments is something far beyond all this. Man's cruelty is limited by the powers of endurance which reside in a mortal life; and, incredibly vast as those powers are, nevertheless they form a limit and they furnish an escape. But the indestructible immortality of a lost soul even

in the tightest grasp of omnipotent anger—this gives
us another measure of the severity of God's punishments. It is a severity not only beyond all historical
record of cruelty, or even the union of all actual
cruelties, but beyond all our imaginations of conceivable
torture. I believe that God's punishments beyond the
grave will completely take His creatures by surprise,
from their exceeding severity. It is implied in the
incredible, profuse, many-sided love of our probation
here. It is implied in the malice of our own rejection
of the Precious Blood. It is implied in the spotless
magnificence of the divine perfections. I believe that
hell will horribly astonish and amaze its victims.
Hence it is that there is something so wounding to
Christian reverence in light words about the chastisements of purgatory. God revealed to B. Henry Suso
His displeasure at them. They come from a want of
appreciation of the divine justice. God's glory requires
a splendour and an exuberance in all things which are
His: in His punishments therefore it requires an immense severity.

The variety of the divine punishments is another of
their characteristics. As God, the one sovereign good,
contains all goods within Himself in their diversity
and in their plenitude, so the loss of God, the one
sovereign evil, contains all evils within itself in their
diversity and in their plenitude. How various are
the pains which flesh and nerve can feel! How
multitudinous the diseases with which suffering can
play upon our bodies, as if it were some musical
instrument! These are but figures of the divine
punishments. God can find unimaginable capabilities
of pain in the immortal body, and yet more un-

imaginable capabilities in the soul. His justice will
tax these capabilities to the utmost, and will exhaust
their almost unfathomable resources. Kinds of punishment undreamed of lie beyond the grave. A world
where anger is as much the rule as love is here, and
severity as prodigal as mercy. Oh majesty of, God!
who can endure the thought? There are the in-
numerable kinds of punishment, and yet there is the
monotony of their insupportable degree. But it is a
monotony which, while it is a separate punishment in
itself, will neither confuse the kinds of suffering, nor
blunt the sense of them by the continuity of its
pressure. The whole soul will be always wholly in
each of these thousandfold torments at once. Alas!
if men would but meditate on God, what an understanding they would get of the sinfulness of sin!

There is another characteristic of the divine punishments which arises out of the perfections of God, and
especially out of His wisdom. It is their dreadful
harmony and congruity with the peculiarities of our
individual character. All that He does, as I have said
before, is efficacious and successful. He knows us as our
Creator. He knows the punishment to which each of us
is most sensible, and He awards that punishment to us.
not simply because it is the one to which we are most
sensible, but because our sins arise for the most part from
that which is most characteristic in us. We all have
a special character. Our keenness of feeling mostly
resides in our speciality of character; and it is precisely by the propensities which are strongest in each
of us that we chiefly transgress the divine laws. Each
man is haunted by some horrors and panics, which
his own character and sensibility exaggerate to him.

Every one has some pain which he can bear less than any other pain, and some repugnances which are in his case peculiarly insurmountable. These particularities coincide in a great degree with our faults, and with the shape of our wickedness. Hence they supply to our omniscient Sovereign peculiar resources for the most intolerable punishment. Just as the mindfulness and minuteness of God's love is such a prolific and perennial source of joy, consolation, and peace to us, so is the way in which He intently individualises our punishment, fits it to us, makes it grow out of ourselves, and takes care to inflict it with a considerate purpose to make it unbearable to our peculiar selves, a source of wretchedness, dismay, and helpless perturbation, to those who have miserably elected to spend their eternity without Him.

Finally, excess is in our way of speaking a necessary characteristic of the divine punishments, as it is of all the divine works. The torments of hell would make our sensibilities sicken if we knew them as they really are. They would probably, because of the tenuity of our grace, offend our sense of justice and moderation. The saints, who have seen visions of hell, appear to have required miraculous support in order to live. The punishments of God are far beyond all moderation in the number of their kinds, and in the intensity of their degree. Neither do they fluctuate. They are always at high tide. Divine excesses are always equable. Omnipotence is at work on both sides. On the one hand, it is sustaining the torture in its unmitigated atrocity and impetuous fury. On the other hand, it is supporting the immortal life of the culprit, so that the heat cannot break it, nor the weight

crush it, nor the blows shatter it, nor the deadliness
extinguish it.   How can we bring home to ourselves
this excess of the divine punishments ?   <u>Some theologians say that the Passion of our Blessed Lord was
a suffering less than the pains of hell.   Can we imagine
an eternity of the Passion, and then add to it the
absence of grace, the inferiority of our souls, the sense
of personal guilt, and the heart's inward storm against
God ?</u>   Surely no one can do so.   It is one of those
few things which can be put into words, but not into
thoughts.   Yet this would give us some idea of the
excess of God's punishments.   A soul, once beautiful,
with the image of God curiously and exquisitely
delineated upon it, all gemmed with graces, all radiant
with the Precious Blood,—behold it, in solitariness,
fallen into the hands of God's everlasting wrath, with
all the flames and torrents of the divine punishments
running round it like an angry sea—is it not a fearful
vision ?   So have I seen a dark rock in the midst of
the stormy waves : leagues of rolling ocean were
breaking upon it ; gathering themselves up they ran
towards it along the level of the sea, like battering
rams of colossal magnitude, and the inanimate rock
groaned as it was struck.   Then another while the
waves sank into a boiling hollow, and rose again like
towers of green water, and leaned over the rock, and
broke themselves in two, and fell upon it as if they
must have crushed it to atoms, and the thunder of
their fall could be heard for miles along the desolate
coast.   It looked like an emblem of the soul in the
ocean of God's anger.   So I thought ; for there was
the power in the waves to lash and buffet, and there
was the power in the rock to bear and to keep its

place. But I saw that no earthly image is without its
accompaniment of gentleness, and so is no fitting type
of the perished soul. For often the waves threatened
and then withdrew, or they leaped towards the rock
and swerved as if they had a will of their own and a
kindly one, or they broke short of the rock and only
laved its sides with soft fringes of creamy foam; the
sea seemed to spare the rock, as I watched it; and
then too the sun made rainbows in the breakers, and the
green of the underwater light was always beautiful.
But God's punishments never miss, never fail, never
intermit, never swerve, never spare. There is always
about them that dreadful unerringness, that dreadful
success, that quiet indubitable efficacy, which makes us
tremble more than any other feature of their adorable
severity.

How happily, how carelessly, how thoughtlessly the
summer day goes round: and so day follows day, and
we are sucked in by this whirlpool of happiness, as if
flowers, and song, and sunshine were the very materials
of our lives, as if we had only to live as the river flows,
lapsing through the green fields in the daylight and in
the starlight, with no other mission than to flow! God
hides Himself till He almost deceives us. We neither
see nor hear His anger. Yet all the while He and His
law and His justice and His wrath go on abidingly;
and by the light of them there is something hideous in
this unseriousness of ours. Are we going to perish for
want of thought? It is not faith we want, but thought.
From various and seemingly opposite texts of Scripture
there is a controversy among theologians as to whether
it is easy to be saved or hard to be saved. There is,
however, no controversy as to the easiness of being lost.

God so hems us in with love, and so fortifies us with
grace, that we may have at some season of our lives to
make an effort to break away from Him, and to stifle
the remorse of our first few sins.   But, if it be an
effort, it is not a difficult effort; and, that first step
once taken, the facility of perdition is something to
take our breath away if we could see it depicted in a
material shape.

Hell is a short word, but it comprehends a volu-
minous science.   The mere fact of hell ought to be
one of the supreme facts of the world.   There is a part
of creation erected expressly for punishment.   The
punishments are beyond human conception.   It is
very vast, and densely peopled.   Its torments are not
only atrocious, but eternal.   Its population is being
increased daily.   The revelations of the saints teach
us that its most fiery abysses are set aside for bad
Catholics, who have known Jesus and have despised
His Passion.   In all probability, there are men there
whom we have seen, to whom we have spoken, with
whom we have lived, and whom we have loved.   We
believe this, and yet we are unserious!

The road thither!   Let us think of that.   There
is not a single difficulty in the way: not a temptation
to be resisted, not a passion to be mortified.   We have
only to do what we are most drawn to do.   We have
only to omit what is irksome.   We have only to please
the world, and to do as the world does.   Indeed we
have only to take life easily, and lo! the road is tra-
velled, and we are there; and yet we are unserious!

What is wanted to ruin a soul eternally?   The
mere leaving undone of many things very hard to do.
A single sin, even of momentary thought, is sufficient,

if the moment were sufficient for deliberation. It is easy to be lost because venial sin glides so smoothly into mortal, because habits of sin are so quickly formed, and, when formed, so obstinate, because temptations are so various, continuous, and violent, because we can only cling to God by supernatural means, because we are too easily contented with our sorrow for sin, because we make too free with God, because of the bad example of others, because vigilance is a great strain upon us, because we have all a besetting sin, which mostly ruins us through our disbelief in it, and finally because of the covert sins of worldliness. Who can deny any one of these propositions? Yet we are unserious!

A God, one of the occupations of whose blessed life is punishment, needs surely to be worshipped with our most humble fears. This needs no proving. Let us pass on to His rewards, and see how they also furnish us with motives for chaste and holy fear. It is vain to attempt to describe the divine rewards. We know already that eye has not seen, nor ear heard, nor man's heart conceived what God has in store for those who love Him. We may say all we have already said of the divine punishments, only in an opposite sense, and the picture will be more than we can take in. But we must remember that God is more wonderful in His rewards than in His punishments. It is more natural to Him, if we may dare to use such a word, to reward than to punish. There are two considerations especially which we ought to bear in mind. In the first place, His justice is not quite free in punishment. It cannot claim all it might claim from the lost soul, because it is already partly satisfied from another source. It is held back by the Passion of our blessed Lord, the exuberance of Whose satisfactions makes itself felt in the dungeons of hell. Even in that region of all woeful things, amid those unutterably disconsolate beings, there is some smoothing of the darkness, some quelling of the fires, which comes from Calvary. But, in the rewards of God, all that holds back His vindictive justice is only a spur, an additional motive, a new urgency to the magnificence of His compassion, and to the abundance of His liberality. The very Passion, which causes hell to be less terrible than it strictly should have been, makes heaven to be a thousandfold more glorious than the most liberal justice could have made it. This is one consideration by which we can measure the glorious excess of the divine rewards over the divine punishments.

The second consideration comes from the very nature of His rewards. When He punishes He has to create the materials for punishment. He has to fashion hell, to gift its fires, to thicken its darkness, to feed its worms, and to invent its nameless unimagined torments. It all comes from without Him. It is all creation. In punishing He is limited by the capabilities of nothingness. But in rewarding He gives Himself. He communicates His own blessedness. He becomes the very possession of the blessed. Himself! All heaven lies in that one word. I believe that the accessories of heaven, the joys of the glorified mind, the loves of the glorified heart, the delights of the glorified senses, the sights, and sounds, and fragrances, and touches, and tastes, the familiarity of the angels, the company of the saints, the intercourse with Mary, the sight of Jesus, amount in themselves alone to an

accumulation of bliss far greater than the accumulation
of the horrors in hell, even comprising the indescribable pain of the loss of God. But we have to add to
all that accumulation of glory in heaven's own proper
joy, the sight, and the possession, and the fruition
of God Himself. There is thus no parity whatever
between the joys of heaven and the pains of hell.
There can be no comparison between them. The
Incarnation which holds back the punishments en-
larges the reward. God punishes with created things,
He rewards with His own uncreated Self. Heaven,
therefore, is not to God's love what hell is to His
anger. It is something incomparably more.

To conceive justly of heaven, we know is impossible. But it is well to meditate upon it, so far as
we are able. The joys of heaven have always been one
of the most powerful motives of the saints, and meditation upon them is one of the most direct roads to
disinterested love. The incalculable magnificence of
the divine rewards is a splendour and a profusion
beyond our thoughts: but we can make enormous
sums of magnificent, beautiful, and refulgent joys in
our thoughts; and to do that, and then to reject
them as being less than a drop to the ocean, is a
fruitful exercise for our souls, over which the things
of earth still exercise far too powerful an attraction.
Their satisfying sweetness furnishes matter for another
kind of meditation, a meditation which grows both in
power, in novelty, and in contentment, as we learn
more and more the unsatisfying hollowness and inevitable treachery of all created things. Even we can
see what an immensity is required to satisfy the
cravings of a soul, and what an inexhaustible pleni-

tude it must be which shall fill up the manifold profound gulfs which there are in the soul, and of which
the huge ocean-beds of the material creation are but
an unworthy figure. The variety of the divine
rewards is a labyrinth in which it is very salutary
often to lose ourselves. It gives us courage when we
despond. It gives us patience to endure. We cannot imagine a smell we have never smelled, nor a
sound we have never heard. Our fancy cannot
decorate a planet or a star, except with fantastic
comminglings of the rarer and the stranger forms of
earth. What must it be to know that there are
millions of pleasures waiting us in heaven, for which
we have neither name nor thought? Most men have
had sweetnesses in prayer. Is there anything to which
we can compare them? Are they not simply things
out of another world? St. Teresa might well say,
that all earthly delights put together, even if they
were made eternal, are mere vilenesses compared with
the tastes which God gives of Himself even in this
life. The exquisite suitableness of the divine rewards
for our own individual souls is another source of
delighted meditation, leading at once to tears, because
it is such a special revelation of the minuteness of
God's love. The gift of a reverent familiarity with
God comes quite peculiarly out of that meditation.
Then, finally, there is the grandeur of the eternity of
these rewards. We can make no images, indulge in
no figures here. Our prayer becomes silence, while
the shadow of eternity passes over our souls, like the
shadow-path of an eclipse over the landscape, trans-
figuring all things by the unearthliness of its gorgeous
darkness. From the passage of that shadow we rise

up more changed than we believe. O heaven! all
calm, and shapely, and orderly as thou art, how dost
thou surpass all the revels of our fancy, all the wild-
ness of our dreams!

But how are the rewards of God a ground of fear?
The question may be answered by asking another.
Have we never felt a sacred fear growing in our souls
as we have been thinking of the joys of heaven?
Have we not felt more as if something were at stake
which intimately concerned ourselves, as if something
of our own were being perilled, as if doubts were like
cold gusts of wind nobody knows whence, and as if
these doubts were more painful and more unreasonable
than usual,—have we not felt all this more about
heaven than we felt it about hell? The truth is, that
the very magnitude of the divine rewards makes us
nervous. We fear to lose what it would be so dreadful
a thing to lose, and yet what we have so little right to
expect. If the reward were less, it would seem to be
more within our reach. A great prize causes more
trepidation in the combatant than a little prize.
This great heaven, whose golden fruit hangs so nearly
within our reach, seems to grow on the edge of a
precipice, and the least breath of wind waves the
bough over the abyss, and seems to take it out of
reach. How near to us it hangs, yet how easy it is
to miss it; and, if it is missed—we dare not think
what then. It must not be missed. We think of
the immensity of God's mercy, and the thought rests
us like the sight of an outspread sea with the sun
upon it, tawnily gilding the sails of the scarcely
moving ships. But when we return to the thought of
the magnificence of the divine rewards, somehow the

thought of the divine compassion loses its mastery over us, and tranquillises us no longer. Who has not felt this?

Moreover what wins heaven? Perseverance; and perseverance is just the grace which cannot be merited. If we are standing by the side of the cross now, how hard it is to keep our footing; and yet we are to keep it perhaps for twenty years longer. We cannot think without dismay of those unevennesses of grace, about which St. Teresa was so fond of speaking. What if God were to take us at the ebb instead of the flood? But it is St. Teresa also who tells us that He never does so, that He calls His elect when they are at their best estate.* Then too these advancing multiplying years, what are they doing to us? Rooting us in the earth, fortifying habits, accumulating interests, magnifying affections. I fear that detachment is a grace easier to the young than to the old. The huge quantity of grace which we receive also comes into the account. It is frightening to think of the obligations we are incurring, of the responsibilities we are multiplying, because of the grace which we receive. To how little of it do we correspond! How little of it do we turn into masculine persistent holiness! How the inspirations of the Holy Ghost fly past us unheeded, like strains of music on the wind! None of this looks like heaven. Here surely is most rational ground for fear. It is heavenly-mindedness

---

* Cartas de St. Teresa. Madrid, 1778, vol. i. c. xxxv. Pues siempre lleva en el mejor estado. The French Jansenist translation falsified this passage. Exception was taken to a similar sentiment in the Creator and the Creature (p. 382, third edition), and I did not know at that time that St. Teresa had taught the same doctrine, or that the University of Paris had condemned it

which is the prophecy of heaven : and see how we are clinging to the ways and loves of earth !

We may conclude therefore that the rewards and punishments of God are both sources of holy fear, and that meditation on heaven leads us to a salutary fear with no less cogency than meditation upon hell, although in a different way. The fear of the Lord is not only the beginning of wisdom, but the fulness of it also. "The fear of the Lord is the religiousness of knowledge. Religiousness shall keep and justify the heart; it shall give joy and gladness. It shall go well with him that feareth the Lord, in the days of his end he shall be blessed. To fear God is the fulness of wisdom, and fulness is from the fruits thereof. The fear of the Lord is a crown of wisdom, filling up peace and the fruit of salvation." *

3

OUR OWN SIN AND MISERY.

If we look at religion from the point of view of our own sin and misery, we see also that it must needs be a worship of fear. Next to the majesty of God there is nothing of which we are so ignorant as the malice of sin. If it is one half of practical religion to learn the grandeurs of God, it is the other half to learn the sinfulness of sin : but St. Teresa tells us that the two lessons are in truth one single operation of grace.

If our minds are rightly balanced in spiritual things, there is nothing depressing in the consideration of our

* Ecclus. i. 17-22.

own unworthiness.   Holy fear brings with it no discouragement.   On the contrary, it is itself the very
vigour of the soul.   The fear which discourages is the
fear which comes of scanty reverence, and of that
offensive familiarity with God which belongs to those
who do not live habitually in His presence, but who
worship Him intermittingly or only on occasions.
The sacred writer says, "The fear of God is the beginning of love;" but then he adds, "and the beginning
of faith is to be fast joined to it."   We may therefore approach the subject of our own sin and misery
without bringing upon ourselves that greatest of all
spiritual evils, discouragement.   Our confidence in
God will rise in proportion as all trust in self eva-
porates from our souls.   There is always something
cheerful in truth, simply because it *is* truth.   What is
practical religion but the conduct which follows from
the sense of sin?   Moreover it is not sin in the abstract,
but our own sin which we require to know.   We do
not want to convince ourselves that all God's creatures
must fear Him, as that we in particular should very
specially fear Him.   Let us now try to learn this
lesson from the consideration of our own sin and
misery.

Unfortunately, the exceeding sinfulness of sin is one
of those matters, which has to be taken in great measure on faith.   It is impossible for us to comprehend
the peculiar horror which there is in a creation falling
from its Creator.   Nothing else is parallel to it.
Nothing else supplies with principles and standards
for forming a judgment.   We do not at all understand what it is to create; and we very imperfectly
understand what it is to be created.   We cannot

measure the ineffable love which was the motive of creation, nor can we comprehend the mysterious sacredness and intimacy of the tie which should exist between the Creator and the creature. The meaning of creation is to be sought in the eternal loneliness of God's self-sufficing majesty, and who shall go there to seek it? He calls creation out of nothing, and it is not free not to be called. He makes it free, when it is already committed to the risks of its life, and then it falls. Its fall is the free use of its own freedom; but it has been a fatal freedom to itself, and it appears in some sense to have impaired the freedom of God Himself. He is not tranquilly supreme, as it looks to us. He has an opponent. He has not undisturbed dominion, in the highest sense of dominion. To crush a rebellion is not to reign in the highest sense of reigning. Sometimes it looks as if another God had appeared, as if the Supreme Sovereignty were actually divided. This is an unbearable thought, but it is one which may assist us to bring home to ourselves the real iniquity of sin. To understand sin, then, we must understand creation, we must understand hell, we must understand God, whereas we can understand none of these things. We know that all God's government is good, and wise, and beautiful, and kind. This is a truth which all who know God are ready to die for. It is not only our faith, but our common sense as well. But it cannot be proved except to love, nor explained except to those who are morally prepared to admit the explanation.

But, if the horror of sin be so inexplicable, is not that in itself a most cogent motive of fear? Imagine the unimaginable sanctity of God.

I. The sanctity of God.
1. His spotless purity — beyond word — beyond thought.
2. The sanctity of angels is but darkness to His light.
3. Even our Lady's holiness is but as a blemish compared to it.
4. He is the Fountain of all other holiness that is.
5. He is the measure of all holiness: it is derived from his character, and He exults in the infinity of His sanctity.

II. Our misery.
1. Our sinful origin.
2. Our extreme weakness.
3. Our past sins, their number, and enormity.
4. The triflingness of the penance we have done, and of the sorrow we feel.
5. Our present state, and our idea of the future.
6. Our meannesses and unamiabilities, and self-loves.
7. The stained, mixed, polluted character of all our good.

III. This is in the hands of God's sanctity.
1. To give the minutest account of forgotten years.
2. With an incredible divine searching of motives.
3. And justice done upon each thing with exactitude.
4. And the divine requisitions immutable, and not to be lowered.
5. And we not knowing at this moment whether we deserve love or wrath at His hands.

Shall we then dare to take liberties with a God like this?

4.

FROM THE NATURE OF GRACE.

I. The world we live in is such an unthought-of world of gifts, if we could only see.

   1. Common mercies would seem to be almost embarrassing us.

   2. Such a section of creation busied in looking after us.

   3. Such a stir because of us in heaven, and such angels thronging round us.

   4. Such showers of wonderful graces, ceaseless, ceaseless, ceaseless.

   5. Such an entwining of the arms of God's loving presence round us.

II. All privileges fill us full of fear, grace most of all from its nature.

   1. What it is in itself.

   2. Its abundance.

   3. Its delicacy.

   4. Its swiftness.

   5. Its individual meaning to ourselves.

   6. A lost grace is always lost.

   7. A rejected grace makes other graces shy.

   8. All grace leaves us worse if not better, harder if not softer.

   9. Grace, each grace has so many unfathomable meanings.

III. How our case stands, as a motive for fear.

   1. Look at our past grace, wasted, or half used.

   2. Our present irreverent carelessness about grace.

3. Our grace may be a fixed quantity, and we may have almost used it up.

4. Many great saints could have been made out of the grace which has only made us what we are.

5. Saint Bernard's three fears (Serm. 54 in Cantica).

   (1) For grace received.

   (2) More for grace lost.

   (3) More still for grace recovered.

      Why these three fears?

Oh, we must be patient with our gifts, their greatness and their number. God is not entrapping us. Our salvation is His sincerest Will, only He will not save us against our own wills; only let us fear like earnest men, and all will go well for our eternity.

5.

FROM THE PERFECTIONS AND CHARACTER OF GOD.

How little we know of God, yet how much we know of Him! And how that little makes us long for more, and how that much makes us fear!

I. The biography of God.

   1. Eternal; this puts creation and the creature in its true light.

   2. The fall of the angels.

   3. The fall of man, and consequent judgments.

   4. The Passion.

   5. The doom, and the eternal sentence.

II. The perfections of God as sources of fear.

   1. His omnipotence—what can we do?

2. His wisdom—how can we hide ?

3. His mercy—what must it be when slighted ?

4. His immutability—we cannot turn Him—*we must turn.*

5. His dominion, beyond all conceivable dominions.

III. What we may call the character of God.

  1. His secrecy.

    (1) Hides his purposes and judgments.

    (2) Acts without our knowing, almost.

    (3) Yet expects us to find Him out.

  2. His jealousy.

    (1) Something more delicate than taking offence.

    (2) More jealous the more He loves.

    (3) Jealous rather of what we prefer, than of our having but a cold preference for Him : hence the misery of worldliness.

  3. His not repeating Himself.

    (1) In other souls, rarely.

    (2) In the same soul, more rarely.

    (3) So that we cannot get on with Him by mere habit, but adoration and *taste.*

  4. His slowness.

    (1) So that He wearies us.

    (2) Sometimes a life is not long enough for His plans.

    (3) Hence exacting great promptitude from us.

  5. His swiftness.

    (1) He suddenly turns to being swift from slow.

    (2) So that this swiftness frightens us.

    (3) Some lives go like lightning flashes, and the results are stereotyped and irrevocable.

Oh once get to Him, and what unfathomable seas

of gladness will all these perfections and characteristics furnish us with!

    IV. Yet could a stranger from some other world
        gather this character of God from the lives we
        are leading?

      1. From its obvious control over our actions.

      2. From our deportment in prayer.

      3. From our conversation.

      4. From our solitary thoughts.

      5. From the objects of our interest, and from our
        tastes.

Oh wonderful holiness of God, how overwhelming,
and yet how infinitely dear! our past lives are some
thing quite terrible in the clearness of its magnifying
light. Nay, there is something so fearfully unholy,
even in our best deeds, that we must shut our eyes,
and fall blindly into the lap of His compassion, and
cry, O Father! Father! mercy, eternal, boundless
mercy!

6.

THE EXCELLENCE OF FEAR.

It peoples heaven, it makes death easy, and it is the
only solid happiness on earth. "Thou hast made his
strength fear."*

    I. Its place in the spiritual life.

      1. It increases and widens our faith.

      2. It gives vigour and activity to our hope.

      3. It deepens our love and is its safeguard.

      4. It leads with gentle compulsion to mortification.

* Ps. lxxxviii. 41.

5. It goes nearest of all graces to ensure perseverance.

II. Practices of holy fear.

 1. To be slow and measured in what we do.
 2. Specially with God's own things, such as sacraments.
 3. Outward reverence both to show and to cause inward.
 4. To meditate on the revealed terrors of God.
 5. To cultivate abiding sorrow for sin.

III. The joys of holy fear.

 1. Because of its safety—and the feeling of safety is one of the most calming of graces.
 2. Because of its fervour—and it has the gift of making us fervent without exciting us.
 3. Because it makes us do all things well and carefully, and this gives an elastic cheerful feeling to our souls.
 4. Because of the power which it gives us over life, and over self, and over temptations, and over all external unhappiness.
 5. Because it is a supernatural joy in itself, and so partakes of the infinite bliss of God.

The grander God is, the more is He an object of adoring fear: but the grander He is, so much the grander will be our blessedness when we possess Him to all eternity; and the more we fear Him now, the more certain will our possession of Him be hereafter! Let us end with the words of David, "What have I in heaven but Thee, and besides Thee what do I desire on earth? For Thee my flesh and my heart hath fainted away: Thou art the God of my heart, and the God that is my portion for ever." *

* Ps. lxxii. 25.

IV.

THE EYE OF GOD.

I. Life with a witness.
 1. Occasional desire all have for privacy and solitude.
 2. Constraining effect of a witness on all we do and say, and even on our thoughts.
 3. If the witness were—(1) observant, (2) silent, then so much the more.
 4. We see the effects of the world's eye upon us; its tyranny.
 5. We wish sometimes to escape from the presence even of those we love.

II. The Eye of God.
 1. Life is in reality thus witnessed, and more than thus.
 2. The beautiful angelic presence; often too the court of heaven sees us in God.
 3. The Eye of God—sleepless, omniscient, omnipotent.
 4. Its continuity, and vision of interior as well as exterior.
 5. It sees us and knows us better than we do ourselves: our self-deceit.
 6. Its overwhelming silence, even at sin.
 7. That silence is a continual recorded judgment of us.

III. The consolation of all this.
 1. If we have really given ourselves to God, this Eye is our joy and consolation.

2. Its support in temptation, injustice, wrong, and perplexities.
3. It makes us real and honest with God.
4. It rouses us out of our tepidity.
5. If we are in sin, it has a converting effect like the Eye of Jesus.
6. The honour of always being looked at by God
7. The look is one of unutterable, unimaginable love.

This Eye was on us in our cradle: it is our joy to think it is on us in darkness and in light—in sin—in death—in judgment through the Eye of Jesus—then purgatory—nay in heaven to all eternity we shall lie in the sunlight of that Ever-blessed and Unsleeping Eye!

V.

THE ONE DRAWBACK OF LIFE.

What astonishes me most in looking at the lives of men is the look of smoothness there is about them; yet is there any one life which is really smooth? As we touch it in society it is smooth: as we see it in faces it seems smooth: as we hear it in conversation it sounds smooth: but in secret, in reality, is life really smooth?

What does it look like to God? To our heavenly Father human life wears an aspect of unutterable pitifulness, of failure, of dissatisfaction, of discontent, of disappointment. He bends over it in unspeakable tenderness, because it is so pathetic, so pitiful, so helpless, and yet to Him so beautiful.

What is the real secret of life?

I. Each life is spoiled by one drawback—one thing which mars to each soul its completeness and its rest.

    1. The great variety of drawbacks, in heart, mind, hand, eye: yet *one* predominates in each soul.

    2. It is with most a *small* cross: nay, often no more than an inconvenience.

    3. It is sometimes from our own fault—often, perhaps more often, not so.

    4. It spreads over whole years of life: sometimes we outgrow it, sometimes we grow into it.

    5. It is always real, however exaggerated.

II. What God means by it: earth is in fact not heaven; and rest is beyond the skies, not here.

    1. I observe that when men get rid of it, they often fall and change for the worse.

    2. I observe also that what is best and most lovable about men is mostly connected with it.

    3. So that it is a law and a love of our heavenly Father, who is secretly sanctifying us by it: oh the secrecy of God's love! His secret mercies —what a marvellous show they will make at the last day! What an incredible amazement of delight in our souls!

    4. Moreover, the noiselessness of God's love! How much He is doing, which we do not hear: the comfort of this reflection when we seem not to be advancing! The one drawback is blessedly and stealthily leading us heavenward!

    5. Lastly, the gentleness of God's love! How is it that so heavy a hand can press so lightly, so sweetly, so soothingly?

Some lives *seem* without a drawback: they are the lives of those who have found God their all, who have made Him their fulness, and found Him such a fulness of contentment, as the full heart can never tell: yet have they not their drawback? If not, why do they of all souls *pine* so? Yes! they have their one drawback, it is that loving God so much, they do not love Him more!

Oh then, my dear Brethren, that we had some of that devotion which the saints seem to have had in so great a degree, and my dear Father St. Philip so especially, devotion to the beautiful providence of God? Is not God wonderful, is He not sweet? How much we love ourselves, and pet ourselves, and legislate for ourselves, and yet God is always doing it much more for each of us. Oh ye that mourn, would ye might be comforted; but is it not comfort to remember that your heavenly Father knows your secret? Oh trust *Him!* Whom shall you trust, if not *Him!* Oh how He loves to see your tears, because quiet tears have so much of eternal life within them, and yet longs to dry them, and with such difficulty refrains. Soft and indulgent as we are to ourselves, God is softer far and a thousandfold more indulgent. This is why He loves so much the kind and the merciful, and those who console the afflicted—because they dry His children's tears which it is not yet His time to dry Himself. Dear God! adorably dear! How is He ever thinking, as if it was His consolation as much as ours, of that day which is spoken of in the Apocalypse, when "the Lamb shall lead us to the fountains of the waters of life, and God shall wipe away all tears." *

* vii. 17.

VI.

HOW IT IS THAT LIFE IS SHORT.

I. We complain that life is short: yet we are always wishing it away in sections. We alternate between the two moods of considering life long, because it is burdensome, and short, because so little seems to come of it. Well, really it is short: this is the religious view of it.

  1. In comparison of eternity.

  2. In face of the work to be done.

  3. Of what our own talents and energy render it likely we could do.

  4. Of what grace seems given us to do: good men always dying with unfulfilled graces.

  5. Because it steals over us so swiftly and so treacherously.

II. Let us examine how it comes to be so short.

  1. Because we waste so much time.

    (1) Sleeping, eating, civility—all necessary.

    (2) Pain and ill health.

    (3) Useless occupations, talk, reading, unnecessary amusement.

  2. So much of life is already gone.

    (1) This is true to all of us, however young or however old.

    (2) Freshness and power past away: *e.g.,* youth, conversion, &c.

    (3) We have got fixed in our groove, and perhaps infelicitously.

  3. So much to do in what remains.

    (1) Evil habits to be got rid of.

(2) Adequate penance for past sin.

(3) Cultivation of graces and formation of habits of virtue.

4. So little to look back upon.

(1) How much should we care to keep?

(2) The past so full of failure.

(3) So that we seem ever *beginning* to try to live holy lives.

5. It seems as if there were nothing to look forward to.

(1) Not a day secured to us.

(2) We are too tired for great changes.

(3) Shall we have better fortune with ourselves than before?

III. The remainder of life; this is in reality the great question.

1. Careful use of time.

2. Determination to be supernatural.

3. Preparation for death, quiet and solemn.

4. Love alone makes up for lost time.

VII.

SELF-DENIAL THE ESSENCE OF RELIGION.

I. The external similarity of the lives of Catholics and infidels.

1. Much of it arises from evil causes—so we must not exaggerate: still after all, the lives will ever be like.

2. Christianity is a religion of motives—ways of acting and reasons of acting, more than actions.

3. The peculiar hiddenness of holiness : its godlike feature.

II. Self-denial the hidden thing, which makes the difference : without it no religion.

   1. The common sense of mankind values self-denial, and puts a price upon actions according to the amount of self-denial which they involve.

   2. The Scripture argument for it: (1) precept, (2) example of Jesus.

   3. Corrupt self is our enemy.

   4. All Christian sanctity, from martyrdom downwards, flows out of this.

   5. It is the special note of the Gospel—the doctrine of the Cross.

III. Importance of realising this.

   1. To prevent self-delusion : *e.g.*, in prayer and devotional exercises, in almsgiving, in benevolent bustle, plans, &c.

   2. It is the test of hypocrisy.

   3. It is an easy way of testing our own progress : it should be the subject of constant self-examination.

Jesus is our model, Who pleased not Himself—how far is this a description of our lives? so far as it is *not*, so far we have reason to fear. Strive to grow in this day after day : do not despise little opportunities; go out of your way daily in search of them. A word on the sweetness and joy of self-denial—one drop of God's consolations : they are free, yet self-denial goes nearest to the direct purchase of them.

VIII.

PERSONAL HOLINESS.

What we want is *power*, and *light*, and *love;* these are not in wealth, how could the power of *poor* Jesus be there? not in political success, that is not His likeness; not in natural talent, that is not His simplicity; not in the control of public opinion, that is ever at enmity with Him; we are only blessed when the world hates us:—but in personal holiness; and by personal holiness I mean

1. Great strictness.—2. Counsels.—3. Prayer.—4. Alms up to the point of self-denial.—5. Sacraments.—6. Weekday mass: for mass is the greatest power of the Church.

I. Why this should be. Supernatural, and therefore holy, is

1. Our end.—2. Our doctrine.—3. Our position. —4. Our sacraments. Almost all failures of the Church in her crises are through want of personal holiness.

II. Holiness is power.

1. Power with God, and the hosts of the invisible world.

2. Power with self, because it so heightens the bravery of our nature, emboldens its aspirations, and deepens its perseverance.

3. Power with men, because it is mysteriously attractive, and gives confidence.

4. Power over evil spirits and bad men, because of the awe wherewith it inspires them, even while they chafe and fret.

III. Holiness is light.
    1. To discern God's will: and so be both cheerful
       and hopeful.
    2. To take the Catholic views of things and line of
       action :—importance of this.
    3. And because it is light, it is patience also.
IV. Holiness is love.
    1. Towards opponents, and so has God's multiplied
       benedictions.
    2. Towards souls as such, and so is never wearying,
       and most liberal to institutions: and at once
       inventive and great-hearted in its works.
    3. Towards God, and so becomes master of the
       Sacred Heart, and does what it will.

IX. .

THE KINGDOM OF HEAVEN SUFFERETH VIOLENCE, AND THE VIOLENT BEAR IT AWAY.

We have often to take serious steps in life, involving
this world, involving the other: *e.g.* as to vocation, and
even things short of that: then sometimes comes a
cold doubt if we have not got entangled in some
tremendous mistake, and so gone the wrong road, and
have to get back into the right one.

Now take another thought. Saints, like the great
St. Antony, have been made saints by one word of the
gospels: what if our Lord appeared and spoke to us?
He *is* going to speak to us now: listen to His word.

If we are in earnest, all our prayers, however various, must be the prayer of the jailor at Philippi to Paul and Silas. "Masters, what must I do that I may be saved?" Jesus answers—

I. The kingdom of heaven suffereth violence, and the violent bear it away.

   1. What fulness in the words! What a silence they make in our souls!

   2. It is our Lord's one view of salvation.

   3. Said *ad turbas* (St. Matt. xi.), not as a counsel to the disciples: on the contrary, the chapter says He had *done* with the apostles. *Et factum est cum consummasset Jesus, præcipiens duodecim discipulis.*

   4. I should like to have seen His Face, whether He looked the Saviour or the Judge—sorrowful or peremptory when He said this,—and heard His tone of voice: He was so persuasive; "Never man spake like this Man."

   5. Sometimes our Lord spoke words, which might have a great many meanings: sometimes words which are like sunbeams, single, self-explaining, unmistakeable darts of eternal light. These words were such.

II. Well! the life you and I are living, Brethren, is it a life of violence? What violence are we doing

   1. To self? its wills, its passions, its cowardices.

   2. To the world? its false maxims, its allurements, its human respects.

   3. To the flesh? in love of ease, of comfort, of sensuality.

   4. To the devil? in temptations, in wearinesses, (for they are chiefly his), in unbeliefs.

5. To God? by prayer, by penance, by the holy audacity of love.

Is violence at all the right word for our lives?

III. But is there nothing to be said on the other side?

1. We must not attempt too high things, above our grace. True, but—the kingdom of heaven suffereth violence, and the violent bear it away.

2. We must not attempt too much, but take things in turn. True, but—the kingdom of heaven suffereth violence, and the violent bear it away.

3. It is better not to begin than to begin and leave off. I doubt that: but—it is useless arguing —the kingdom of heaven suffereth violence, and the violent bear it away.

4. We are not saints; true—we are not talking of saints, but of salvation:—the kingdom of heaven suffereth violence, and the violent bear it away.

5. Slowness is the great thing in grace. Partly true—but not altogether, *for*—the kingdom of heaven suffereth violence, and the violent bear it away.

This kingdom of heaven—is it a thing I can do without? If I must have it, I must put up with the terms—the kingdom of heaven suffereth violence, and the violent bear it away. O dearest Brethren! when we think how idle and how cowardly we are, is it not plain that we cannot pray for a better or a safer grace than this—all through life, when we are idling or when we are shrinking, to see by faith the well known face of Jesus, and to hear His voice, the voice of our dear Judge, one while thrilling through the silence of our solitude, and another while mastering all the clamours of the outward world, with that tremendous axiom of eternal life—the kingdom of heaven suffereth violence, and the violent bear it away.

X.

LENT A CALL TO PENANCE.

I. The occupations of the Holy Land in the days of St. John Baptist.

   1. Parties among the Jews: foreign Jews: proselytes: strangers.

   2. Apparition of the Baptist on the banks of Jordan; mixed success and failure of his mission.

   3. Lent a similar call to similar duties; with similarly mixed success and failure.

II. Characteristic offices of Lent, a season of the year on which the Church lays especial stress.

   1. Heaven is more open, and grace more abundant.

   2. It is a time of conversion and of renewal, that renewal which is often more difficult than conversion.

   3. It is especially a call to penance, and a help from our desperate worldliness.

III. Our state as regards penance.

   1. Does the world look as if it were doing penance, or even acknowledged the obligation of it?

   2. Do professedly good people look as if they were doing penance?

3. We ourselves—are we not living as though we had never lost our baptismal innocence—and have we not lost it?

Have we no cause to fear? are we quite sure we can do without this austere virtue of penance, with all its incommodious details and stern realities? to several among us it will be our last Lent! and how many deathbeds all through the year depend on *last Lents ! ! !* The words of Jeremias: "Hear ye, and give ear. Be not proud, for the Lord hath spoken. Give ye glory to the Lord your God, before it be dark, and before your feet stumble upon the dark mountains" (xiii. 14, 15.)

XI.

PUTTING HAND TO THE PLOUGH AND LOOKING BACK.

I. Wisdom to be learnt from conversing with the lost. St. Philip said, "He who does not go down into hell while he is alive, runs a great risk of going there after he is dead."

   1. All or almost all are surprised by their sentence; they died not expecting it.

   2. They had at some time begun to be religious, and would at one time have been saved.

   3. They are surprised to see by how little and in what half insensible ways they had missed. They put their hands to the plough and looked back.

II. "Hand to the plough and looking back:" this was

spoken (St. Luke ix.) as He was on His way, "steadfastly facing" Jerusalem.

1. All of us have had our call, an inward call as well as an outward one.
2. We go on some way after the call.
3. Then we begin to get tired.
4. Then to go sorrowfully, sullenly, ungracefully, querulously.
5. Then our heart gets behind us, and lags.
6. Then we turn round and look back, only intending to *look* back.
7. The plough jolts, and falls : and we, for the most part quietly, as if half asleep, not by a great sudden sin, go another road.

III. "Looking back."

1. Why is it so fatally displeasing to our Lord ? It seems so pardonable.
2. How it reveals His character ! *He* in His work for us never looked back.
3. He must have the heart with its brightness, alacrity, and promptitude.
4. These are hard terms. Is it better then not to put our hand to the plough at all ? No ! for that would be certain damnation.
5. Are we looking back ? For it is dreadful to think we may be without realising it. We do so chiefly—
   (1) By worldliness rather than by sin.
   (2) In little things rather than in great ones.
   (3) After efforts, such as feasts, new beginnings, &c., as if a reaction followed them.

IV. How to avoid it ?

1. Keep your conscience well examined.

2. Meditate more often on the joys of heaven.

3. Depend more upon grace.

My brethren! I want to put before you a frightening thought, which it is wholesome for us to reflect upon. Men speak and write as if *we* had to choose Jesus or to reject Him. Well! it is most true: but it is not quite *all* the truth. We must not forget that He also has a choice, and very clear partialities to determine His choice, and quite a distinct view in choosing us. Many are called but few are chosen. The grand thing is—TO BE CHOSEN.

XII.

JESUS CHRIST AND HIM CRUCIFIED.

When our Lord set His face to go up to Jerusalem to His last passover, His disciples were amazed. Also He walked quicker than usual, and rebuked St. Peter with a vehemence startlingly unusual with Him. Yet His whole life was in fact a going up to His Passion.

I. The example which this is to us.

    1. A man's character must be formed by an object he is always gazing on.

    2. So with the human character of Jesus, in desire for the glory of His Father, zeal for souls, sweet gravity.

    3. Thus the Passion must colour all our lives, if we are to be like Him.

    4. Tendency of man to variety, to *many* and *different* things; it is this which makes the

practice of the presence of God so peculiarly hard.

5. Whereas Christian life is a gathering of all things into one, which is God.

II. The apostle meant to express this fundamental truth of spirituality, when he said he would know nothing but Jesus Christ and *Him Crucified.*

    1. The crucifix is the meaning of everything to us.

    2. We must view all things in its light, and judge all things by its principles.

    3. It must be the object of our imitation.

    4. And to be so, it must be the subject of our daily meditations.

    5. The world is in all things the opposite of the crucifix.

    6. And hell simply the result of forgetting the crucifix.

    7. And heaven the end of remembering the crucifix.

    8. And saints simply striking likenesses of the crucifix.

    9. Hence there must be a total break with the world —nothing but Jesus Christ and Him Crucified.

III. Practical questions.

    1. What is it to be crucified?

    2. What is meant by an interior crucifixion?

    3. What is it to be crucified to the world?

    4. Can we name any one thing to which we are crucified?

    5. Have we ever taken any pains to be crucified?

    6. Have we any object in life which we think more of than being crucified?

    7. Are we quite sure then that all our devotion is not simply a delusion?

O great God! how many souls are ruined by delusions, ruined for ever by delusions which their self-love can hardly bring itself to suspect—and how many people's piety is nothing better than delusion! Alas! it is not austerities that are so hard to shrinking nature; it is this extreme, lifelong, divine simplicity of faith, this one thing needful, this single matter of importance, this Jesus Christ and Him Crucified!

———

XIII.

TO-DAY.

Dum Hodie cognominatur.—HEB. iii. 13.

I. General considerations.
1. Use of our time of immense importance in the spiritual life.
2. Life, though long in feeling, is too short for work.
3. Concentration the only way to meet the crowdedness and multiplicity of life.
4. God is all in the present—this in itself makes the present of consummate importance to us.
5. The present time.
   (1) Its own duty. (2) Its own grace. (3) Also its own opportunity. (4) It is a divine and human conjuncture of things visible and invisible, which never may return again.
6. We want, then, (1) attention for the present—(2) room for the present—(3) readiness for the present.
7. The want of these three things the cause of huge evils in the spiritual life.

II. Phenomena.

    1. Time passes and nothing is done.

    2. Time passes, and too much is done, out of which too much comes nothing.

    3. Time passes, and everything is done very unsatisfactorily.

    4. On the whole, great increase of venial sins, not so much in kind as in number.

    5. In other respects a general stoppage.

    6. So many things tried superficially that interest is gone for all.

    7. General feeling of unwellness and unwashedness and dustiness in life.

III. Causes of these phenomena.

    1. Doing things before their time; so with precipitation.

    2. Procrastinating—so with precipitation also.

    3. Taking life too passively.

    4. Not getting our life into our own hands; want of self-knowledge.

    5. Letting past and future encroach on present.

    6. So nothing done with cleanliness, clear-sightedness, and vigour.

    7. So fraudulence, negligence, slovenliness in God's service—we are always under the mark—our life a failure in detail.

All this comes from want of attention to the present.

XIV.

ON FRITTERING.

I. What is frittering?
    1. As distinguished from idleness.
    2. As distinguished from procrastination.
    3. As distinguished from actual dawdling.
    4. It implies want of earnestness.
    5. Its religion has no spirit of penance in it.
    6. It comes from weakness of character.
    7. Too great an indulgence and repose in the present.
    8. Dull sense of the presence of God.
    9. Want of application to particular examen.
  10. General want of system in devotion.
II. Its symptoms.
    1. Always busy.
    2. Yet always ready for what may occur.
    3. Fondness for plans, and full of them.
    4. Days gone no one knows how.
    5. Feeling that we are not grasping ourselves.
    6. Cloudliness of conscience rather than reproaching of it.
    7. Always on the eve of taking a step, like a stone carried to a building, and left there for a hundred years, a mockery and a sadness, or at best a pathos and a moral.
III. Dangers of it.
    1. The evil of the day.
    2. Manifestations.
        (1) Frittering of time, (2) of mind, (3) of money, (4) of influence, (5) of conversation, (6) of study, (7) of thought and originality.

3. So self catches and becomes impregnated with the spirit of the age.
4. It destroys the reality of prayer.
5. Intercepts grace all day long.
6. Unnerves the sacraments.
7. Prepares a trying deathbed.
8. Interferes with reality of contrition.
9. Makes faith's vision unclear.
10. Works of mercy few and scanty.
11. Want of zeal for souls.
12. Life one overflowing fountain of venial sins.
Cure of it a frightened use of time.

XV.

TENDERNESS IN RELIGION.

I.

NECESSITY OF IT AND ITS NATURE.

I. Two classes of persons, trying—(1) to get out of sinful habits—(2) to advance to perfection—they are kept back and know not why—describe their state and efforts, high sense of duty, disgust with sin, appreciation of high things, &c.; yet they make no way, have got to a wall and can go no farther: in many cases it is from want of tenderness. This shows its necessity.

II. The nature of Christian tenderness—it does not mean a mere facility of tears.

1. Sorrow for sin, without the thought of hell.

2. Touchiness about the interests of Jesus.

3. Great docility to director.

4. Not feeling things strict, or keeping to obligations.

5. An *incipient* love of humiliations.

III. The Gospel a religion of tenderness, shown by the manner of our Lord's coming.

1. Helplessness.

2. Unnecessary and unobliged suffering.

3. Sacrifice, not of goods, but of self.

4. Abasement.

5. The position in which He has placed His Mother.

6. The style of His teaching.

7. The way in which He has trusted Himself and His truth to the world.

IV. The advantages of this tenderness.

1. Love the safeguard against sin, more than fear.

2. Tenderness renders conversion more easy.

3. It attracts Jesus, who will not be outdone in tenderness.

4. No spiritual growth without it.

5. It renders duty easy.

6. It gives Christlike instincts, love of suffering, &c., so as to be like Him.

7. It deepens sorrow for sin.

It is a great gift of God; we must never rest till we have it. We must ask Mary and the holy angels, by devotion to them: they like to see it; it looks to them the right return for the Incarnation.

2.

THE TENDERNESS OF JESUS.

The whole mystery of the Incarnation is one of tenderness—the Infancy—the Passion—the Blessed Sacrament: but take the common life of Jesus among men.

I The tenderness of His outward deportment.

  1. Palm Sunday—bruised reed—way with disciples —with sinners.

  2. The tenderness of His looks.
    St. Peter's conversion—the young man whom He looked on with love.

  3. His tenderness in conversation.
    Tone of His parables—absence of horrors in His sermons—abyss of forgiveness which His teaching opens out.

  4. His tenderness in answering.
    When accused of being possessed—when struck on the face—and so all through His Passion.

  5. The tenderness of His reprimands.
    The woman taken in adultery—Magdalen— the Samaritan woman—Judas.

  6. The tenderness of His zeal.
    Rebuke of John and James about fire from heaven—also about seats in heaven—also setting a child in the midst—cleansing the temple—sweet meekness of His divine indignation.

    Compare our own conduct with all this.

II. His work in our souls is a faithful reproduction of this in all its details continually ; how then

can our service of Him be anything but a
service of tenderness ?

O Jesus ! Thou art unknown.   Men will not
fathom the abysses of Thy love and Thy forbearance :
make us know Thee, and melt our hard hearts every
hour before the touches of Thy grace.

3.

HOW TO GAIN IT.

If tenderness is of such importance in religion, and
the only true imitation of Jesus, we must consider how
to obtain it.

I. Means.

   1. Frequent confession and communion.
   2. Familiarity with the mysteries of our Lord's life,
      especially the Passion.
   3. Colloquies with our blessed Lady.
   4. Affectionate use of pictures and images.
   5. Devotion to the holy souls, and angels—this
      takes away hardness and worldliness.
   6. Alms or self-denying courtesies.
   7. Some bodily austerity, regular and under obedi-
      ence.
   8. Sedulous worship of the Blessed Sacrament.
   9. Asking it by special prayer.
     (1) Of the eternal Father, by His tenderness for
         His Son.
     (2) Of the Holy Ghost, who fashioned the Sacred
         Humanity.

II. Cautions.

1. Not to be cast down if the gift seems long in coming.
2. Not to make constrained efforts, as if it was in our power.
3. Not to say or act one jot more than we feel.
4. Never to flag in praying and working for it.
5. Not to criticise it in others, even when it manifests itself in disagreeable developments.

The worship of the Sacred Heart: the wish of Jesus that these latter ages should be marked by tenderness—the spirit of the world opposed to it—the intense happiness of it—how it unites us to God!—The spirit of the Oratory at once reverence and familiarity with Jesus.

XVI.

THE DELICACY OF THE OPERATIONS OF GRACE.*

How little there was to lead the kings, and yet what they would have lost if they had decided not to follow the star. It may be taken as an illustration of the doctrine of vocations and inspirations.

I. The particularity of God's Providence over us.
  1. He has a special work for each of His creatures to do.
  2. His outward Providence does not altogether settle what it is.
  3. The great cases of calls to the priesthood, and the religious life.
  4. But beyond this, every one has a sort of vocation.

* Octave of the Epiphany, 1856.

5. And inspirations are a further development of God's special design.

II. Yet the nature of these operations has much in it to breed a holy fear.

   1. The extreme delicacy of them; they escape unperceived if we are not interior.

   2. Very often they require other eyes than our own to understand them.

   3. Many of them do not solicit us, but go away if not welcomed, and return no more.

   4. Yet our sanctity, perhaps our salvation, may be much concerned in them.

   5. We shall see at the last what a life of inspirations we have had, and what immense holiness we might have gained with comparative ease.

III. What we must do to make the most of these things.

   1. We must not suspect God of laying snares for us: all is broad love.

   2. We must make especial prayer for the light of the Holy Ghost.

   3. Be very accurate and punctual in the habit of examination of conscience.

   4. We must seek for spiritual direction, and submit to it with docility.

   5. Above all we must lead lives of prayer, and then we shall dwell in light, and in the companionship of God, and understand His way with us.

Oh many a star has risen to each of us in the clear blue night of faith, and we have not followed it! Many a one has stood over where the young Child was, as it were beckoning to us with a brightness, in which we felt there was something heavenly, and yet we have turned away, and have now clean forgotten it! Oh that we had hearts to feel, and eyes in our souls to see, where we really are! There are good angels round us, and graces are raining down upon us, great and small, all our lives long, and inspirations are falling upon us, thick as snow-flakes, and almost as softly and as silently, and we are fastened with a thousand fastenings, to great unknown eternal purposes, and we feel them no more than a strong man feels the cobwebs and the gossamer on the autumnal grass, and all the while we are closed all round and walled in, not so much with the sun and moon and stars, with the air and the floor of our own planet, as with the living inevitable tremendous presence of our omnipotent all-holy God, Who will not spare us one moment from His sight, and Who even while we sleep expects us to do His work, Whose love of us, and therefore jealousy of us, is as everlasting as Himself.

XVII.

GOD'S LOVE OF PRAYER.

"And it came to pass, that as He was in a certain place, praying, when He ceased, one of His disciples said to Him, Lord, teach us to pray, as John also taught his disciples."—ST LUKE xi. 1.

The disciple watches Jesus—and then says, Lord, teach us to pray: evidently he had looked most beautiful at prayer, as the disciple (we should love to know what disciple it was), gazed upon Him.

I. It is very natural that many things should surprise us in God: one of the things which surprises one most is His intense love of prayer.

1. The overwhelmingness of His immensity.
2. The blessedness of His self-sufficiency.
3. Yet His vast pleasure at being asked—at being prayed to by creatures so low. .
4. His desire to give—yet curbed by and subjected to His love of prayer.
5. What immense things He does for prayer: *e.g.* at Ninive—miracles, often doing no mighty works because of unbelief.
6. Yet prayer seems to alter Him, to obscure Him, His will, His unchangeableness, &c.
7. And after all, what sort of prayer is it which He gets from us ?

II. The life of prayer.

1. If God's great love of prayer surprises us, I could think that, if anything could surprise God, it would be our little love of prayer: for it is surprising to ourselves when we come to think of it.
2. Prayer is by far the greatest power in the world.
3. A life of prayer is a life without disappointments or failures ; a life of victory.
4. It is a life of incessant progress in sanctity.
5. It turns everything into itself, temptations, even falls—all life comes to prayer—and this is easier than it sounds.
6. It leaves a scarce perceptible amount of unanswered prayer.
7. And its unanswered prayers are its greatest gifts, its heavenliest favours.

III. Practical conclusions.

1. Do we dwell enough on this remarkable feature of God—His fondness for prayer ?

2. How is our prayer in respect of quantity ?

3. How in respect of reverence ?

4. How in respect of perseverance and importunity, which is our greatest reverence ?

5. How in respect of its sincerity ? can we be insincere in prayer ? Yes ! perhaps in nothing more insincere.

6. How in respect of fervour and of fulness ? To an angel what a strange thing cold prayer must seem !

7. How in respect of faith ? Oh to pray believingly . it does away with the necessity of faith—for at once we touch God, we feel Him, we lay hold of Him, His arm is wound round us with a pressure which, when we have once felt it, we can never mistake for anything else.

XVIII.

HOLINESS IS AN INWARD SILENCE.

Midlent Sunday ! We ought now to be feeling the effects of Lent in our souls, when God has drawn us so far into the wilderness.

I. Holiness is an inward silence.

1. Scripture represents it as a solitude; God's chosen time and place and *chance*, so to call it, as if He was too bashful to speak in public, or as if it was below His dignity, or as though what He had to say was meant only for ourselves.

2. It is crowd, and noise, and many objects which hinder our realising God.

3. Holiness has the same effect on the *mind* as the mountain, the forest, dan the wilderness.

4. This seems to show that worldliness, even more than sin, hinders us from seeing God.

5. Certainly the effects of grace are to produce an inward silence.

II. The silence of God; represented by the Nativity at midnight, the Resurrection before dawn, and the Second Advent at dead of night.

1. This is one of His most adorable perfections.

2. The multiplicity of His operations—yet no voice. The trees and the streams, the winds and the waves, the volcano and the thunder, they have voices—but He has none! Silent as the grave —nay, eternity is more silent than any grave.

3. The unimaginable outstretching of His infinity —yet no voice: all sounds flow over Him, all sounds are uttered in His ears: all music is from Him, yet He Himself is an Uncreated Silentness.

4. The tremendous might of His inward jubilee— yet all breathless silence.

5. Look at Him, as over a boundless ocean, an expanse of numberless perfections—each losing itself interminably in another in infinities of white light—yet not a sound is heard upon that uncreated indistinguishable Sea!

III. The silences of holiness.

1. Conversion: silencing the world—sins—passions.

2. Growth: silencing human interests—human loves —human pleasures.

3. Sorrow—pain—and sickness, all sanctify in so far as they make an inward silence in the soul.

4. So also shame, calumny, hatred, and all forms of human persecution : they make a solitude and a silence round us, and so give room for grace.

5. Prayer : a speaking to God in silence—a hearing of God in silence—it grows to be a speaking to God by silence : silence is the height of worship ; what is ecstasy but the silence of the soul struck dumb with the beautifulness of God ?

IV. The last silences.

1. The silence in which we die.

2. The silence the moment after death—deeper ; the silence of change, the silence of astonishment, the out-blaze of a new world upon our bodiless souls.

3. The silence in which the judgment is pronounced.

4. The silence immediately after the doom—a tingling hush, as if all the stars and worlds had stopped rolling.

5. The last silence—the silence round the Throne !

XIX.

THE PLACE OF WEEPERS.*

God does wonderful things for those who love Him. The Red Sea and the Wilderness : the entry into the Promised Land : the death of Josue.

* Judges ii. 5.

I. The Place of Weepers.

   1. St. Michael came up from Galgal.

   2. The Wood in the Valley of Raphaim, on the west side of Jerusalem.

   3. The Israelites were to have overthrown the idols, destroyed the false gods, and made no league with the wicked people.

   4. The angel's reproach.

   5. They lifted up their voice and wept, and offered sacrifices to the Lord.

II. All this is a beautiful figure of Lent: the Church in Lent is the *locus flentium :* we have not overthrown the idols, nor destroyed the false gods, but made a league with the world, the enemy of God. Let us look at our past.

   1. Past sins—many—grievous—reiterated—peculiarly guilty in us with our peculiar grace— what penance has been done ?

   2. Past graces—countless—wonderful—constant : what correspondence ?

   3. Past mercies—so loving—so much what we wanted—so sweetly given ; what gratitude ? nay, what amount even of common remembrance ?

   4. Past crosses—how borne—how profited by ?—a terrible thing is a cross which has *gone* and left us unsanctified—yet there are many of us whose whole lives are thus.

   5. Nay, past virtues ! yes, a virtue past, lost, good habits gone.

III. All this we have to weep.

   1. We have an angel with us, our own, the angel of Lent, and St. Michael also, the angel of the

Church, the same who was at the Place of
Weepers: heaven is open, it is the time of
God's great annual pardon.

2. How happily the Israelites returned home from
the Place of Weepers.

3. So to us our spiritual weeping will be more a
joy than a sorrow.

4. Joy of humility—comfort of peace—pleasantness
of thinking better of others, because we think
worse of ourselves—the feeling of inward purity
which contrition brings—the sweetness of being
nearer to God.

5. What is our Lent grace, our Lent gift ?   A great
love of God !   Love is what we want—lack of
love has caused all our past mistakes—but it
must be a great love, not a little one—we have
tried that, and it has not been enough.

Oh my Brethren, how much more God is longing
to give us at our prayers, if only our prayers would
ask for more, and would ask it more boldly, more
hungrily, and more believingly.

XX.

PROSPERITY.

To call things by their right names, and to know
their right value, is half the science of life.   Their true
names are the names God calls them by ; their true
value is the value He sets upon them.

True view of prosperity.

I. An account of prosperity.
   1. The value men set upon it, and how they count it a blessing.
   2. What it consists in, absence of pain, &c., in fact, a life least like that of Jesus.
   3. The class of people who are most prosperous, not saints, nor great sinners, but mostly a middle class of good kind of people who act on natural motives.
   4. A description of quiet domestic English prosperity.

II. The dangers of prosperity.
   1. Its tendency to wean the heart from God, and to fix it on creatures : mutual worship of members of an English family.
   2. Habit of esteeming others according to their prosperity.
   3. As prosperity increases, so does anxiety to keep it, and this makes men restless, selfish, and irreligious.
   4. Effeminacy of character which it produces.
   5. Vanity from praise of those around us.
   6. Low temporal style of prayer and religion which it produces, *e.g.,* Anglican family prayers.
   7. It unfits man for the high virtues of the Christian character ; saints introduced rough penances to counteract this.

III. Possible or probable meanings of prosperity.
   1. Absence of chastisement is anything but a mark of God's love.
   2. If your prosperity is in any way a blessing, it is as a condescension to your weakness.
   3. *Accepisti mercedem tuam*——fearfulness of this, yet

its likelihood when we consider the class of characters which usually prosper.

This view changes the aspect of the world, yet it is not really a gloomy view. You cannot have both worlds; men start all manner of contrivances to serve both God and mammon, but none have ever succeeded, none ever will. Choose which world you will have. Oh happy they who say, not this, not this, but that where Jesus and where Mary are!

XXI.

INWARD PEACE.

I. Our Lord's voice.
  1. How exceedingly sweet in the ears of the disciples.
  2. Sound takes us to the past and not to the future.
  3. Each had operations of grace connected in his mind with that voice.
  4. After the Resurrection association must have made it doubly sweet.
  5. And then his favourite word was *peace—Pax vobis.*
II. Inward peace.
  1. It seems to rise upward as from some depth in the soul.
  2. It is not forfeited by activity, but rather collects us for fresh activity.
  3. It gives light also, and makes things clear in our minds, especially supernatural things.

4. Yet it is forfeited by indocility to grace, or undue interest in worldly things.

5. And goes suddenly, whereas, though it *sometimes* comes suddenly, it *generally* comes slowly.

III. The want of it

1. Is the cause of most of our sins.

2. And of most of our unworthinesses.

3. And also of most of our unhappiness.

4. Nothing wastes grace so much.

5. Hence the want of it is the chief obstacle to progress in holy living—contrast lake and sea, the last images not heaven.

IV. How to gain it.'

1. By having few wants, and thus few irritabilities.

2. By not meddling with other people's business, nor setting them right.

3. By not judging others.

4. By some sort of exercise of silence.

5. By looking particularly after humility.

V. Fruits of it.

1. Robustness in practice of virtues.

2. Great sweetness to others.

3. Sensible sweetness in devotion.

4. Facility for realising the presence of God.

5. Enjoyment of it in itself—something beyond words to say—it is a TOUCH OF GOD.

XXII.

HEARING SERMONS.

I. Christ made the spread of His gospel to depend on the foolishness of preaching.

  1. Yet it is but the repetition of a faith already known.

  2. And that by men of various abilities, and still more various powers of expression.

  3. Yet its effects are very wonderful, and indeed on human principles inexplicable.

  4. The unction of the Holy Ghost goes out with the words.

  5. It must then be a matter of consequence to hear sermons well.

II. How to hear sermons well.

  1. It is coming to be told something about God from one who knows better than we do.

  2. And then going to put this something into practice.

  3. We have to give a separate account at the last day of every sermon we have heard, though long since forgotten.

  4. Every one brought grace, to which we were bound to correspond.

  5. It is God waiting on us to speak, and to enlighten, and to inflame, and to bless.

III. How as a matter of fact do we hear sermons?

  1. Either as a simple weariness.

  2. Or to criticise, and talk, and pretend to be frightened, &c.

  3. Or to see how it applies to our neighbours.

4. Or to seek mere consolation—to find out the least we can safely do for God.

5. Or because we are pleased with simple fluency and the excitement of listening.

How few hear them humbly, or wisely, or reverently: yet the true love of hearing sermons is actually enumerated by spiritual writers as one of the signs of predestination.

The best test of sermons is whether they make good people uncomfortable.

XXIII.

DEVOTION TO THE POOR.

There are some thoughts so overwhelming that we cannot take them in all at once, we have to grow to them; and even then we never become familiar with them: here is one—that the world was made by God and belongs to Him, and yet that He and we come to quite different judgments about it. One great part of religion, therefore, is to reform our judgments on the judgments of God.

I. God's view of poverty.

1. He chose it when He came among us Himself.

2. He has given all His saints a similar instinct.

3. He has revealed Himself as having a special love for the poor—and God's love is true riches.

4. He has pronounced a solemn blessing upon the poor for ever.

5. He has made poverty the easiest road to heaven.

II. What is poverty ?

   1. It is hard labour, like the punishment we inflict on criminals.

   2. It is difficulty in getting sufficient food, and also domestic discomfort.

   3. It is not having our own time at our disposal, nor our own movements.

   4. It is being without means to satisfy the dearest affections of our hearts, children, in illness, &c.

   5. It is having to live from day to day, without the comfort of a settled future. All holiness is a simulation of poverty—for it is utter mortification of body, or of will.

III. It is one of Mary's special worlds.

   1. Because of the choice of Jesus—and of God's divine predilection for it.

   2. Because of her own endurance of it.

   3. Because of its multitudinous wants and woes.

   4. Because of the immensity of hidden virtues which it contains—though externally it does not appear to do so.

   5. Because of the means it gives the rich of saving their souls—and the rich also are her children.

IV. What are the rich ?

   1. A class of people, who for no other cause have a woe standing recorded against them in the gospel.

   2. Who have more ties to earth than others, making death bitter.

   3. Who have less opportunity of exercising their faith in God.

   4. Whose state was never sanctified to Jesus.

   5. Fewer of whom, as a revealed fact, are saved. Oh what a change it would make in the world,

if the rich only knew truly how dreadfully hard it is for the rich to be saved !

V. Almsgiving. Give alms, and all things are clean —astonishing word !

1. It exactly meets the disadvantage the rich labour under.

2. It is precisely God's will concerning the rich, and precisely so because they are rich: a rich man not giving alms is like a man resisting an infallible divine vocation.

3. Not a mere counsel; there exists regarding it a certain obligation under penalty of grave sin.

4. There is no point of practice in their lives more needing legislation and provision.

5. With what amount of generosity ? One word answers that question—God.

I conclude with one more grave truth—I said fewer rich were saved than poor: I now add that the great multitudes of the rich who are lost are lost principally because they are stingy, irregular, or fanciful—I beg of you to mark the three words ! stingy, irregular, or fanciful, in their mercy to the poor.

XXIV.

THE SPIRITUAL ADVANTAGES OF HAVING A BAD MEMORY.

Wherever we turn, even in the most unlikely places, there are spiritual advantages, means of uniting ourselves more closely to God. I will take the common complaint of people as they come to middle life, that they cannot trust their memories as they did before. Some have naturally a bad memory: with others it weakens as life advances. Well! let us make the best of it. It comes from reading more than we *think* —and from the encyclopædical character of our modern education.

I. The pleasures and advantages of memory.

   1. It fills our minds with pleasant pictures, softening and brightening realities.

   2. It makes us loved, by making us mindful of the past, and grateful for it.

   3. It makes the experience of life more handy and more useful to us.

   4. It keeps up a spirit of thanksgiving by keeping up the remembrance of past mercies.

   5. It imparts a remarkable and winning tenderness to our characters.

   6. It saves us from the look of insincerity, which unretentive memories give to us.

   7. It makes our spiritual life more clear by keeping it before us in accurate recollection.

II. The other side of the question: bad memory is part of the process of sanctification in old age. Read St. Francis of Sales (Esprit, part i. sect. xxxiv.) on bad memories.

   1. Nearly one half of our sins are committed through memory.

   2. All custody of our senses is intended to keep the memory empty. F. de Ravignan says, " *On oublie beaucoup; car Dieu veut qu'on oublie.*" *
Also in his last illness at St. Acheul, "*oubliez*

* Vie, i. 160.

_tout sans cesse, autant que possible, et jetez-vous dans une pure joie de l'esprit._*

3. Contemplation, and all higher graces, require the memory empty as far as possible. St. Teresa had a bad memory.†

4. Destruction of particular classes of recollections has been a gift of God to some saints, as to St. Ignatius. Instance of high grace effacing the memory in the life of Mere Esprite de Jésus.‡

5. Half the mischief our past sins do us is through memory.

6. Memory is less under our control than any other faculty, even than imagination.

7. Writers say that God fills an empty memory as a matter of course, as air or water fill an empty vessel. Wonderful passage in Blosius on the good of spiritual reading which you forget.§

III. Distinct spiritual advantages to be gained from a bad memory.

1. Use of time, not losing the present in past or future : real holiness is all in the present.

2. Humility—not remembering praise, or past work or graces given.

3. Charity—not remembering sores, nor brooding over them, not being critical or suspicious; how needful love of enemies is to spirituality.‖

4. Peace—because no vivid remembrance of past disturbances, or wrongs.

5. Prayer less teased by distractions; keen remem-

---

* Vie, ii. 412. † Bouix, Vie, cap. xi. also cap. xv.
‡ Giry, Paris, 1860, vol. viii. p. 557.
§ Newsham's edition, p. 37.
‖ Aggiunta al Combattimento, cap. xxxvii.

brances of family history and domestic incidents
are seldom found in a man of prayer.

6. Temptations—less material for the evil one to
work on; and less delusion possible.

7. Faith—eternal things less obscured, and we more
simple, and more unworldly.

Thus a bad memory may be made to do for us the
work of very high graces, and may enable us to say
with St. Paul—"*One* thing I do; forgetting the things
that are behind, and stretching forth myself to those
that are before, I press towards the mark, to the prize
of the supernal vocation of God in Christ Jesus." *

XXV.

SINS OF THE TONGUE.

We cannot better sanctify Passiontide than by a
distinct attack against some one of our besetting sins;
and the silence of our Lord in His Passion will be a
supernatural power to help us against our tongues,
wherewith we *all* offend.

Nature and characteristics of sins of the tongue.

I. Almost all the virtues are wounded by some of the
following things.

1. Calumny wounds justice.
2. Detraction charity.
3. Falsehood truth.
4. Self-praise humility.
5. Exaggeration simplicity.

* Philippians iii. 13.

6. Profaneness religion and reverence.

7. And all of these are scandals.

II. Characteristics of these sins.

    1. Their number.

        (1) Number of words each day. (2) Proportion of criticism. (3) Of self-laudation. (4) Of exaggeration. (5) Of simple frivolity.

    2. Their facility.

        (1) Speaking seems to hinder our thinking at the time. (2) Others lead us on. (3) What is wrong is easiest to say. (4) Cheap cleverness of criticism.

    3. Their gratuitousness.

        (1) We mostly gain nothing. (2) But lose by getting ourselves into scrapes. (3) And wound charity, without wishing to satisfy malice.

    4. Their being forgotten.

        (1) How hard it is to remember what we said. (2) How often we are surprised when told it. (3) This hinders penance for these sins.

    5. The invisibility of their effects.

        (1) We do not see the hearts of our listeners. (2) Nor can we trace their telling others. (3) Nor see what actions come of it. (4) Nor discern the deterioration of our own souls.

    6. The lastingness of their effects.

        (1) A whole life. (2) Future generations. (3) Eternity. (4) Our places in heaven or hell. (5) The duration of our purgatory.

    7. The chief objects of their attack are the two

divine virtues of justice and charity. Impossibility of holiness without these two virtues.

8. Their invariable result is to hinder holiness, which is the special will of God.

(1) In the victim, because of bitterness, &c.

(2) In the listener; they defile his mind, destroy his sense of the presence of God, &c.

(3) In the speaker, most of all.

9. An unbridled tongue is therefore more like diabolical possession than any other sin.

(1) It is the plenitude of the devil, with abundance, persistency, irresistibility.

(2) The whole man goes to the tongue; eyes; hands, feet, mind, will, voice.

(3) We almost seem to lose our free will.

Take one gaze at the awful, unbroken, beautiful silence of the Majesty on high!

XXVI.

A CURE FOR DETRACTION.

Detraction.

1. Its commonness—it forms almost the staple of conversation.

2. Its facility to clever people, and to stupid people; it is the only interest of worldly people.

3. Its amount, so far beyond belief, unless we practice particular examen.

4. Its peculiar cancerous nature—tainting all our

graces; it is not merely local, but a disease of the whole soul.

5. It is so peculiarly the vice of religious people.

Remedy.   Meditate often and formally on our own faults.

I. Our sins.

    1. Their number.   2. Their weight.   3. Their shamefulness.   4. Against grace and light.   5. Our little penance.

II. Our natural faults.

    1. So many in number.

    2. So little and undignified in character.

    3 After so many years so little impression made on them in the way of improvement.

    4. So much worse than the faults of others round us.

    5. New faults rising with new circumstances, as if they were nothing but a possibility of faults.

III. Our unworthinesses.

    1. Meannesses and stinginesses.

    2. Falsehoods of a hundred varieties.

    3. Plots, indirectnesses, and sneakingnesses.

    4. Jealousies, suspicions, and inward ill tempers.

    5. Conceits, quite monstrously absurd; we had almost rather tell our sins than detail our castle-buildings.

IV. The world of temptations in which we live.

    1. So prolific, and yet so humblingly peculiar.

    2. So much our masters.

    3. Implying so much corruption.

    4. The pleasure we could take in them, if we chose and if we might.

    5. Each has some he would give worlds to keep secret.

Yet all this will be made plain to all men at the last day.

Now consider—

1. If we grow in grace, we shall come one day to see ourselves worse than this.
2. The saints in heaven see us worse.
3. Our guardian angel now at our side sees us worse.
4. But oh! how much worse are we in the sight of God!

If we keep our minds full of this, we shall be very charitable to others; whereas now, most probably, there are several of us who, if we died this moment, would, to our terrible surprise, find ourselves lost for ever, because of our detraction.

XXVII.

JEALOUSY IN GOOD WORKS.

A fault to which good people are subject, unless they have the natural gift of nobleness of heart. Picture of good people curbing and clipping the little good there is in the world; compare this with the conduct of the blessed. Picture of one of the blessed enjoying the bliss of all the other blessed as if it was his own.

I. How this comes to pass.

1. It is a fault of middle life, and so comes after people are good.
2. Zeal, which is apparently opposed to it, in fact leads to it.

   3. We think God's work must be done our way.

   4. There is more of self than we think for in all the good we do.

   5. Few are holily indifferent to success, and the success of others diminishes ours by diverting attention from it.

II. Features of it.

   1. Extreme narrowness of mind.

   2. It leads to a wish for news and gossip.

   3. Also to talking about self and plans.

   4. Also to tyranny towards those we work with.

   5. It takes the shape of cold praise or of ungenerous silence.

III. Miseries of it.

   1. So much of God's glory squandered.

   2. Mens' hearts cowed by want of sympathy.

   3. Many other men hindered from joining in good works; this harms ourselves, the men hindered, the work hindered, the souls to be helped, and God also.

   4. It affects banefully the whole of our own spiritual life, and is the negative of prayer.

   5. Horror of the unknown evil it does, which will meet us at the last day.

IV. Rules for its cure.

   1. Steady contemplation of its baseness and vulgarity.

   2. Openness about it in confession.

   3. Punishment of the feelings.

   4. To speak against our own feeling, not untruthfully, but *with* our convictions and *against* our feelings.

   5. Never to seek praise for our own works.

6. The practice of intercessory prayer—what a magnificent spirituality it moulds in us.

7. To avoid in religion all party, local prejudice, and *esprit de corps.*

The fact is, we must in this, as in so many other things, pass through what seems like insincerity in order to a cure. All men whose good and evil nature is struggling must look false.

Especial opposition of jealousy to the spirit of ' Jesus.

XXVIII.

CHILDISHNESS.

Where does sin come from ? On the whole from the lower part of our nature. There it is prepared in littleness, in unworthiness, in imperfection, rising up to sin at last. Therefore, this inferior part of our nature is especially to be looked to.

I. Our nature.

  1. Its dignity from being the image of God.

  2. Its immense powers.

  3. Its capability of immense graces.

  4. Human nature from God's point of view.

  5. Our end is to see God ; our magnificence in the Beatific Vision.

II. Now look at our realities.

  1. What interests us ?

    (1) Hardly ever religion. (2) Ends of quite a ludicrous smallness. (3) Things so transitory. (4) Things so really uninteresting. (5) Things

we should be ashamed to say interested us, not because of wrongness, but of childishness.

2. What amuses us ?

(1) An amusement seems no amusement unless it is undignified. (2) Seeing fine sights. (3) Dancing, though it is surely mysterious how this can be amusing. (4) Crowded rooms. (5) The fatigue we go through to be amused.

3. What tempts us ?

(1) Irresistibleness of very little temptations. (2) Nice clothes to put on. (3) Nice things to eat. (4) What others have and we can't get. (5) The notice of great people.

4 What rests us ?

(1) Leaving God. (2) Wasting time, doing nothing. (3) Gossip and criticism. (4) Thinking of ourselves. (5) Dreaming over novels.

III. The difficulty of being good consists, then, precisely in its being an effort.

1. Importance, therefore, of not intermitting the habit of the effort.

2. Jealousy of the puerility that we find in ourselves.

3. Importance of Church services, High Masses, sermons, and all externals of religion.

4. Directly sanctifying our recreations.

5. Realising unworthinesses as undeveloped sins.

The childishness of my nature frightens me almost more than its corruption.

XXIX.

INDIFFERENCE.

What have you been doing, how have you been living all last week.

All day long and a good part of the night, taking an interest in things! All life looks like a denial of indifference, like a protest against indifference. Such an interest, and in so many things, and for so long a time, and in such a succession of things! It is scarcely credible you are not worn out. Indifference is only the occasional weariness or collapse of our intense and laborious interests. But what are we interested in? Nay, rather, what are we not interested in? Well! are we much interested in religion? But why many words? I ask you this—you have often taken a vivid interest in spreading a piece of gossip or in discussing a neighbour's character: I do not say that has been your highest or greatest interest—oh no! but have you ever taken *as much* interest in Jesus Christ? have you ever been as keen, as quick, as busy, as loquacious for Him?

I. Human life is full of interest: look at the Human Life in the Tabernacle, the Sacred Heart of our most Blessed Lord.

   1. The adorable activity of Its countless and intense interests.

   2. Its passionate interests in the glory of God and the cause of holiness.

   3. Its unutterable occupations and sensitiveness about and in behalf of the salvation of each one of us.

And our indifference! Does not hell itself look to light a punishment for indifference?

II. Description of indifference.

    1. A dying man is unable to taste or feel, he cares about nothing: even human respect may go, though it seems the last thing to go.

    2. Imagine a man indifferent at the Crucifixion or a spirit indifferent in heaven.

    3. So a Catholic indifferent among the doctrines, sacraments, spiritual presences, historical grandeurs, or present conflicts of his religion? Does such a man look as if he were predestinated?

III. The sources of indifference.

    1. Worldliness, with its opposite interests, heartlessnesses, its vulgarising of the good of natural character, and its manifold suffocations of grace. Worldliness is a supplying of ourselves with interesting things which are not God.

    2. From habits of past sin, especially sins of thought.

    3. From a bad use of sacraments, whether sacrilegious, invalid, or slovenly.

IV. The dangers of indifference.

    1. It hinders present repentance, and prevents growth by stunting everything.

    2. It makes future return to God immensely difficult, specially by making us deaf to calls and inspirations.

    3. It is the worst form of tepidity, which is so hateful to God, and becomes incurable sooner than any other spiritual disease.

God hates it! and is it not hateful? Oh, is it not

enough to rouse the whole boundless meekness and
benignity of God into divinest storms of holy abhor-
rence ?   Indifference !   Was God the Father indifferent when He gave His only begotten Son to die for
men ?   Was God the Son indifferent when He hung
upon the cross, and every beating of His Heart was a
martyrdom of intensest love of sinners ?   Was God
the Holy Ghost indifferent when He sprang down
from heaven, shaking the strong foundations of the
temple with the mighty wind, and filling apostolic
hearts and tongues with fire that they might convert
the world ?   And the creature, the puny mean uninteresting creature, to whom God might well be indifferent, the creature who should be prostrate, shivering
in the extremest terrors of a most reasonable adoration,
dares to be indifferent, to care more for his money, his
honour, nay, I will say it, for his carriage, his food,
and his dress, than for the Majesty on high—nay, who
has found out a lower depth still, who does not care
less for God, but who does not care for God at all.

Well! the indifferent must die like others.   You
may die distracted and despairing, but most likely will
not—quite quietly—stupefied like an animal, indifferent to the last; is that any comfort to you ?   I
think not, but you may take it so if you will.   But
will the indifference be eternal ?   No! you will wake
up in God's eternal prison-house of fire—and there will
be no indifference *there !*

XXX.

THE AWFULNESS OF SIN.

A word has been whispered on the earth—sin! What is it! we know not what its awfulness can be, because we know not thoroughly what God is. Let us come aside from the world—cross Cedron—climb the Mount of Olives—enter the garden of Gethsemane—see the Easter moon above the olive trees—Jesus, His pallid countenance—His prayer—agony—bloody sweat—He was God—with the sins of men upon Him. Devotion of St. Charles to this mystery. Pray to enter in your measure into the interior dispositions of Jesus in the Garden.

I. The awfulness of sin in its effects.

1. The blighting of the soul by original sin; its unwearied kind of omnipresence; its mysterious transmission; the exile of unbaptized children from God transcends our comprehension, yet gives us a terrific view of sin.

2. One mortal sin—the ease with which it is committed—shortness of the act—it may be all interior—yet it is the death of grace, the instantaneous separation from God—the loss of all former merit—inevitable perdition—the rupture of good habits of years—the germ of everlasting hatred of God.

3. One venial sin—penances, illnesses, instances of God's wrath, fires of purgatory—so detestable before God that hell and purgatory might not be emptied, nor all heathen lands converted, by one simple falsehood.

4. Consequences even of remitted sin, mortal sin, remitted *quoad culpam ;* for all the Blood of Jesus, for all the mysteries included in the confessional, the forgiven sinner leaves it owing a terrific debt to God, a debt really not short of terrific ; he goes to communion, still that debt remains, the debt of purgatorial flames.

5. The consequences of sin to others—scandal— bad example—propagation of sin—its fearfully prolific nature—one man a devil to another— recriminations before the Judgment seat, if the awful majesty of the Judge hush them not.

6. The remedy which it requires—the Blood of God made man : Oh, it is awful to think that He would have taken that Precious Blood, yet need not have shed it if we had not sinned.

II. The nature of sin.

1. Its power against the abundant grace of God.

2. Its punishment—hell, and that is *citra con- dignum,* less than it deserves.

3. It is in its malice an attempt to dethrone God ; the revolting horror of this, to the angels especially, who see all sins as shadows of their brothers' first sin.

And we—how often have we sinned—how gravely ? Are we prepared to sin again ?

XXXI.

LAMPADES NOSTRÆ EXTINGUUNTUR.

Whatever it costs, we must be saved. Certainly—but from the lives we lead it does not seem as if salvation was costing much. Is it? If it is, then to you I do not speak. If it is not, then one of two things: either it is a mistake that salvation costs much—or else we are not in the right way to be saved. Of the two alternatives, the last in my judgment is most likely to be true.

Is a careless, inattentive, easy-going good person better off in his chances of salvation than a downright sinner? Let us see if we can get an answer to this question from Our Blessed Lord Himself.

Read the history of the Foolish Virgins.

I. *Lampades nostræ extinguuntur!* The horror of this cry: all that is compressed in it: what secrets of slovenly lives which only half suspected their own slovenliness; numbers of dying people are uttering it daily: if it could be heard and understood, it would surely hush all creatures into silence, it is so thrilling, so significant, a whole boundless eternity echoing it so wildly.

II. You see they had got lamps; they had been at the pains to buy oil: *once* their lamps were *not* out; good works you see, but not enough, not persevering.

III. They had been watching and wakeful nearly all their lives; it had been the object of their lives to wait for the Bridegroom. You do not look to me as if you were doing even so much as that.

IV. And now they did not go away, go after the world: they only slept, *i.e.* they took things easily: it was troublesome to be always on their guard: they relaxed the wakefulness of prayer: they let their consciences get indistinct But the good slept also: yes! and even they ran a hideous risk: but before that they had done penance, good works, mortifications, not trusted to faith, to feelings, and to outward devotions. The midnight cry takes *all* by surprise!

V. The haste to buy oil: the Bridegroom comes: the doors are shut: *Domine! Domine! aperi nobis!* He can but just have gone in! He will hear.

VI. The voice from within! yes! He *has* heard: the voice! such fearful words in so sweet a voice: I know you not! Not even know us: why! we believed in Him, we prayed to Him, we waited for Him: yet He is truth and cannot lie—oh! it is only to try us, to reprove us: it can be nothing more.

VII. *Domine! Domine! aperi nobis!* oh the agonising cry! for what is it to be left outside? it is misery, despair, madness, hell! *Domine! Domine! aperi nobis!* All is still: no voice comes again. He spake once, and He confirmed it with His amen, the gentle positiveness of which had been heard by the lake side, and on the green hill, and in the cornfield, and in the temple court. Oh those shut doors!

how fair, how beautiful is all within those doors, a land of golden light, of purest happiness, of everlasting life! *Domine! Domine! aperi nobis.*

O foolish, foolish Virgins, those doors will never open more!

XXXII.

*QUONIAM ADVESPERASCIT.**

Our Lord is gone—how old thoughts about Him return—this is always the way with love—parents die, and *then* we think of things—it is the same with divine love—the Holy Ghost's office was to bring Jesus to mind. Now He is gone—and we think of the *quoniam advesperascit*—because it is towards evening.

I. True of old age, and of all lapse of time.

  1. All proves itself to be vanity.

  2. We trust Jesus more.

  3. He is more all in all to us.

  4. Things and times are coming when we cannot do without Him.

  5. He is grown a necessity to our hearts, to our greater love of Him.

II. True of all growth in grace.

  1. Growth in grace is like old age, inasmuch as it is a disenchantment.

  2. An increase of tenderness is an inseparable accompaniment of all growth in grace.

* Sunday within the Octave of the Ascension, 1859.

3. Prayer makes death and eternity always near, more even than mere age does.

4. Sense of dependence on Jesus grows also with grace.

5. Our life passes into His, and is hid with His in God; the world slips from us, twilight of heart is coming on, the shades of evening thicken, the sense of exile presses, the feeling of home-lessness is heavy. We *must* have Him. Like the disciples we must "constrain" Him. All the instincts of our love combine in the one sweet petition, Stay with us, because it is towards evening, and the day is now far spent.

XXXIII.

DUTIES OF PARENTS TO CHILDREN.

Astonishing how much of evil is from tradition, and not simply from inward corruption of nature; family traditions are often the strongholds of sin, poisoning whole generations.

I. Duties of parents.

1. They can have no other duties on which their own salvation will turn more exclusively.

2. The position they occupy to their children is that of God.

3. Their children are much less their own than His.

4. They lose their own liberty of action by having continually to act so as to be a living law to their children.

5. They must have a definite system, and carry it on in the light of prayer.

6. Their influence is inevitable and continuous: they cannot be passive if they would. You cannot really *neglect* your children, you can *destroy* them.

7. Their mistakes are not easily discerned, and are almost impossible to repair.

II. The commonest of these mistakes.

1. Careless education of children, which is quite a characteristic of the day.

2. Not regarding them as *souls*.

3. Inconsistency of indulging and thwarting them as variable temper leads.

4. Crotchets of individual character practised upon them.

5. Praising them and saying foolish fondnesses to them, as if they were dogs or cats.

6. Not cultivating their confidence enough—this is a most fruitful error so far as after consequences are concerned—it is often fallen into by not giving liberty enough.

7. Making a personal luxury of children.

Necessity of not fidgetting, but having a huge confidence in God.

Sweet shadow of Mary's office! how many millions in heaven at this hour delightedly confess that of all God's natural gifts that which had most to do with putting them there was His gift of a wise and thoughtful Mother!

XXXIV.

DUTIES TO SERVANTS.

I. Relative duties.
1. They are as it were the private revelation of God to each soul.
2. They are our most undoubted obligations.
3. They take precedence of our own personal attractions in piety.
4. They will form in a special manner the subject matter of our judgment.
5. Hence nothing is so practical or so important— I will select one—duties to servants.

II. Duties to servants.
1. The idea of family—servants as children—house a sanctuary—a home even for them.
2. They are persons, not things, their character and salvation depending much on us.
3. Masters and mistresses are in great measure responsible before God for the sins of their servants.
4. Their sanctification should be a distinct principle in the arrangement of households.
5. Neglect of them is a source of unsuspected sins, which will be eternally fatal to many at last. So much for omissions, now for commissions.

III. Carelessness of a more active kind.
1. In point of time, inconsiderateness, unpunctuality.
2. In point of religious superintendence.
3. In point of illness.
4. In amount of work.

5. In wounding language, or even sulky manners.

IV. How we may sanctify ourselves by our duties to our servants.

 1. By making them our masters in some respects —the absence of government of temper—a specially modern deficiency.

 2. By deference to their weaknesses.

 3. By seeking their happiness, and finding a pleasure in making them happy.

 4. By looking on them as equals, or as most likely superiors in grace.

 5. By not thinking the personal service of a fellow-being a thing which is purchaseable by money; we purchase things, not persons, except in slave-dealing.

 6. By teaching our children carefully about this matter.

V. The good we may do by the right discharge of these duties.

 1. It is a sort of apostolate, to sanctify and convert souls to God.

 2. Of the number of servants who go wrong, most do so through the fault of their masters and mistresses.

  (1) Either by neglect. (2) Or by unkindness. (3) Or by want of prayer.

 3. The good to society will be very great.

 4. It is also the best way for ourselves, to avoid the dangers of wealth and station.

 5. We can hardly conceive a thing which, as entangling so many duties of justice and charity, will be more searched into by God at the judgment.

Yet what is your conduct as masters and mistresses ? It is known to Him who will judge you for it !

XXXV.

THOUGHTS FOR ACTIVE MEN.

I. We must do—
1. What comes to hand to do.
2. What belongs to our station in life.
3. What we are told by competent authority to do.
4. Not falling short of our grace.
5. Looking about to find good to do; much good lies hidden under us, like gold—under all positions in life, even under the most common-place.
6 Even making it for ourselves.
7. Our tasks should be exuberant and run over.
8. Never being content, nor thinking that we are to stop where we are.
9. Listening for inspirations to do more good.
10. There is a sort of holy restlessness—but we must be careful about it.

On the whole we do too much in life rather than too little; and a great proportion of our activity is often waste of precious time.

II. To leave undone—
1. What is too much for us.
2. Or too frequent for us.
3 Or unreasonable now.
4. Or beyond our grace.
5. Or not in keeping with our vocation.

6. Or unsuited to our character.

7. Or doing now what should have been done before.

8. Or anticipating what ought not to be done till afterwards.

9. Or doing good without reference to its suitableness to us.

10. Or selfwilled good—which often usurps the better place of commanded good.

11. Or the good which it belongs to some one else to do.

12. Or the good which we can do, but which commits us to what we cannot do.

13. Or the unnecessary good likely to be mistaken, and not harmlessly so, by others.

14. Or good done only because we want to be active and do something—we had better *pray* then.

15. Or good to which we have no actual inspiration.

Two maxims about our time.

1. Never put off. Never put off till to-morrow what you can do to-day.

2. Never anticipate. Never do to-day what you can put off till to-morrow.

Both have their time—their place—their character. The one should preponderate which is most against our natural disposition. They produce different varieties of holiness.

"Work your work before the time and He will give you your reward in His time." *

* Ecclus. li. 38.

XXXVI.

HINTS FOR VALETUDINARIANS.

1 Not to aim at making long meditations.
2. Not to kneel for long together, but to pray in postures which do not incommode the body.
3. To avoid burdening yourself with many vocal prayers.
4. Not to perform spiritual exercises shortly after meals.
5. To avoid long church functions, as lassitude brings on indevotion.
6. To be much given to spiritual reading, and that pausingly, as a compensation for long mental prayer.
7. To go very frequently to confession, and so make examen of conscience less onerous.
8. Not to have set times for more things than experience shows to be necessary.
9. To meditate chiefly on the Incarnation, not on the four last things and the like.
10. Never to attempt mortifications connected with eating or sleeping.
11. To devote yourself to ejaculatory prayer.
12. Never to keep a journal, or note down spiritual sentiments on paper.
13. To surround yourself with holy pictures and images.
14. To ask at all communions for a childlike humility, and for the gift of the sensible Presence of God.
15. To think as seldom as possible of past sins.

16. To avoid solemnity of manner.
17. The government of the tongue is the great field of valetudinarian mortification.
18. Considerate gentleness to servants should be an especial virtue of valetudinarians.
19. Thanksgivings after, or preparations for Holy Communion, should not be prolonged when they require much effort.
20. Touchiness of temper and inordinate desire for sympathy must be guarded against.
21. If you have fixed mornings for communion, do not scruple to change the morning if you feel unwell, or have a presentiment of unwellness.

XXXVII.

SHORT PAPERS.

I.

LAY PIETY.

Hearing sermons.* *One* great good of them is, that lay persons have to *listen* as inferiors, as to an oracle, and this is much to those whom nobody else dare thwart.

High Mass, and great functions.

Weekday Mass.

Spiritual reading, chiefly lives of saints.

Almsgiving, not out of whim, systematic, secret, with prayer, and with the intention of satisfaction.

* *See* pp. 233, 234.

Carefulness to be in sympathy with the Church.

Valuing outward things of our religion, and outward professions of faith.

Regularity, at considerable personal inconvenience, in keeping to times of frequenting the sacraments.

Some annual retreat, if possible.

Cultivating the sense of sin as an antidote against the unsuspected insidiousnesses of human respect and worldliness, and meditating often on purgatory.

Diligence, because indolence is half, and the better half, of worldliness.

Some very moderate and *exceedingly secret* bodily penance.

Profession of faith extremely open—devotion extremely secret: this is the lay rule.

2.

I. The horrible condition of a man who leads no inward life—between whom and his God there is no privacy.

He does not know where he is—like a man at sea, or in the wilderness, or rather in the forest where he cannot see the sun

He is open to all manner of delusions—nay, all things turn to delusions to him.

He has not even the initial grace of suspicion and self-distrust.

Death—eternity—God—all will be *surprises* to him—horror of this.

Only one thing about him is certain, viz., that

he is not as God would have him be, nay, that he is without God in the world—excommunicated.

II. How to mend.   By—

1. Daily examen of conscience.
2. Particular examen.
3. Distinct carefulness about each single confession.
4. Some *mental* prayer.
5. Much (at first greedy) spiritual reading.

3

OUR WAY WITH GOD.

We try Him last, having tried all else before Him.

We cast Him away when we have done with Him.

We claim Him as our right as creatures without giving Him His rights as Creator.

We think we may piece ourselves on with Him after any amount of intermission.

When we are with Him, He is to do all—and to be content with our profession of allegiance.

We account Him as some one to be cautious of.

At best we reckon Him an intervening God, not an ever-living, ever-present, ever-claiming God.

Contrast an adoring angel with this!

4.

THE WONDERFUL REVOLUTION WROUGHT IN US BY CONTINUALLY KEEPING OUR SINS BEFORE US.

It comes with *time,* but is most amazing when it comes.

It renders difficult virtues easy, and especially brings within our reach the heights of humility.

It gives us patience with others, with self, with God, great sweetness in intercourse with others, and a facility of judging well of all men.

It gives quite a new keenness and freshness to our gratitude to God, and a modest surprise at little kindnesses, which enables us to win the hearts of others.

It ensures final perseverance and a safe death sooner than anything else.

5.

EXPENSIVENESS.

· Fallacy of " I can afford it."

Life of immortification in little successive details of life.

Spending money weakens all our spiritual nature.

Immense work to be done for God. Disproportionate littleness of our alms to the poor: I doubt if it comes up to what theology says is obligatory. Obligations of charity are apt to slide into obligations of justice.

It is astonishing how childish we are at bottom, Expensiveness shows us this, and alas! hardens us in it.

The saints were magnificent souls, but was there ever one who was not parsimonious in personal expenses?

Money is a terrible talent to give account of.

6.

HEAVEN IS NOT ON THIS SIDE THE GRAVE.

Yet good people commonly make the mistake of thinking it is.

They think religion brings only privileges, and not responsibilities.

They expect consolations, and those at once, and in all things.

They use sacraments for self's ends.

Penance ever centres in self.

How few seek God.

Now on this side the grave God lives in crosses, and is only sweet when He is making us suffer also.

It is the saddest time for us when He is not trying us.

Is there then happiness in religion?—Yes! when our faith is so simple and so pure, that God being God, and we being we, we feel experimentally that all responsibilities are in reality condescensions and privileges.

7.

The apostles, who lived with our Lord continually and were imbued with His spirit, are recorded to have asked only two spiritual things of Him—prayer and faith.—Increase our faith.—Teach us how to pray. How much is implied in this?

8.

COMMON THINGS NOT REALISED SUFFICIENTLY.

That there is a huge invisible world.

That it is close to us.

That we have some day to be part of it.

That it touches us already.

That we may fall through into it any moment.

That the moment of this change is uncertain.

That all in it is fixed, doomed : it is a world of dooms.

That it embraces the extremes of weal and woe.

Any moment—and we are stopped by some one—and we look up : it is God.

Would any one seeing our lives dream we believed all this ?

———

9.

The best part of a man's treasure of merits are the things he has left unsaid.   Have *we* many ?

———

10.

A saint is simply a man who can act as well on what he only sees by faith as on what he sees with his eyes.   Faith is the most real of the two to him.   What we *see* leads us away.   The saint *sees* what he believes in, and so goes ahead.

Part Sixth.

MISCELLANEOUS.

SECTION I.

OLD TESTAMENT HISTORY.

I.

THE FALL OF THE ANGELS.

LENT is come again with its graces: but of what use are the growing years if the love of God grows not also ? But to love God more, we must learn God more. Let us select therefore some of the wonderful actions which God has done, and by which He reveals His character.

I. The fall of the Angels. Only the awe-stricken eye of contemplatives can see Him alone, an outspread formless solitude, a life not flowing nor noted by time, a grandeur unmeasured by space: now see Him surrounded by His new creation, leaping like waves in the brightness of the morning.

1. Beauty of this creation.

2. Immense joy of God in it.

3. Immense tenderness, like a mother's over her first-born.

4. First act of worship and love, made unanimously.

5. A third part fall in love with their own beauty —recoil at the Sacred Humanity: beautiful as they were, God had yet a more beautiful beauty in store—and it is an offence to them.

6. Duration of trial unknown—but very short suiting angelic intelligence.

7. Contest of the good angels with them—an intellectual one.

8. The moment expires, and they fall.

9. Unutterableness of their ruin.

II. Analysis of their sin.

1. They rested on self and loved it.

2. Attachment to their own opinion.

3. Want of promptitude to submit and adore.

4. Contentment with natural beatitude.

5. No wish to attack God, but simply to be apart from Him.

III. Lessons learned about God.

1. The singleness of His sanctity.

2. The swiftness of His justice.

3. His adorable recklessness; no consideration weighed with Him but that of His own glory.

4. Secret individual justice to each fallen spirit, meting out to each its exact punishment.

5. His blessed tranquillity amidst the irrevocableness of so vast a ruin.

This is the God with whom We have to do—to Whom we make our promises and resolutions—and from Whom alone we look for our eternal life.

II.

THE FLOOD.

All hearts have Edens from which God's justice drives them, or, if not His justice, even His very love; and yet all hearts linger fondly on the frontiers of the Edens from which they have been exiled.

I. The history.

1. Was it not in the evening that God blessed the world? Hence came evening peace, the suspension of the punishment of labour.

2. So on Adam's first evening out of Eden.

3. His nine hundred years of penance: we believe him to have been a great saint.

4. Two races: and mixed marriages between them.

5. Giants in those days, as though growths of the fresh earth.

6. Increase of wickedness—Adam's death—then seven hundred years.

7. Noe, the preacher of justice: secrecy of his immense holiness.

8. Noe building the Ark and preaching.

9. Animals going into the Ark.

10. God shutting him in: evident miraculousness of the whole account.

11. Hill tops, and waste of waters: a slow judgment not like the Fall of the Angels: and effected chiefly by agony of mind and breakings of heart.

12. The waters rise with their inexorable increase: the bridal songs are hushed; there are fearful intervals of silence and of wailing; the strange calamity is scarce believed even though it has come; the voices of children are extinguished, and the women's lamentations die out feebly in the cold greedy water, and the awful woeful sounds of men in their last agony; there must be sorrow even in the Ark, and a fear of the silence which has usurped the many-voiced dear earth of God. The flood surges against the

keel of the unearthly ship: there is now no
other sound.

II. Lessons.

1. Patience of this judgment: He treats men
   differently from angels.

2. Mercy in the midst of it: St. Chrysostom says
   that most were saved.

3. Yet there is still the same adorable recklessness
   —judgment on a vast scale.

4. There are giants now as then—science, politics,
   wealth, trade, progress, civilisation—but God is
   a greater, taller giant.

5. Saints now, as then, are the saviours of the
   earth.

6. Mixed marriages are mentioned as the seeming
   motive for the Flood.

7. Our Lord's description of Noe's times, like the
   times before the day of judgment; sins of
   omission: just as with the angels, not so much
   revolt, as a wish to stand apart: in these days
   it is God's interference which annoys men; the
   world wants to belong to itself.

God on the first Friday evening blessing the varie-
gated virgin earth—now He looks through the rents of
the wild ponderous clouds, and the whole scene is a
boundless plain of turbid and resounding waters: a
strange trouble of the dull crimson sunset is forcing
its way through the volumes of dense mist, and making
the waters look like a field of some blood-coloured
metal; only, like a black spot, there floats the single
Ark far away amidst the slanting rain in the red
light of that unnatural sea!

III.

THE TOWER OF BABEL.

I. We now approach one of the strangest events in the history of man, and one of the strangest judgments of God.

1. Devastated scenery after the flood: gradual gauzelike greening of the earth, from vales upwards.

2. God's ardour of love at Noe's sacrifice: He binds Himself to curse the earth no more.

3. Noe and his house lived among the mountains of Armenia for fear of floods, loving the sight of Ararat, where the curious Ark still lay.

4. Sweet sights of rainbows spanning the green Armenian valleys.

5. Noe's preaching: but Nemrod his great grandson seduces the people from him, as they multiply; and they begin the heresy of star worship, also *hunting* instead of *tilling the ground*.

6. Under Nemrod they move to the mighty plains of Sennaar: by the swift Tigris and the slow gliding Euphrates, with its smooth lips on a level with the sward—black buffaloes spotting the dark green morasses—rivers fringed with evergreen plumes of date palm, populous with doves, pelicans, and multitudes of waterfowl—bitterns in the pools of the marshes—men hawking gazelles upon the plains.

7. This was the beginning of politics. " When the *nations* had conspired together to consent to wickedness." *

* Wisdom x. 5.

8. They determined to build the tower, with bricks of clay, chopped reeds, and bitumen, of immense height, with a carriage road winding on the outside—covering it with a yellowish white glaze.

   (1) As an observatory temple for false worship of stars—heresy.

   (2) As a refuge against another flood—no faith in God's promise.

   (3) To make themselves a head and centre, and to have fame—pride.

   (4) As a beacon to get unity if they were scattered over the vast plains—politics: to frustrate God's precept of going out upon the earth.

9. How they knew beforehand the scattering which followed—traditions were still vivid—precept to Adam, twice repeated to Noe. They could not bear that God should get hold of them singly or in little parties—ah! we are always single with God.

10. God comes down to see, implying care, and almost, if God could have it, wonder.

11. The confusion—one talks to another—awfulness of no outward portent—causeless, unaccountable, the sun still shining—all like sudden stammering—each seeking out some one who could understand him—humbling and childish punishment. They had sacrificed all for society, and now they were cast back into an individual isolation which was horrible.

12. Inward anguish of soul and mind, rage and despair, fearful prospect—the *feel* of God's

hitherto *unfelt* hand, like man's hand to a quick-pulsed scared bird.

Pentecost—make a picture of it; the upper chamber was nearer to heaven than the tower, though not so high—then was the opposite of all this—but it was also to destroy the tyranny of states by Christian unity: states are the great enemies of God; there seems to be an inevitable ungodliness in politics.

II. Lessons.

1. The little impression which divine punishments make; we do not know God because we have no memory to realise how we have tried His patience in life: incurableness of sin: the tower was barely two hundred years after the flood.

2. Boldness also of sin, in aiming to reverse all God's intentions about His own world: rebellion against God is mostly a wrong *fear* of God.

3. Stupidity and childishness of sin—to escape flood! All sins are towers of Babel.

4. Sin encouraged by multitude, cowardly when dispersed.

5. A worse sin than the sins before the flood, yet so mildly dealt with: God was bound by His promise—also it is as if He were learning man's helpless badness by experience: He uses sin to carry out His law, so now to help His Church.

6. Here we get from wanting to *avoid* God to actual defiance of Him: so is it with all of us —we become bad with a badness we never could have believed.

I hardly know a more monumental sight in all history than the picture of the evening after the confusion: night comes down over the huge Babylonian plains: silence after the great Babel—the innocent stars come out and shine over the unfinished tower which would have so dishonoured them. Noe sitting by Euphrates' side—the low-voiced river gurgling faintly—the night wind in the palms—the grinding of the tall sedges one against another in the marshes, and the fitful stirring of nocturnal animals—the thoughts in Noe's mind, the man of God uncrowned by the proud hunter Nemrod—allowed to live almost out of contempt—yet now he has twice saved the earth, twice been the saviour of mankind. Dives wished one from the dead to go, yet Noe was *more*. His thoughts are an inward crown of thorns to his head: the staff of his neglected age is as the sceptre of reed in his hands: like Jesus in the guardroom of the Roman soldiers, Noe sits by the river side, silent in the grandeur of his unangry sorrow, in the magnificence of his incredible disgrace, while the great river takes its waters slowly to the sea with a plaintive sound, as if it was the voice that came from the broken heart of the man of God.

IV.

THE CITIES OF THE PLAIN.

"Behold this was the iniquity of Sodom, thy sister :—they did not put forth their hand to the needy, and to the poor."

EZECHIEL xvi. 49.

This history expounds God's dealings with great saints, great sinners, and ordinary believers.

Scene I.

1. Abraham and Lot on the heights near Bethel and Ai—Abraham's grandeur of holiness. View from near the tent—to the south-east a woodland vale, like " the paradise of God," or watered verdant Egypt—foliage of Jordan—scarlet anemones—song-birds—blue lakes ramparted by mountains.

2. Wickedness of its inhabitants — five cities— prosperity and ungodliness mostly go together —success worse than riches—dangers of a very successful man—prosperity based on underground fires.

3. Lot chooses the south—selfishness of the choice —see what it leads to.

4. God's reward to Abraham when he was left silent and alone—he moved to Mambre near Hebron, and built his altar there.

5. War of the four kings—Lot in trouble—Cities warned—Abraham's unselfishness ; he will take no reward, but will only be " enriched by God." Awful appearance of Melchisedec—he blesses Abraham—how instantaneously God always rewards generosity.

Scene II.

1. Noontide at the tent door at Mambre—the widespreading evergreen oak—three angels, Michael represents our Lord, and reveals the secret to Abraham—Abraham's five prayers not enough. The faith even of the Father of the Faithful could not take in the immensity of God's compassions.

2. Lot's life in the wicked city—it vexed his soul

daily, yet he stayed—Lot sitting in the gate of the city—hospitality of the angels—nocturnal flight—cowardice about the mountains—Segor, he gets by his selfish prayer what Abraham did not get by his unselfish intercession—how God accommodates Himself to our lowness.

3. Yet in the midst of mercy what strictness— Lot's wife, her irreligiousness—God's love of secrecy—there stands the pillar to this day, on the lower heights below the salt mountains of Usdum.

4. Nothing escapes God, nothing goes unrewarded, nothing unpunished, and all this in His own way, not in ours.

5. All moreover is so calm, so orderly, so un-precipitate; yet so sure, so obstinate, so in-veterate, and at last so suddenly overwhelming in the march of God.

Scene III.

1. The white light of the dawn coming up over the mountains of Hauran, struggling in the dark precipitate gorges—peacefulness of it—the night-bird of the country sings, but this is to be the last sunrise for the doomed cities of the plain.

2. Night of revelry and wickedness in the cities— no warnings seen—property looks so sure; who can wither the steadfast glory of all that beautiful nature? Arabian wind—air filled and reddened with sand, the stars like spots of blood through it, the moaning of the mountains, the storm.

3. The lightning sets the bitumen on fire—bitu-men! How despised things work for God!

Ark, tower, cities, in all three bitumen was used! Fountains of fire spouting upwards, crackling of the burning forests, thunderbolts in the cities, hissing of the Jordan, vast clouds of angry steam; the earthquake driving its colossal chariot wheels, like muffled thunder, underground—the wakening of the sleep-bound, half-drunken people, dying in sins, yet hardly half themselves; how often on quiet beds single sinners die thus!

4. The bed of the river, lake and plain, give way—vast subterranean beds of salt melt and give way into the cauldrons of fire, and all sinks down, with a terrific throe, deeper than the bottom of the sea; God has burned His victims, and burned them in this mysterious trough, which still seams the earth like the scar of a great wound, or the wrinkle of a fearful anguish, the most wondrous and awe-inspiring thing on earth.

5. Abraham rises very early in the morning—perceives clouds of fine ashes and a fetid smoke—adores the judgments of God, and marvels at His hatred of sin. Lot flies in utter poverty from the very Segor he had prayed for, and dwells like a hunted robber in the desolate caves of the mountains; while the inhabitants of the cities, each with the torturing consciousness of his own separate soul and separate guilt, lie in the terrible arms of God's justice, and are lying there to this hour, as if the morning of their destruction were yet unpassed, a morning to which there comes no calm of evening, no intermission of sweet night.

The scene now—the intense blue—the violet haze—the lifeless waters, with no life, but the bitterness of God's anger in them—sparkling spiked crystals of salt—yellow-foliaged canes, as if it were always autumn there—salt-frosted plants, and leafless ragged shrubs of thorny acacia—the ragged limestone clefts upon the west, and on the east the red mountains of Moab, as if they were on fire in the summer sunset—sunk in its hollow caverned trough that eye of shining water looks up through its violet haze to heaven, and the sun burnishes it—and the moon silvers it—and the stars shine deep down into it—and the winds ripple it, and the rain patters upon it in beaded drops—and the scene itself is a silent worship of the magnificent anger of our Heavenly Father. There is no horror in the place, only an inward gloom of heart in spite of the outward radiance of the landscape. It is as if God had painted a picture of the Universal Doom, and then had drawn this weary brightness of silent desolation like a curtain over the horrors of the painting. O terrible beauty, O terrible sunshine of that Blue Dead Sea! God's majesty never cows us more than when it looks so imperturbable.

V.

JONAS AND NINIVE.

I come to-day to that Bible history which, more than any other, touches my heart, and gives me a special devotion—the story of Jonas and Ninive.

A man coming down from the mountains of

Zabulon, close to Nazareth and Sephoris, with his face towards the sea—with hasty, unquiet look: the man almost of all men the greatest type of Jesus, and one of God's prophets: Jonas, who had prophesied * to Jeroboam the Second his recovery of his old dominions from Damascus to the Dead Sea: it is 807 B.C.

I The Flight.

What is the errand of this Galilean? He is flying from the omnipresent God, he a prophet and a saint! How childishness lies close to grandeur in human souls! God's word to him among the mountains: magnificence of his mission, like Jesus, to call the Gentiles. Jonas refuses, just as Moses strove to decline his mission: he had studied the character of God well, and has an instinct that mercy will be shown to Ninive. Perhaps his prophetic spirit warned him that it would repent.

II. The Shore.

He comes to Joppe: takes ship to Tarsus: will he escape from God over those blue waters? Strange! He refuses to convert the heathen and flies to Joppe where St. Peter had the vision of the Gentiles, and he pays his fare to Tarsus, where the Apostle of the Gentiles should be born! How God makes game of man!

III. The Ship.

Deep sleep in the ship like Jesus—storm—the prophet taught by the heathen shipmaster, Call on thy God! The lots; Jonas prophesies against himself with heroic charity: like Jesus, thrown over

* 4 Kings xiv. 25.

into the storm of God's anger : like Jesus, he makes
a calm : the goodness of the heathen sailors might
have shown what God could do even in heathen
hearts : men were converted and sacrificed to the
true God—so even here Jonas against his will
converts heathen.

IV. The Fish.

God "prepared" it as He did the gourd—he was in
it three days and three nights—his prayer and
hymn—he professes faith in the resurrection of
the body : he sees the temple ever before him : he
must have had a special devotion to it, as most
of the prophets had : "but yet I shall see Thy holy
temple again," heroic faith—he was cast out on the
lone seashore near Beyrout—a type of the Resurrection of our Blessed Lord and of our own : who
would have thought that lonely mystery was to
judge the Jews ? This is God's way.

V. The Preaching.

1. The second word of God ! God does not abandon
His purposes, but returns to them again and
again : this is a great mercy, His not taking us
at our word, or making our petulance final.
Possibly it came to him in the temple, when
making his thanksgiving.

2. Ninive—its immense size—huge population—
luxury—intense sin and corruption—idolatry :
he is to go and preach to all this, and threaten it,
like the apostles sent out to destroy the Roman
empire—like St. Peter when he had his vision of
the conversion of the Gentiles at Joppe. He
goes a day's journey into the city, and preaches,
"Yet forty days, and Ninive shall be destroyed."

VI. The Penance.

What a colossal grace! Graces mostly, like dew, small; but some large, as the first conversion of some nations to the Gospel.—The Ninevites *all* believe—*all* repent—even Sardanapalus—fast, wear sackcloth "from the greatest to the least"—the king sitting on ashes for a throne—proclamation about the cattle—all "cry with all their strength "— the beasts lowing from hunger—and it was acceptable to their Creator. There must have been a grandeur and an unaction in the preaching of Jonas: he could not have preached *penance* obviously—therefore he described God! Some have been preachers of penance, some of justice, Jonas simply of God ; and see how converting his preaching was—then how the heathen teach us Christians— faith of "Who can tell if God will turn?" *we know* He will turn. God hears: oh power of penance!

VII. The Prophet's Trouble.

Trouble of Jonas—men, even saints, cannot fathom God's mercy, cannot understand God's patience— Jonas' beautiful confession of God's character—how we always long to see God exercising His justice and interfering—he who knew God's character so eminently is also the most human of all the saints —how self-love mingles with high sanctity. God reasons—Jonas in his booth on the east side of the city, waiting and watching, sulky with God. The gourd—Jonas exceedingly glad of it—God like a mother spoiling a peevish child! The worm and the heat,—Jonas speaks—God questions—Jonas answers—God treats him like a wayward child, yet as if He wished to stand well with His creatures

—half apologises for the immensity of His compassion as if it were a scandal—His beautiful conclusion—"*May* I not save," *Et Ego non parcam Ninive?* * as if Jonas had some kind of right to his reputation and God would fain have his leave. See St. Teresa's remarkable excuse for Jonas, that since it is the Spirit of God (that speaks in us) it is very fit that we shew this fidelity to Him, to desire that He be not accounted a liar whereas He is the Supreme Truth.† Oh incredible joy to have a God like this! I have no words to tell, but I have a heart to feel what a God He is. O my God! it is the dearest thing to me in life that I belong to Thee, and that Thou wilt do to me not what I please, but, which is far better, far sweeter, far tenderer, what Thou pleasest

VIII. God beaten.

Magnificent sight, the men of Ninive driving God back by their humility; a frustrated judgment— and God more glorified in this appearance of defeat than in the surges of the Flood, or the thunderbolts of the guilty cities of the Plain: He sets His power in array and draws out the army of His vengeance, with the banners of His intolerable holiness, the music of angels, and all the pomp of His omnipotence, to that central plain of Asia, His prophet going before Him as His Herald. And the sighs of a hungry people, the lowing of the famished kine, the ornament of the sackcloth, and the sight of the king in ashes, the fair vision of hearts brought low, and of consciences ashamed, disperses Him

---

* Jon. iv. 11.
† Interior Castle, 6th mansion, chap. 3.

like the hoar frost of the morning—Oh how beautiful is this! Oh how wonderful is God?

IX. Jonas' Future—St. Ephrem says the king sent him back to Jerusalem—he would not have been so honoured had he been a more successful prophet —apparition of him related by St. Gregory *— his empty tomb at Geth Opher amid the green solitudes of Galilee—Jonas, risen in body, the body that was in the fish, that was fatigued with preaching, that loved the shade of the broad-leaved gourd, and that was scorched with the heat, that very Jonas ascended from Olivet with Jesus on Ascension Day, and is at this hour one of the splendours of the highest heaven.

Let us go and linger in thought on the battle-field where man's submission defeated and disarmed the vengeance of his Creator. How mournfully, how desolately, the evening comes amongst the treeless mounds of Ninive, scarred with excavations: the Tigris rushes by, half choked with the ruins of ancient causeways, hurrying its cold splashing waters as if it longed to be far away—and the coming out of those once worshipped stars is greeted now not by the idolatrous cadences of the dark priests on the watch-tower balconies, but by the long howl of the wild beasts, heard by none but the few marauding Arabs in their black tents, who are almost nocturnal beasts of prey themselves: yet to us with our faith, to Jonas looking out from the bosom of God over that faded turf and those tawny mounds, there lies, more than over any spot on earth but Calvary, the beautiful unfading splendour of the Divine Compassion, a

* Dial. Lib. iv. c. 34.

gracious, pathetic disclosure of that all-powerful Creator who has no power to harden His heart against the humility of His frightened creatures!

———— .

VI.

BALTASSAR'S FEAST.

I.—1. You must come with me again into the middle of Asia, to the river side, where the Tower of Babel stood. Nabuchodonosor on the palace roof—the magnificent city lying below—a huge square, fifty-six miles round, in the soft heated air—a hundred brass gates—the quiet Euphrates lapsing through, hemmed in by quays—tiers of sculptured palaces—hanging gardens, intersected with silver runlets of cool gurgling water—perfumed air of the gardens comes quivering up—huge parks, lawns, pastures and cornfields, enclosed within the city.—Is not this the great Babylon which I have built? He goes mad that very hour— is driven out—lives in wind and wet, eats grass, with hair like eagle's feathers, nails like bird's claws—for seven years—then he repents, and is restored: the Divine Master teaching kings their lessons.

2. The usual fate of divine lessons—look at his grandson, not twenty-five years after Nabucho-donosor's restoration to reason; Baltassar's hall — night falls on Babylon — apparent security—the banquet of a thousand guests—

magnificence of Asiatic state—it is as if there were no God, or as if none were needed, or as if He were far away.

3. The night in the city—in the lower dwellings are the captive Jews, by the river and its willows, or in dark chambers poring over parchment scrolls, or on palace steps of alabaster or varnished tiles, watching the wavering pillars of light reddening in the river from countless lamps, feeding their souls on the great mysteries of Genesis or the thrilling grandeurs of the Exodus, as if they could almost hear the sound of Miriam's timbrel coming up the long ages from the wreck-strewn sands of the Red Egyptian Sea, or sorrow finding its voice in the psalms of David—or with dark hope and fiery faith revolving the prophecies of Isaias. Is Cyrus "the man of God's own will from a far country?" Thinking of the hills around Jerusalem, the silent Olivet—the tumbled masses of ruined masonry, which once were the ramparts of their dear Sion—the broken walls—the desolate temple—they say, Sing us one of the songs of Sion—how shall we sing the song of the Lord in a strange land? Better to their eyes the stony waterless bed of Cedron, than the brimming and exulting waters of Euphrates!

4. The Medes and Persians lying two years outside the walls—blockade impossible or useless —they divert the river, hoping to be able to force the water-gate—God brought them there

—they represent His judgments—that night their works are ready.

5. Back to the feast—now drunkenness has come —the king sends for the sacred vessels—the guests drink out of them—praise their own gods—with an excess of boisterous mirth awful in sinful creatures—the quiet God listening without a sign.

6. Change in the king's face — his knees, in drunken fear, striking one against another— he sees a man's hand over against the candle-stick, and writing on the wall—he cries aloud for his magicians, who cannot even *read* the writing, which glows on the walls in characters of steady flame.

7. The Queen Dowager comes in—proposes Daniel —the king did not even know him—Nabucho-donosor's dream had been forgotten like one of those family histories people are so fond of putting away from their minds.

Mane. God hath numbered thy kingdom and finished it.

Thecel Thou art weighed in the balance and found wanting.

Phares. Thy kingdom is divided and given to the Medes and Persians.*

8. Procession by night of Daniel in purple, with gold chain, appointed the third in the kingdom —surprise of the people.

9. Meanwhile the soldiers on guard are neglectful —the city all in revelry—the river turned— Cyrus enters—confusion in the hall—the gold

* Dan. v. 26-8.

and silver vessels gleamed angrily in the lamp-light, as if they were bearing witness—Baltassar is slain—the Assyrian empire, that wonder of the old world, is blotted out in blood.

II. Lessons.

1. Drunk! worldliness makes us all drunk.

2. The three words—how they apply to us all.

3. Sacrilege—how God rises up to judgment, when His Church is touched.

4. Daniel paraded about, when he knew what a few hours would bring forth—so the saints always view all earthly things: a strange, peculiar picture, which shows how theatrical all life really is.

5. God's habit of interfering in unexpected times and places: the knowledge of this trait of God's character is a constant antidote to a false security of worldliness or unbelief.

6. Warnings vary—some give long notice—some are almost part of the very judgments they denounce: we have been judged while we did not suspect it.

7. Recent frequency of sudden deaths. What an unutterable thing a sudden death really is—the instant silence—the instant sight—the smooth velocity of the irrevocable doom.

Thus earth has yet another midnight to see, foreshadowed by that of Babylon.

Think of that night in Babylon—the immense size of the city giving time for the spread of rumours—word goes out that Euphrates has shrunk, and only trickles like a summer rivulet in his huge bed—all rush to see—cries of the fugitive and wounded—red

glare of the burning palaces—the war-cries of the
foreign people—canopy of black smoke momentarily
increasing in volume—reflecting the crimson confla-
gration—no stars as after Babel—no starry river, as
when Noe sat there under the date-palms fifteen hundred years ago. When God judges by Himself, all is
beautiful and dread and still: when He calls man to
His aid, all is clamour and confusion. On one side all
is panic and misery, on the other the excitement of
intoxicating conquest. In all the city there is no heart
at peace but that of Daniel. Look at him in his little
chamber praying at his open window as was his wont
—one of those little habits by which each saint is
known—he has laid down the purple mantle and the
golden collar—the lurid gleam of the burning city lights
up for us his face of supernatural youth and virgin beauty
—Oh look how it beams with God! He hears no
trampling of the multitudes, no rushing of the fugitives,
no falling in of burning palaces, no cries of murderous
victory, no wail from the women that cluster by the
empty bed of that treacherous Euphrates. Babylon is
burning! the grand Assyrian monarchy has gone to the
ground with a crash which the whole earth shall hear
—but the spirit of Daniel is far away, rapt into heaven,
fastened in the magnificence of prayer, as it were asleep
in the peace of heavenly contemplation. Wonderful
type of the Church and of the world! The gorgeous
Assyrians have become a nation of terror-stricken slaves
—the conquering Medes and Persians are themselves
the slaves of their own passionate triumph—only the
captive Hebrew, unconscious of the fiery city round
him, walks at large and at liberty in his soul within
the peaceful immensity of God! There is no freedom
in the world but sanctity!

Part Sixth.

MISCELLANEOUS.

SECTION II.

SPECIAL OCCASIONS.

I.

SUNDAY AFTER THE OPENING OF THE CHURCH OF THE IMMACULATE CONCEPTION, FARM STREET, 1849.

I. THE Church and the large towns of modern times. Influence of Paris over France. Growth of the influence of London.

Problems.

1. Absorbing and irreligious character of politics.
2. Intricate morals of trade and commerce.
3. Antichristian bent of literature and philosophy.
4. Degraded and vicious poverty in almost uncontrollable masses.
5. Luxury and indifferentism in the higher classes.
6. Want of method in well-intentioned energy.
7. Low principles and mere worldly prudence in the faithful from daily intercourse with unbelievers and heretics.

The power of evil in London—hopeless look of all this to all but Catholics.

II. London in Lord George Gordon's riots compared
  with London now. It is as if Jesus were weeping over the city, and the saints, one by one, were coming down to do His work, St. Alphonso, St. Philip, St. Ignatius. There is hope for

London in the energetic spirit of St. Ignatius. He was the saint—

1. Of common sense.
2. Of simplicity.
3. Of confidence in God.
4. Of boldness for truth.
5. Of carelessness for human respect.
6. Of urging on us our own sanctity first of all.

III. Thoughts which naturally come to mind on this occasion.

   1. View of the conversion of England in the spirit of St. Ignatius.

     (1) His love of concealment.
     (2) Not looking for great things. The *way* of the Spirit.
     (3) Waiting on God's will and grace.

   2. Not strangers in the land, as Redemptorists and Oratorians are, but linking us with the days of domestic persecution.

   3. Joy at the Church being under the Immaculate Conception, the *Virgo Prædicanda.* The sweet persuasiveness of truth—openness-loving Saxons.

Let us conquer for Mary—with Mary's name burning on our lips, and blazoned on our banners—what better eloquence to persuade Jesus to fight our battles, than that the nerve of our courage and the fruit of our triumphs should be the glory of His Immaculate Mother?

———

II.

THE ECCLESIASTICAL TITLES BILL.

I. Good always comes out of every evil which God permits on the face of the earth; so good has come, and more is yet to come out of the ordeal which English Catholics have had to pass through during the last half year or more. It comes in the shape of lessons to ourselves.

1. It has surprised us to find how old prejudices, misconceptions, and dislikes have come up just the same, and as virulent as before.

2. It teaches us by this that it does not do to smooth down or explain away our doctrines—no good comes of it.

3. It convinces us of the essential antagonism between the world and the Church; we must take our side with one or the other; the war will never end till the day of doom; the wrongs are unpardonable, the hatred unextinguishable.

4. It shows us the necessity of internal union, and of avoiding jealousies, lest through ill temper we get on the wrong side and so offend God.

5. It ought to drive us to our supernatural weapons of prayer and sacraments; for there is our strength, and by them we shall prevail.

II. We now see before us the prospect of the battle commencing once again, how shall we meet it?

1. By showing that we have not been studying our dearest Saviour's Passion in vain.

2. By humbling ourselves perpetually under the hand of God.

3. By gentleness of word and demeanour.
4. By frequenting the sacraments, and using intercessory prayer.
5. By remembering that it is the Month of Mary.

III. Consolations.

1. Numerous conversions, and growing trouble in thoughtful minds.
2. Weakness of Protestantism shown in its recurrence to mere force.
3. Number of scandals contrived together show the devil is alarmed, and has a plot, and he would not be frightened for nothing.
4. It has knit us together much more in England, and shown us whom we can trust.
5. It has bound the Irish and English Catholics together in a closer bond.

Pray, be gentle and loving, think well of your enemies, and leave the matter in the hands of Mary.

III.

CONFRATERNITY OF THE BLESSED SACRAMENT, ISLINGTON.

I. Picture of a true Catholic parish.

1. Confraternities suiting each man's taste.
2. Chapels in the church under their care.
3. Cultivation of different interior devotions; intercession and thanksgiving founded on them.
4. Works of mercy divided among them.
5. Their three loves. (1) The beauty of the

parish church. (2) The comforts of the poor. (3) The reconciliation of feuds.

II. The position of confraternities in a parish.

   1. What religious orders are in the church: they satisfy a kind of vocation.

   2. Their twofold life. (1) Functions. (2) An interior spirit. Neither must be neglected ; they are related one to another.

   3. They give unity to a parish, and are the strength of a pastor : they blend the parishes of a city.

   4. How they are indulgenced by the Church.

   5. The help they are to perseverance, needed as the *parochial* grace : many more than you think for are watching *you* now, sympathising or criticising ; so *persevere.*

III. Peculiar spirit of the Confraternity of the Blessed Sacrament : necessity of keeping to this spirit, as in religious orders.

   1. Sacrifice, as He is in this sacrament.

     (1) In bountiful alms to the poor.

     (2) In decoration of the altar.

     (3) In personal toil of mercy.

     (4) In some allowed mortifications.

     (5) In giving up your own will in confraternity and parochial matters.

   2. Joy, simply because He is there, shown—

     (1) In sweetness of manner.

     (2) In frequentation of the sacraments.

     (3) In delight with functions.

     (4) In zeal to get rid of sin and self.

     (5) In untiringness to get rid of it in others.

Patronage of St. John. Worship of the Immaculate Lamb—caught and glassed in the Church on earth—

so be it here—and when London is converted, sweet mass-bells sound, &c., people shall think of how parish glories began, almost at a birth with the hierarchy, in the church of St. John of Islington.

IV.

AT THE PROFESSION OF A SEPULCHRINE NUN.*

I. It seems simply the most natural thing to give our hearts utterly to God—an act of sheer justice—and that no pomp or solemnity should be made about it, because—

    1. It is His right.   2. The gift is so poor.   3. It is our own interest.   4. The attraction is His own grace.

II. Yet the Church, the Spouse of Christ, does make a solemnity of it, and why ?

    1. God, while blessing the earth with its beautiful and precious things, wants only for Himself the spirits of angels and the hearts of men.

    2. The value which by the gift of free will is imparted to the gift of ourselves to God.

    3. It is the carrying out of the Incarnation, and each such sacrifice is a new triumph for Jesus.

III. Hence the life of a religious is not so much a life of duty as a life of love; it is heaven begun on earth, because it is a death to the world.

IV. The vocation of a Sepulchrine shadowed in the Burial of Jesus.

* Preached at New Hall, 1852.

1. Mary prepared Him for the tomb, and left her heart with Him.
2. The bright city, the guilty city keeping feast hard by.
3. The tomb is in a garden of fruits and flowers and aromatic herbs.
4. Jesus makes no use of His senses.
5. Angels watch the precious deposit with adoring love.
6. It is cloistered, the stone rolled up against it, and the world watches it with fear.
7. Yet the body is all the while God, united to the divinity, and so deserving of worship.

V. Thus must a good Sepulchrine

1. Die by inches hour after hour in little things.
2. To the world without.
3. To selfwill within.
4. Even to spiritual sweetness and the caresses of Jesus.
5. And this death must be by the love of a hidden life of modest obedience.

Therefore it is that the Church makes a solemn pomp when a heart sacrifices itself to God; but the pomp is not concluded here; there is a function one day in heaven which will correspond to this, and be its true conclusion—Jesus receiving there the heart that dedicates itself unto Him this day. As it is on our Lady's feast here, so will it be her feast there: Heaven is the perpetual feast of Mary. Remember then the hour of which this hour is prophesying, whether it be night or day, after earth or after purgatory, when this heart shall kiss the five glorious Wounds of Jesus, and find its home for ever in the

wonders, and the joys, and the surpassing peace of
that same Eden wherein the Holy Trinity finds
ineffable delights, the Sacred Heart of the Eternal
Word, of God made Man.

———

V.

THE SECULAR CLERGY.*

St. Philip discerning the young priest; so let me
discern for my own profit rather than yours the
dignity of the secular clergy, and their vocation.

I. The secular clergy the divine patron of all
　　religious orders.

　　1. The vocation of the Incarnate Word to His
　　　　apostles—it began in abjection—He was
　　　　thought mad.†

　　2. Jesus Himself at once Founder and Member
　　　　of the secular clergy, though God.

　　3. The papacy a perpetuation of Jesus, in mixed
　　　　majesty and weakness on earth.

　　4. The secular hierarchy a shadow of the celestial—
　　　　just as mass is our real worship of the Imma-
　　　　culate Lamb.

　　5. Dignity of the apostles.　Our Lord died leaving
　　　　His work unfinished, so did St. Edmund.

II. History of the secular clergy.

　　1. Secular clergy in apostolic times—the whole
　　　　work of the world's conversion done by them.

　　2. Age of martyrs, and early councils.

* Preached at St. Edmund's College, Nov, 16, 1850.
† Mark iii. 21.

3. Parochial system in the Middle Ages, uncele-
   brated, but like the Hidden Life at Nazareth.

4. The relation of the secular clergy to religious.
   (1) Precedency in the spiritual hierarchy. (2)
   Religious orders borrow their priesthood. (3)
   A bishop requires greater perfection than a
   religious. (4) Religious are devoted to special
   ends. (5) The secular clergy represent the
   vita communis of the Incarnate Word.

5. How much it has to do in England just now!

III. If the secular clergy is an order, then it must
   have a cognisable spirit of its own.

1. Its attraction to Rome an instinct as well as a
   defined duty.

2. Love of Mary an essential part of the sacerdotal
   vocation.

3. Spirit of prayer—not too much activity—no
   hurry—all supernatural.

4. Dogmatic theology, which is more necessary as
   science spreads, lest physics should exclude it,
   and so the sacred science of the Incarnate
   Word be lost.

5. Fight with the world, of which fight celibacy is
   the symbol—it is easy to fight with force, but
   our most dangerous warfare is with the subtle
   moderation and masked deformity of low
   principles.

Present tumults show that the world is not dead, or
changed. The world in its badness changes just as
little as the Church. May I suggest a devotion? The
weariness of Jesus at the well!

VI.

CLOSING OF THE ORATORY IN KING WILLIAM STREET.

The one great lesson taught in this chapel has been that God is our Father—and so to be loved and trusted. Now we are all of us called to practice what we have been taught.

I. The immutability of God.

   1. When we realise God as our Father, all His perfections are so many consolations.

   2. None so great as His unchangeableness; for the pain of earth is its change.

   3. Yet in a way God Himself seems to change on earth.

   4. And reveals Himself especially in the past, as in the cases of Jacob, Moses, and Elias, and at Emmaus.

   5. Yet the gifts which He has given when we hardly knew it are solid and enduring.

II. Yes, the great overshadowing thought of life should be God.

   1. To have personal relations with God is an unspeakable delight.

   2. To have received private and personal marks of favour from Him.

   3. We love the place where He spoke—listened—appeared.

   4. All these are so many signs of our predestination.

   5. If memories of earth live in heaven, these will.

III. All this is but a description of what you and I feel about the Oratory.

1. Present feelings. (1) Love and confidence in St. Philip. (2) Daily word of God, customs, ways, hymns, look of things. (3) Voices and faces familiar to us are now about to pass away.

2. Four years ago, we came here as strangers and converts with a new and untried institute, bringing apparent novelties and foreign ways.

3. What you have given us. (1) Confidence. (2) Forbearance. (3) You have made us your home.

4. What are we to do? (1) We for our uncertain future must trust God and dear St. Philip. (2) You too must do the same. God cannot leave you; St. Philip will not. Put up his picture. (3) Lesson of to-day's feast, the Name of the daughter of the Eternal Father—Mary pondering things.

Conclusion : a chapter is closed—a day will come when we shall be in heaven, tranquil and safe for ever. The work begun in the Oratory will have ended in that —we shall be near St. Philip and can tell him so. Vision of earth—planet now purified and brightened by fires of doom floating sweetly on its track—the great city passed away, like a blot effaced—an image comes before us amid the beautiful fires of the Beatific Vision, and the songs of angels, and the soft flashings of the light of glory, and the magnificence of Jesus and the queenly splendours of Mary—the old chapel, with the echo of its long silenced hymns, and the poor ornaments of its well-remembered festivals—St. Philip by the altar-side busy with his Mother, our Lord dwelling there, like the Ark of God, for four years—nay even

the worn benches and the dingy stains upon the walls,
which are tokens and witnesses of the presence and
freedom of the poor. It will not mar the vision: it
will be full of God, of Jesus, of Mary: and we shall
see that it and all that was in it and about it, which is
a silliness to the world perhaps, was nothing less than
a thoughtful gift, a heavenly compassion, an act of love
to rouse, to cheer, to help, to soothe, to bless, a sweet
personal kindness to every one of us out of the abounding tenderness of our most dear Eternal Father !

VII.

OPENING OF THE ORATORY AT BROMPTON.

I. Picture of Catholics in the first ages of the Church.
  1. Men with a single dominant master interest,
     Jesus Christ and Him crucified.
  2. Their position with respect to literature and
     philosophy.
  3. Their political position: vague horror of unsocial
     tenets, &c.
  4. Suffering, for the most part, their method of
     meeting their difficulties: yet St. Paul gives an
     example of using what may be called consti-
     tutional rights.
  5. Possessed of doctrines out of harmony with all
     around them.
  6. Yet teasingly initiated by heretics without.
  7. Their position felt more as a duty than as a privi-

lege, though it was both. This is exactly our position as Catholics in England.

II. Tactics of those opposed to us,—inconsistent, yet necessarily and naturally so.

   1. Fair and honest controversy.

   2. Exciting feelings without appealing to reason, as at meetings.

   3. Exaggerated expressions of panic : as the Ecclesiastical Titles Bill, &c.

   4. Then the opposite—denying our numbers, and being scornful, the contempt not hiding real fear.

   5. Ignoring us and being silent about us, as in Tertullian's time.

III. Our warfare.

   1. Gentleness—not getting out of temper—believing the best where we know there is so much that is good.

   2. Teach our own doctrines—show their reasonableness and connection—and give a body of positive teaching.

   3. Prayer—silent life of the Church, growing day and night, like the grass in the gospel, men know not how.

   4. Cheerfulness, union, finding good in every one, trust in God, no set policy, fears, or coldness.

   5. Care of Christ's poor.

To look at St. Joseph, who would have said that he was trusted with the Treasure of heaven ?—so we in this mighty land as Catholics. England so dear, is yet lost, engulfed in material interests, with so much talent, and so little of it for God, with such a vast colonial empire, and so little planting of the cross in it. Think of her woods and fields, her hills and hollows, and running rivers, and sweet corners of domestic peace, which the quiet sunshine is lighting up, and think what it is to love her dearly and yet fear for her, lest one we love should haply be in all the wide wide earth the enemy of God.

.VIII.

FOR THE POOR SCHOOLS.

Who loves Jesus so little that he would not rejoice if his Lord met him, and asked something definite of him, and asked it by His Sacred Heart?

I. History of the Sacred Heart.

    1. A Human Heart fashioned of Mary's blood, assumed by God, and to be worshipped as divine.

    2. The mysteries It traversed.

    3. All were mysteries of love.

    4. And in all we were present by minutest and intensest love.

    5. So that the Sacred Heart is the perpetual rapture of spirits and of souls.

II. By the Sacred Heart we have our highest knowledge of God.

    1. Enjoyment of this knowledge.

    2. Value of it.

    3. Misery of being without it.

III. By the Sacred Heart we have the gift of faith.

    1. Enjoyment of it.

    2. Support of it.

    3. It is hell on earth to be without it.

IV. By the Sacred Heart we have grace, and sacraments, and Church.

    1. Enjoyment of them.

    2. Abundance of them.

    3. Who are more pitiable than those without it?

V. All these things how much are they to us?

    1. In sin.

    2. In sorrow.

    3. In death.

Eternity depends upon them.

VI. Statistics.

    1. Thousands are lost for want of these things.

    2. They are without them because of schools wanted.

    3. The fearful littleness of what is done.

VII. The fearfulness of the Sacred Heart trusting so much to us; the greatness of what is in our power.

VIII. Shame of other measures than those of the Sacred Heart.

    1. Generosity.

    2. Sacrifice.

    3. Expiation of your own sins.

    4. Each of such calls hardens the hearts it fails to open.

    5. Lent—Easter—May—Corpus Christi have gone by. I must take what you do to-day as the measure of your advancement in them.

Could you see a soul falling into the hands of its Judge for eternal doom, and not rescue it if you could, the Judge Himself looking wistfully at it the while? O my brethren! do not be angry with me, if I implore you to turn for one moment from the bright life of earth's abundance which you are leading, from the sweet sights and cheery sounds of domestic peace and love, to the drear horrors of the everlasting hell—the hell to which so many travel daily, even from this huge city, to which in a thousand ways the city's annual festive season sends so many fresh and additional victims, the hell to which you must not forget that you may go yourselves, and to which you are by sin actually due; and then conjure up to yourselves, as if in one vision, the bright eyes, and the young open brows, and the pretty downy cheeks, and the smiling mouths, and the fair childish hair, and the ever changing light of attractive infantine intelligence of all those thousands of dearest little ones; and then, rather than make some sacrifice of worldly goods and gains, will you let the dark spirit steal all that from the Sacred Heart, and sweep it into his night of eternal fire and pain, while Jesus, the Children's Lover, stands weeping by?

IX.

THE WORKHOUSE GRIEVANCE.

The Cardinal's mandate for the collection.

St. Francis of Sales, looking over his gifts and graces, thanked God most for the preservation of his faith, though he lived among those who were out of the Church, and read their books.

I. Let us consider the gift of faith.

    1. Its marvel—why it is given to some and not to others—its self-evidence which cannot be put into words.

2. Its mystery—it is so strange and unearthly, like another sense, a supernatural sight.

3. Its being a mark of God's election and pre-destination.

4. Its abounding joy, because of all these accompaniments, and also in itself.

5. Its incredibleness because it is so exceedingly grand.

II. The value we set on this gift.   The Apostles only asked two things, Teach us to pray, and Increase our faith.

   1. Of all our gifts it is the one we should most fear to lose: yet we *may* lose it, impossible as that may seem.

   2. It is a gift hardly ever given a second time.

   3. It is the gift on which the success of all our other gifts depends.

   4. It is the gift this age is specially trying to take from us: there is now a look of the last times: in days of Antichrist, there will be the apostacy of two-thirds of Catholics: should *we* persevere ?   This ought to fill us with a most salutary fear.

   5. The best way of keeping this gift is by using it, especially in devotion to the Church.

III. The workhouse grievance.

   1. It is a matter which turns simply on the question of faith.

   2. It is a hidden wound: for those outside the Church cannot even understand what we feel about it; our conduct seems to them either a pertinacity or an exaggeration.

3. It is a spreading wound because of unborn generations of children.

4. It is an evil so immense that it seems beyond
us and our strength : hence it is just an evil
which demands faith—for it is only to faith
that all things are possible.

5. It is an evil to which God is calling our special
attention, because He has put it into so many
minds and hearts.

A deathbed without faith—oh what a very wilderness it is—nothing can make up for it—all other
beauty only darkens it—have we not all or nearly all
of us griefs of this sort in our hearts ?   How comfortless they are! for some griefs *are* more comfortless
than others.   The dismal deathbeds of many of these
poor perverted children—though we have no kith or
kin, could we bear to see them ? yet they might have
been hindered by us !   And have we none, none in
our mind's eye now, whom we love and for whose
last hour we fear?—Oh give, give to these poor
children now, and the Father of the Fatherless will
give the gift of faith to those dear ones for whom you
would lay down your life, to get them the light of
faith.

Part Sixth.

MISCELLANEOUS.

SECTION III.

LIFE.

LIFE.

I.

THE NATURE OF LIFE.

I. ALL day long we live, and hardly ever think of living.

  1. Life is the most intimate feeling we have: so intimate we can hardly realise it.

  2. Outside of ourselves we see nothing but life: creation seems to be simply multitudinous life.

  3. But the life we see is nothing to the unseen life: earth is so full of life, that science is growing almost afraid of its own discoveries.

  4. Spiritual life: the realms of angels.

  5. God Himself is best defined as a boundless ocean of being, an inexhaustible abyss of life.

II. What, then, is the nature of our human life?

  1. It is a mystery.

    (1) Physically: never yet discovered, and probably never to be discovered.

    (2) Intellectually: here are fresh mysteries.

    (3) Morally: full of strange problems, of grandeur and of meanness.

  2. It is a joy.

    (1) It is the greatest of all joys: the visible joy of animals is like a visible expression of God's love of them.

(2) The joy by which alone all other joys are possible.

(3) A joy even amidst intensest sorrows.

3. It is a responsibility.

(1) It is not our own, but a charge.

(2) Difficult to understand, and yet more difficult to manage.

(3) Incredible exactness of the account we have to render: what God wants is *increase*, not burial of the talent.

4. It is a probation.

(1) This is the indelible character of every hour and of every action of life.

(2) Revelation is the making known of the terms, and the manner, and the *singleness* of this probation.

(3) It is a trial for an unknown life which will be very unlike this one.

(4) Strange elasticity of life, not to be permanently crushed by the unrelieved pressure of this sense of probation.

5. It is a martyrdom.

(1) Because it is a suffering, quick or slow, while on earth.

(2) Also a perpetual, inevitable witnessing to the life, and rights, and grandeurs of God.

(3) It will to all eternity, in weal or woe, be a trophy and a manifestation of the Divine Perfections.

6. It is a vocation: great necessity of bringing this home to ourselves.

(1) It is a special work, which each has to fulfil.

Members of one religious order cannot understand those of another.

(2) The call to it is a divine one.

(3) Hence an objectless, lapsing life is the worst impiety—the greatest frustration of a divine purpose: work is the divine condition of the gift of life.

7. It is a worship.

(1) Its beauty and its defects, its powers and its helplessness are alike prayer and praise to God.

(2) Life is worship in the mere living of it, it is so intensely divine a thing.

(3) It is our dignity to make life an enthusiasm by putting love into this worship, and by daring to copy God.

III. Conclusion.

1. To understand life we must look at God.

2. What He wants is increase: we must trade with life, and multiply it, and broaden it, and deepen it, and purify it.

3. It is fearful to think of the unsuspected capabilities of magnificence hidden in the humblest.

4. The buried talent is the sunken rock on which most lives strike and founder.

5. To the angels what a fearful sight is the foundering of a single life: to God, who understands it in all its terrible reality, how inexpressible is the horror of the vision!

Yet what is earth to look down upon but a storm-blackened ocean, covered all over daily with the foundering of beautiful predestinated lives!

2.

THE CHARACTERISTICS OF LIFE.

I. Preamble.

1. Variety of lives: each single life is a species—
   never repeated.

2. Yet they may be classed: some lives are poems,
   some histories, some contemplations, some sufferings, some enthusiasms, some pastimes.

3. But all lives are actions, whether we will it or
   not; and all serious whether we will it or not.

4. No man can *quite* understand another's man's life,
   however nearly he may do so; nay, who will
   dare to say that he understands his own?—this
   is a great source of charity. We all live secret
   lives—our only true publicity is in the mind of
   God: we are secret even to ourselves.

5. Under all this dazzle of diversity life, considered
   simply as life, has universal characteristics, life
   as life has its differences, life as life its same-
   nesses.

II. What are these characteristics?

1. Its shortness.

   (1) Not time to do all which we have to do: and
       time to do nothing with a satisfactory com-
       pleteness.

   (2) Time is always promising to go slower, but
       seems really to grow precipitate with years.

   (3) We do not get used to its shortness: it
       always equally takes us by surprise.

2. Its length.

(1) It seems long even at the very moment it feels short.

(2) It is long because it comes in chapters—because it is crowded with risks—because it makes such deep impressions—because it is so varied—because it is so uniform.

(3) The yoke of perseverance makes it seem long: hence the lives of good people often seem so weary, especially when grace leaves nature a little more than usual to itself.

3. Its independence of ourselves.

(1) We have so little power over it—hardly any rudder at all.

(2) Yet in some ways we have such a terrible power of inflicting irreparable injury upon ourselves: so that our present selves are hardly ever free, being dependent on our past selves; grace is the only thing like an emancipation.

(3) Yet on the whole, in matters of conduct, and especially in great things, life feels as if it were somebody else's life rather than our own.

4 Its dependence upon others.

(1) The way in which it is enchained with things, persons, times, places, and circumstances: and generally so that the outward seems to give the law to the inward.

(2) The most accidental events are those which seem most lastingly and critically to affect our freedom.

·(3) And this thraldom, meant in an unfallen world for a beautiful thraldom of love,

affects even our eternal destiny : the tran-
sient makes a deep dint upon our eternity
—and our predestination seems often to be
accomplished by that which seems most
wayward and accidental in what befalls us.

5. Its vicissitudes.

   (1) It never rests ; even time varies a state
       seemingly the same.

   (2) Its constant changes weary us, and also
       interfere with the growth of habits : and
       that purposely, for life is a deeper thing
       than an affair of habits.

   (3) We seem to live out and finish several lives
       in one, by reason of this changing : we
       learn the extent of life, and get that dim
       suspicion of its infinite capabilities, out of
       which heroisms come when wanted.

6. Its uniformity.

   (1) There is a uniformity in the very perpetuity
       of change.

   (2) Life seems more uniform than it is, because
       present years prophesy of the future, and
       assimilate the past, and so all life is always
       being lived twice, if not thrice over.

   (3) All life is a being overworked—and the feeling
       of fatigue simulates the effects of uniformity.

7. It has a distinct divine meaning.

   (1) This is true of all varieties of lives : the
       business of our life is to find it out.

   (2) Grace is to some a prospective, to others a
       retrospective, to others a piecemeal revela-
       tion of this meaning.

   (3) Thus all life is strictly providential to us,

and most so in least things : and least so
to those who have, or when they have,
much developed self-consciousness. Too
much self-consciousness oversets the truth-
fulness of life.

III. Conclusion.

   1. This life, thus characterised, does not pass so
much in an outside world, as within the temple,
which is God.

   2. How intimate beyond thought or word God is
to it all ; right fear and right love hinders this
feeling from becoming a superstition.

   3. We must be weary of life, and yet love it—
resting in it, yet yearning for heavenly things
—accounting it as little, yet reverencing it as
great—husbanding it with thrift, yet spending
it with generosity.

   4. We must live life by *unliving* it—*i.e* by living
for something beyond, something different from
it—and we do this in penance, in mortification,
in prayer, in works of mercy, in suffering, and
above all in contemplation.

   5. Our life must be an unretracted supernatural
love, as if it were part of God's life rather than
our own.

3.

THE STATES OF LIFE.

I. Preamble.

   1. The light and shade, the weather and the seasons
make the mountains always new : so is it with

the picturesqueness of human life, as the procession of circumstances drifts over it.

2. The very shallowest life on earth has always some unexpected novelties to disclose.

3. This is because of the strange mixture and mutual imbedding of the natural and supernatural, which belongs to every life, and is its secret rudder.

4. The way in which men's lives change under the quiet or the sudden pressure of providence is a continual new and double revelation of God and of humanity.

5. We shall only consider states which belong, not to the individual, but to human life in general.

II. The states of life.—Its theological states.

  1. Nature.

    (1) Nature is ever a likeness to God, in degree and proportion and fitness.

    (2) No rational creation has been in a state of nature.

    (3) We must not underrate the goodness and beauty of nature.

  2. Grace.

    (1) Its wonderful character, which grows incredible as we think of it.

    (2) Its strife and harmony with nature.

    (3) The state of grace in fallen creatures is not one of peace but of conflict.

  3. Glory.

    (1) The most natural of the states of life, because the one for which we were created.

    (2) The most supernatural, because the attainment of it is wholly the work of grace.

    (3) It is stable, enduring, and contented—and it alone brings out life, and all that is in it, giving life unity by making it entirely and only love.

III. States of age.

  1. Youth.

    (1) Its freshness and unworldliness.

    (2) Its sensual and imaginative character.

    (3) Its empire over our future.

  2. Middle life.

    (1) Its worldliness: yet to the unworldly it brings increased sense of vanity of the world.

    (2) Time of changes and crises: its sensual character becomes more animal because less imaginative.

    (3) The way in which new passions domineer: it is the time when sweet, kind, and gentle things perish.

  3. Old age.

    (1) Life withdrawing its forces, and living more slowly.

    (2) It is a time when life is very secret, secret even to ourselves.

    (3) When nature does not withstand grace, but conspires against it and undermines it.

IV. States of circumstances.

  1. Happiness.

    (1) It improves the good, but spoils the mediocre character: it makes the holy humble.

    (2) It broadens the character, however, rather than deepens it: but breadth is best for some.

(3) To the loving it is a new power of making others happy, a new power of loving.

2. Sorrow.

    (1) To most this is normally the sanctifying state, but it requires great grace.

    (2) Its action is so energetic that it hardens the hearts which it does not soften and ennoble.

    (3) It is the world in which grace finds and multiplies its capabilities: it is the beautifier of all life.

3. Temptation.

    (1) This comes by seasons, or in storms, or in epochs, sometimes almost or wholly life-long.

    (2) It is the action of living invisible evil upon the strength and feebleness of our nature.

    (3) In no part of His providence is God so watchful, so minute, or so partial to our interests.

V. Religious states.

   1. Conversion.

    (1) Enthusiasm must be its law, else its effort will be insufficient.

    (2) It should commit itself, like James and John, with a discreet indiscretion.

    (3) It is a season when our duty to God seems through our unskilfulness to thwart our duties to our neighbours.

   2. Penance.

    (1) It should be abiding yet cheerful, brave yet cautious, shamefaced but trusting.

    (2) It should have seasons of rigour, as the Holy Spirit seems to guide us.

(3) It should be very secret, and silent, and be the basis of all our successive spiritual states.

3. Habits of virtue.

(1) Life often gets out of the groove now without our knowing when or how.

(2) Vigilance over our character is apt to be one sided, and so neglect to correspond to inspirations.

(3) There is often a want of delicacy in our appreciation, and we get *too* natural after having exaggerated against nature.

4. Conclusion.

(1) In all these states there is the same inexorable activity almost fiercely imprinted upon life; it is as if we were being carried down a stream; life is a loom which plies of itself, and is playing day and night.

(2) At the bottom of the soul there is a thirst for God, always insatiable.

(3) How a man makes his own life by his own individual past—in all these different states.

(4) No mistake irreparable so far as regards our eternal interests—but often so with regard to this world—yet there is grandeur in silently sacrificing a life which for God's sake has irretrievably missed of its success in this world.

(5) What may not life be in the world to come, when it can be what we thus see it is on this side the grave, whether multiplied by joy, or magnified by sorrow, or deepened by temptation ?

4.

THE MEANINGS OF LIFE.

I. Preamble.

   1. Picture of the angels studying human life, a life so dissimilar to their own, yet so closely associated with it.

   2. Their astonishment at the romantic destinies of men, as visible in history.

   3. They see all human life in God's preference of human to angelic life in the Incarnation.

   4. One of the chief joys of angelic life is to be under human government; Jesus their Head, and Mary their Queen.

   5. They see human life, and all human lives in God: how marvellous must the vision be!

II. The meanings of life: each of its meanings is threefold—(1) To ourselves. (2) To others. (3) To God.

   1. In regard to eternity.

     (1) Looked at with reference to time it must seem incomplete, as it was not meant for time.

     (2) Indeed it has not only an obscure significance, but no significance at all, except in regard to eternity.

     (3) Every aspect of life, when dark, is full of a wistful look of eternity—when bright is simply reflecting eternity.

   2. In regard to the world, and its problems.

     (1) To life the world means exile, separation, and conflict: the whole world cannot fill the vacant heart of life.

(2) Absence of curiosity with regard to the problems of the world (or at least patient withholding of judgment), for we are in the crowd, and cannot see the look of the whole, the shape of the Cosmos.

(3) Yet the world, evil as it is, is a revelation of God, which is very needful for us, and enlightens even where it bewilders.

3. In regard to others, far off or near.

   (1) Life is meant to be communicative, a communication of God to all.

   (2) No one comes near us or across us, but it is through an intention of God, that we may help, soothe, or cheer him.

   (3) We must see God in all men, good or bad, and treat them as His representatives: human life is the Divine Mercy multiplied and made visible in all manner of little inventive tendernesses.

4. In regard to its own time and place: this regards individual lives.

   (1) It has a special work to do, which will not be done if we do not do it.

   (2) Relative duties are a most certain private revelation of God's will about it.

   (3) Time and place both pass—so life must be prompt to seize and fulfil the vocation of the hour.

5. In regard to grace.

   (1) Grace is meant to be the truth and the complement of life.

   (2) Nature is to give place to grace—sometimes to be supplanted. sometimes to be ruined by

it, sometimes to be voluntarily put to pain
because of it.

(3) Yet our grace is our own grace, in kind, in
degree, and in shape: we must keep to it
as to a vocation: *our* life means *our* grace:
each life means its own grace, and only its
own grace.

6. In regard to glory.

(1) Glory is our proper state—our sole satisfaction—God's sole satisfaction for us.

(2) Hence our work is not yet begun: it is only
preluded, if even so much as that.

(3) Our exile means that we should quicken the
impatience of our desires, and make our love
burn us more inwardly by restraining it:
this life is only the first chapter of life, pre-
fatory and of secondary though needful
import.

7. In regard to God.

(1) Our life is His from first to last—it is to Him
the realisation of a very sweet and eternal
thought.

(2) It is an incense to be burnt before Him for
ever, the glory of which is in being consumed.

(3) It is to be for ever losing and for ever finding itself in the abyss of His blessed and
bliss-giving Sovereignty.

III. Conclusion.

1. A picture of animal life—intense joy of it in
insects—fishes—reptiles—birds—beasts, wild
or domestic: thrills of their peculiar sensations,
exquisite senses, and above all, their light-like
instincts: quantity of outpoured joy, varieties

of it, intensities of it—hidden divine signet upon each animal pulsation of delight.

2. Angelic life—so broad, vast, so multitudinous, so impetuous, so peculiar—yet one sparkle only as it were of God's jubilant life.

3. Next to God I most revere a human life: the Life of Jesus upon earth, the Human Life of the Incarnate God.

4 God's inner Life—all love—as it were three oceans of light lying one within the other, one unspeakable, illimitable, incomprehensible unity of Life, one only Life but in a threefold jubilee.

5 God's outer Life—all love—as Creator, Redeemer, Sanctifier: to each one of us His seeming recklessness, yet His delicate tenderness, and the patience of His sensitive yearnings for our lives —a threefold love, a threefold ministry, but in one single unbeginning and unending love: threefold to Himself, He is one to us, and His oneness is eternal love gifting us with eternal life.

Life then is a grandeur; for it is half eternal. Each human life is as it were a divine thing expatriated from heaven, that in its exile it may learn to love God more, and to win a right to His further love. Human life is divine love, and the meaning of self is God.

Part Seventh.

THE LAST THINGS.

SECTION I.

THE FOUR LAST THINGS.

I.

THE LIGHT OF A DEATHBED.

THE feelings of Balaam on the rocky heights of
Moab, when he cried out, "Who can count the dust
of Jacob, and know the number of the stock of Israel?
Let my soul die the death of the just, and my last end
be like to them." St. Ignatius' rule to do everything,
as we should wish we had done it when we come to
die. Deceitful glimmering twilight of the world;
death the dawn, the sweet aurora of eternity; the
light which then streams in upon the soul.

I. The difference which the light of the deathbed
causes in our judgment of things.

    1. The extreme difficulty in life and health of
realising the soul, and looking at it apart and
separate in the multitude of sensible objects:
even good men feel this; such is the bewilder-
ing multiplicity of the world, and its almost
countless beautiful distractions.

    2. The exaggerated value we set on earthly objects,
or, which is the snare of holy souls, on doing
good on earth; we are so beset with the present that we cannot get to see God's side of the
question.

    3. The difficulty of bringing home to ourselves how
hard it is to save our souls; we cannot get the

solitude and silence required for realising this:
we really make far too light of this, and
acquiesce in much lower views than we think:
what if the number of the elect *be* so small, as
the *words* of our Lord, and as the views of many
saints and theologians would make it?

4 Death gradually, as bodily weakness increases,
and self-love ebbs out, unveils the Great
Eternal God—His interests, claims, views of
us, &c., &c.

II. We have all to die; it is not a something which
happens to this man, and not to that, but to all:
—the last illness of a good man.

1. Its beginning—slight symptoms—no prognostics
of its fatal ending—the devils prepare for the
fight—so does the guardian angel—Mary prays
—all is preluding in the invisible world.

2. News of his danger—sorrow of those who love
him—his own dispositions—perhaps not instantaneous calmness—trembling in the sight of
God's judgments—his view of how much goes
to the salvation of a soul.

3. The last Sacraments—Confession—Viaticum—
Extreme Unction—Plenary Indulgence—as if
earth had done, and could do no more; all is to
be supernatural.

4. Aspirations for death—the fortitude he has
received in the Sacraments gleams out thus—
danger of presumption—effort to calm himself
—earthly thoughts put away, the world is
going on around him as usual, he heeds it not,
and it heeds not him—it is God's hour—all is
supernatural—the world has done with him.

5. The last temptations—he enters into his eclipse: now Mary, Saints, Angels, come to his aid— despair, presumption, desire to get well, scruples: peace restored.

6. The last breath—describe the agony—life's energies are rallied to die—the soul sits on the lips—look! it has gone. That thing on the bed is not a man—whither has he gone?

II.

BAD DEATHS OF THOSE WHO HAVE ONCE BEEN GOOD.

If the material world is beautiful for its wisdom and its power, the spiritual world is yet more beautiful for its mercy and its compassion; but there are some mysterious apparent exceptions to this universal rule of mercy, which are full of doubt and fear, and which we must not omit to study. We shall be least safe from their happening to ourselves, if we wilfully refuse to consider them. The bad deaths of those who have once been good, and good for the greater part of their lives; the opposite of deathbed salvation.

I. Considerations on the phenomenon.

1. Our eternity depends on the state in which we are when we die—death fixes it—bad life with good death is secure—good life with bad death is perdition.

2. Thus the hour of death, its time, manner, and circumstances, is one of the most, or positively *the* most, decisive of God's providences over us.

3. As to whether such deaths are common, we are left in uneasy ignorance.

4. It is curious that wisdom was the gift of some of the most startling instances, Solomon, Origen, Tertullian, Hosius.

5. We are to pass the time of our sojourning here in fear.

6. The fearful mystery involved in so dire a dispensation.

7. It does not seem to happen to those who are devoted to Mary.

8. There are three classes to whom it does happen :
   (1) Either those who have been really good, and have not persevered.
   (2) Or those who have been in delusions all along.
   (3) Or those who have got into a rut of slovenliness and tepidity, and so cannot fight through the last hours.

II. The roots and origins of this awful visitation.

1. Carelessness about little things.

2. A spirit of self-trust, and a want of self-knowledge.

3. A habit of criticising others.

4. Want of special prayer for the gift of perseverance.

5. Some secret fault, like Judas.

6. A hidden covetousness, which is idolatry.

7. A habit of taking our own advice and opinion.

8. Absence of works of mercy to others.

9. A want of being thoroughly sincere with God.

Oh, how manifold and inscrutable are the clouds which are round about the judgment seat of God!

When I look on this dispensation of an evil death, my head turns dizzy with the thick close darkness into which I look. It is fearful that all things should depend on *one*. It must be a strong rope at the end of which all eternity is to hang, and it shall not break. Whether any of us shall die such a dog's death, I know not; but I know that if we do, it will be our own fault, and only ours; and I know, moreover, that if we do not take pains, and great pains, and persevering pains, there will be fearful darkness round us in that hour when we shall most need light.

III.

THE PARTICULAR JUDGMENT.

We have come to the shore of eternity—what will it be like?—what sounds shall we hear?—what will be the first sight to meet our eyes?—the looks of dying people—the look that comes after death—who shall unlock the secret of those looks?—all depends on our living so that that moment should not take us by surprise.

I. The last hum of worldly sound passing from our ears: the act of death probably not *very* painful.

II. The disembodied soul—the world, the flesh fall off—it sees plainly—its acts of renunciation of any venial sin it may have upon it unremitted —this act not meritorious.

III. Judgment. Into whose hands does it fall? Who is judge?

1. Would it not seem awful to be judged by God? Through His mercy we are not judged by God as God; though He who judges us be God.

2. Could we trust a fellow creature? almost not—even if God allowed it.

3. To the beautiful Human Soul of Jesus is this judicial power given.   Oh joy and consolation!

IV. The act of judgment: Jesus comes not down, nor is the soul caught up to His corporal presence; it is raised to Him intellectually: He flashes a light upon it—reveals all sins, motives, inexcusableness, &c.   Guardian Angel and Tempter waiting.

1. The soul sees the discussion.

2. Hears the sentence.

3. Thrilling awfulness of its instantaneity; no time to explain; or to set matters right—not even the delay of colloquy, as at the Universal Judgment.

4. The sentence, irrevocable and fixed, rushes upon the soul; now at last the creature is in the hands of the Creator—no medium, no gobetween, no world, no distractions : the tingling silentness of eternity all round.

V. This is actually to happen to each one of us here present; stay ! let us realise that for a moment.

VI. The sentence! what was it? what will it be? Listen—can you not fancy you hear the dear, dread, most dread yet most dear sound, of the voice of Mary's Son, like His Mother's voice, penetrating the depths of the clear soul?   O Jesus! what wilt Thou say? what will it be? He is there in the tabernacle! He knows! He might speak if He would! But He keeps it to Himself! His Blessed Mouth is there—but His Lips are closed.

O Jesus! For Thy sweet Mother's sake, speak gentle things to our poor frightened souls in that tremendous hour!

IV.

ETERNITY.

I believe in the life everlasting. Amen.

I. Picture of life; all classes living, scheming, building, planning, as if all was to go on the same without end. An Angel comes down, stands on the shore of the sea—proclaims, No more time!—startled horror of people! then what begins? Nothing begins. We fall into the dreadful arms of eternity, which never did begin, as if we fell off from the round world into space.

II. What this proclamation imports to us, who are used habitually to time,—now time is to be no more.

  1. Time in a material sense, no clocks, no bells, hours, days, nights, seasons; all still and stationary for evermore.

  2. Time for pleasure in earthly things.

  3. Time for meriting.

  4. Time for repenting.

III. Let us walk through London: what will become of all these people? they will live for ever! But Father! they never think of God! Live for ever!

What will· life be like when time will be no
more ? We are so used to time, what can we
do without it ? it is like air to us, or like water
to a fish. Yet an Angel drives us out of it,—
into what ? awful ! what is this new thing ?
this eternity ? we do not know. True ! our
ignorance is more awful still : but are we ready ?
are we getting ready ? are we going to get ready ?
If we slept our last sleep to-night, when and
where would our awakening be ?

IV. But this eternity ! souls still live,—oh yes ! live
for ever ! The builders of the Tower of Babel, all
those the flood drowned are alive, fearfully alive,
fearfully strong ! Those of Sodom and Gomorrah,
whom the fire licked up like the tongue of a cruel
beast—those that crucified our Lord—your own
ancestors—all of the last five thousand years.
Did you see your father or your mother die ?
They are alive still. And we *must, must, must*
live for ever ! This day one hundred thousand
million years hence we shall be strong, fresh,
immortal, so immortal that fire cannot kill us,
blaze it ever so cruelly.

V. But this eternity—what is it ? It moves not,—all
else moves.

1. We die—survivors go on journeys, eat, sleep,
   wake, change,—we, if we are lost, burn : at
   every change and every turn we are fixed
   somewhere and doing something—O my God !
   that we could be sure it was not living in fire !

2. We cannot perish, even torture cannot consume
   us. All, all in eternity is irrevocable.

3. How can we bring this home to ourselves ?

Drops of water, grains of sand, leaves of trees, pulses of men.

4. And then it ends? Oh no! it is only beginning.—Oh poor damned souls! could we not almost pity them? and our own relations, our sister's eyes,—our child's voice,—our mother that bore us, and the father that toiled for us, perhaps!

5. Imagine endurance of pain, hot coals, or quick lime in the eye, spikes under the nails, for a million years!

6. And each moment is all eternity at once, like the pressure of a weight.

VI. But really, really, will it never end? Hush! let us speak gently, it is such a dreadful thing to say! Can we get at God? Where is He? Can we touch Him? Can we hold Him fast? Can we tie Him on His throne? Hush! let us speak lower. Can we kill Him? O my God! that we should utter the words! then, then there might be a chance of ending eternity!

VII. Good God! what shall we do? We cannot get out of the way of eternity: we cannot turn the corner of it. My Jesus! where shall we flee? No wonder sinners at the day of doom will call on the mountains to fall on them—what shall *we* do? Make friends with eternity! Oh, then, that God would send us an angel to tell us on what eternity, a good eternity, depends. See! the heavens open: it is not an angel. Hear! a voice! not of an angel but of the crucified God. He tells us—a good confession! Once more let us go to the damned and learn—they would give all the world for five minutes at the feet of a priest! Now count up the sins of your past life—look at that damned soul—how it struggles—oh, how sick it is with fire—how the flames roar through that crowded dungeon. See! how it tosses and bounds! what convulsions— oh, horrible! Then will you make up your minds that you will not go to hell? Lift up your hands, in the name of God! lift up your hands, all ye who will not go to hell—now on your knees—look at the crucifix—now say with me aloud—O Jesus, mercy!—now again once more, louder, from your hearts—O Jesus, mercy!

VIII. Dearest children! God bless your good resolutions! Oh this eternity is a tremendous thing. I wonder people do not faint when they think of it. Soon, soon shall we set sail upon that boundless sea—we know not how soon—it may be this very night! It is no fairy tale, it concerns both you and me. Each of us is to be either an angel or a devil, either saved or damned; on rolls the wheel of time; death steals on with a dreadful swiftness, and then bounds upon us, like the going of a train upon the railway; nearer still and nearer does it come. It is not a long work to die, it is not a hard thing to die, albeit a little painful, and tight, and cold, and suffocating; and when, my dear Brethren, it is past, what and where shall we be? aye—what and where shall we be when the day has come and gone, and all is still—fixed—wonderful—eternal?

V.

THE MISTAKE FOUND OUT TOO LATE.

The difference between putting ourselves into the position of our Lord's mysteries, at which we never can assist, and into positions where one day we most infallibly shall be,—as death and judgment. Well! now I will suppose what is really going on somewhere while I speak.

I. Life over—plans at an end—the illness—the agony—all is over. This must come to every one of us, good or bad—there is no exception: we are judged, and sentence is passed, one of eternal condemnation; this too may happen to all of us, and will, unless we are careful.

II. There we stand where we are judged: our feelings.

1. Death is over—it was not so very bad to bear—however, it is over, and will never come again.

2. Surprise—it has all come so suddenly,—things are so odd and strange,—is it really all over? and have I seen Jesus,—and the Angels,—and the devil?

3. Without my body, such immense power,—such ability to feel things, pleasure or pain, so intensely. Now I realise what I am of myself; I can do well without my body;—what wonderful life, what terrible life there is in my soul: death could do nothing to it.

4. Without creatures,—awful silence,—breathless wilderness,—not a sound,—not a friend,—not a creature,—stripped of all,—and fallen just as

I am into the hands of God. All I lived for
has left me, or I have left it: it matters not
which. I could not have believed it. It is
terrible: people on earth never could believe it:
it could not be explained to them.

5. I have seen Jesus too,—the Babe, the Boy, the
Man, the Blessed Sacrament. Oh! it was most
beautiful—and I have seen Him speak. I wish
I could see Him at my ease, not all trembling as
I naturally was at judgment—I have seen Him,
however, but all is vain. It was of no good to
me. I must try to be calm, if I can, but this
is unutterable: I have only seen Him to be
condemned: condemned,—what do I mean by
condemned when I say it?

6. What then really are my prospects? Fire, pain,
agony, imprisonment, tyranny of devils, to go
on fathoming unfathomable depths of pain, and
find no bottom in them to all eternity. Well!
I must make up my mind to it! No! but I
can't. O God! Jesus! come back again just for
one moment—I have one word to say. No!
all is silent, more silent than the grave.

7. Change of views about—(1) Sacraments, (2)
Pleasures, (3) Penance, (4) Prayer, (5) Lukewarmness leading to mortal sin. Good heavens!
why did I not see this before? Why say, good
heavens! There are none for me!

8. Novelty of despair—What is this new feeling
coming on me,—a new kind of life? Oh,
dreadful! I feel it stealing first into one faculty,
then another,—it is mastering me, hope is going
out of me. Oh! death was nothing to this;—

for ever, for ever, for ever! It cannot be.—I
can't live this life.—It will crush me to pieces
—Oh! how strong it is!

Every moment some one is in this predicament,
which is as common as a man digging in a field, or
whistling in the road, as a clock striking, as a train
starting;—our turn for this risk must come.—We do
not know when; and nobody is sure of coming safe out
of it. If this does not make us religious, what will?

VI.

THE JUDGMENT OF THE REPROBATE.

I. There is an end of the world to each of us in our
own death and immediate judgment.

   1 The uncertainty of the time, but the certainty
that it must be very soon.

   2. Very likely we shall have no warning, or an
insufficient one.

   3. All that is involved in passing out of time into
eternity.

   4. The startling indifference and practical unbelief
of men.

   5. The tremendous reality they will fall into all at
once.

II. The judgment of a worldly man may be taken as
an illustration. Interest of it—daily is it acted
in *substance*.

   1. Our Lord's inquiry concerning—

     (1) The greatness of His Passion. (2) Works of
mercy. (3) Sins of commission. (4) Sins
of omission. (5) Bad thoughts and pur-

poses. (6) Idle words. (7) Temporal goods. (8) Relative duties. (9) Use of time.

2. The accusers.
   (1) Conscience, with its clear view of sins, and of the corruption of motives heretofore secret even to itself.
   (2) The devil, with unspeakable ability, and desperate malice.
   (3) Place and accomplice as it were appearing against us.

3. The witnesses.
   (1) The Creator. (2) Guardian Angel. (3) Stain of sin visible on the soul.

4. The assessors.
   (1) The Apostles. (2) Martyrs. (3) Patriarchs and Prophets. (4) ·The voluntarily poor.

5. The executioners.
   (1) St. Michael directing demons to torture. (2) Demons torturing. (3) Heavenly spirits applauding. (4) Instruments of torture, fire, cold, &c., created expressly for torture.

6. Intolerable sentence.
   (1) Bitterness of pains, mental and bodily. (2) Their variety. (3) Continuity. (4) Eternity.

III. Differences of this from the particular judgment.
   1. The soul knows its fate beforehand, and so has no hope : thus it is an execution rather than a judgment.
   2. The unutterableness of the pains.
   3. Increase of pains from union with the body.
   4. All the publicity of it.
   5. *We* shall see it.

What will be our fate then? what our share of that pomp? Should not this thought cover all our lives? We resemble men in prison waiting for trial; the issue is uncertain, because our guilt is clear, and mercy not quite so sure. This is a picture of our condition; we should think of nothing but our trial.

VII.

THE LOSS OF GOD.

Forgive me if I pain you very much this morning. Bear with me, peace will come out of it. Suppose Jesus has not spoken gently to the disembodied soul, what comes of it? Let us follow it on. Heaven is closed, Jesus gone, vanished; but the terrific sound of the Voice of Mary's Son rings through the depths of the lost soul—lost, lost, eternally! O misery! O misery! what has it gained? fire! what has it lost? God!

I. How many of the two millions and more in London live without God in the world; yet what is the end?

  1. Picture of hell at this very hour existing, active, full of life, while we are here!

  2. The inexorableness of God's Majesty, while the cries of lost souls rise up clamorously before Him—it simply glorifies Him—proof of the intensity of His hatred of sin.

  3. This is the destiny of those who lose God.

II. View of the pain of loss.

  1. The instant the soul is disengaged from the body, it has a terrific attraction towards God

through the *radical* love it has for Him, and the
exceeding sweetness and beauty of the Divinity.

2. The efforts it makes.

  (1) In rage, it would fain murder God and
      destroy Him.

  (2) In agony, it would fain suffocate its own
      interior thirst for God.

  (3) In fury, it would fain break its tight fetters
      of gnawing fire.

3. The state of the lost soul in this respect.

  (1) It lives a horrible life in the simultaneous
      commingling of the three effects just named.

  (2) Its imprecations against God, Whom it is
      powerless to hurt.

  (3) Its writhing under the sense of its being its
      own executioner.

  (4) The sickening, overwhelming sense of all
      being eternal.

4. The four views which it continually takes of its
   own state.

  (1) The union of all the pains of sense with this
      vast central pain of loss.

  (2) Its view of the graces it has received.

  (3) Its view of the grandeur of the bliss it has lost.

  (4) When it seeks God it meets terrors—it cries,
      where is God? and it embraces keen
      flames; where is God? and it meets hide-
      ous demons; where is God? and it dashes
      into an affrighted crowd of damned souls.

Think, (1) One mortal sin can send us there.
(2) Venial sin and trepidity dispose us thither.
(3) We ought to be there at this moment. (4) Many
are there at this hour who have sinned less than we.

Oh the beauty, the beauty, the ravishing beauty of God! One sunbeam of His beauty falling athwart the outer darkness of that land of everlasting curse, and it would be lit up into a paradise of peace and a home of joy! O Beauty! O uncreated Beauty! show Thyself, show Thyself but ever so little to our poor hearts, that they may leap forward with longing love, and unite themselves eternally to Thee!

VIII.

WHY OUR BLESSED LORD SAID SO LITTLE ABOUT HEAVEN.

Exiles love to talk of home—friends who part of the home where they shall meet—those who love each other of the joys they have prepared for those they love. Why does our Lord say so little about heaven? It seems as if His disciples so needed it, and it would have cheered them so much.

I. That we might love Him for His own sake. He was jealous lest the very beauty of His rewards should steal our hearts from the pure love of His own beauty.

II. Because it is simply He Who will make the immense delight of heaven.

III. That we might reach higher in heaven by loving more disinterestedly.

IV. Because the joys of heaven are so surpassing, that our present understanding is not capable of comprehending them.

V. Because we should scarcely have been able to believe it. It would have been a standing temptation against faith, especially when we considered our own unworthiness.

I recommend meditation on the joys of heaven, because of the encroachments of worldliness upon our spirits in these times. I do not tell you to forget hell. Oh no! from time to time, my Brethren, feed on those fires, till your blood is cold and your flesh trembles. You, I think, run less risks than many others, but the mere chance of going there is enough to make us tremble. But for once you think of hell, think ten times of the bright heaven which your Father has prepared for you. Each one's place is ready at this hour—your name is fixed to it—the angels pass it by—they admire its beauty and its joys —but they think of the beautiful throne which was ready for Satan, but on which he never sat, and where St. Joseph, or the Baptist, or St. Peter perhaps is sitting now—and each time they pass your own beautiful home in heaven, they tremble lest you should never come to live there, and they breathe a sweet prayer that you may persevere!

IX.

ENTER THOU INTO THE JOY OF THY LORD.

The Christian lies upon his deathbed—sacraments over—his strength ebbing—with full consciousness, facing eternity—all his good disappears from his eyes —the Passion of Jesus grows—now the great mercy of God is all he sees—the end—he is too weak to suffer much—he wakes, oh, with such a new freshness of awakening—it is the vigour, and the health, and the alacrity of immortality—angels singing—the Face of Jesus wearing such a smile—the words, Well done, thou good and faithful servant, enter thou into the joy of thy Lord. This has happened to more than one since Mass began.

I. His feelings.

    1. Of surprise at such a salvation for so little a service. Lord, when saw we Thee hungry? &c.—he argues against himself.

    2. Of jubilee at the first feeling of eternity, so new, so strange, so surpassing a thing.

    3. Of ecstasy at the new raptures of love of God, which fill his soul.

II. I see three crowds of souls to whom this sweet word is daily being said—*daily*, while the sun climbs and descends the sky, and we do our ordinary actions.

    1. Those who are in love with God, and though with many faults, have no taste but for Him, and have laid up their treasure in His love.

    2. Those who from a sense of duty do their ordinary actions for Him, correspond on the whole to His grace, and persevere in their spiritual exercises.

    3. Those who have suffered much, and, though complaining, have been patient and obedient to His will, and to His stripping them of the joys of earth.

How beautiful is life when it is the way to God! How sweet is death when it is the gate of heaven! How welcome to us the thought that Jesus is occupied so many times a day in saying that glorious word,

Well done! How welcome too the thought that there is a thrill of love in His Heart this hour, in thinking of the time when He will say to each one of us, Well done!

Conclusion.

1. You sorrow, and you seem to murmur, and not to bear it well—yet you *wish* to bear it well—your honest wish will do—you shall one day hear that word, Well done!

2. You are in temptation—seem overwhelmed—hardly know if you have resisted, but you *mean* to resist—you are trying to resist—you too shall one day hear that word, Well done!

3. You have fallen, fallen back into sin, dearest souls, souls whom Jesus died for—be of good cheer—have faith. Do you not sorrow?—would you not it were otherwise?—in humblest dependence upon grace, do you not fully purpose now to sin no more?—then lo! the angels are singing over you in heaven even now—you too shall one day hear that word, Well done!

O my Brethren, my Brethren! you who love Jesus with a true love, however poor a love, listen to my words. Do not fear to die, you will find it-very easy and very sweet—do not fear the judgment, you will find it very gentle, very kindly, very safe!

X.

WE WITH JESUS AFTERWARDS.

Some day the sun will rise on London: the Lent exercises will be going on, the Exposition in some church, and we no longer there; a hundred years ago we may have passed away; nay, a day will come when there will be no London; all, all will be done away, and God be all in all—where shall we be then? That day will soon be here—the end of a boy's holiday seems to be close on its beginning—where shall we be? Hope whispers, with Jesus! Oh if it be so, how little hard will strictness seem! how we shall joy that we have been generous with God on earth! Now let us talk of Heaven.

I. God knew and loved us from all eternity: Heaven is the end and satisfaction of that love. What manner of place it must be, if God made it for this. St. Paul says, "Eye hath not seen, nor ear heard, neither hath it entered into the heart of man to conceive what things God hath prepared for them that love Him."

II. The beauty and wonderfulness of creation: the Incarnation would have taken place if there had been no sin.

  1. The silence of eternity broken because of it.

  2. How it rises—stones—plants—animals—men—elect—saints—angels—Mary—the apex of all creation the Sacred Humanity, which touches God.

  3. Heaven the crown of it all; the treasure-house of its beauty and its sanctity.

III. The wondrousness of the mystery of the Incarnation, as a remedy for sin.

  1. God still could not resist His thirst to share in His own creation, by assuming a created nature.

  2. All redemption was—(1) to redeem Mary, (2) to redeem us to fill heaven.

IV. Heaven a home for Mary.
   1. The love of the Most Holy Trinity for her.
   2. The Divine Maternity.
   3. The ravishing beauty of her sinlessness
V. Heaven the court of the Sacred Humanity: the
   same heaven as ours.
   1. The beauty of it because of His merits.
   2. The magnificence of the Sacred Heart there.
VI. The place of the disclosure of the Vision of the
   Omnipresent God—*our* heaven.
   1. Beauty—peace — joy — love — wisdom — un-
     changeableness—eternity.
   2. Weary yourself with picturing and wishing—it
     is unspeakably more than all that.
   3. The gifts of the glorified body—pleasures of the
     pure senses, how sublime they are.
   4. The power, wisdom, and love of the glorified soul.
There are souls there this hour that love us dearly
—the saints worshipping there—the angels at their
melody—Mary on her throne exercising the magnificence of her sweet Queendom there—Creation's crown
and end and gem and miracle and unspeakably divine
beauty, the Sacred Humanity is there—the voice is
heard that cried in Bethlehem, and that preached upon
the mountain, and by the well, and that strove for us
in the anguish-trembling accents of mysterious prayer
—what is that Voice saying now? And there too is
the Eternal Show, the Vision of Visions, gleaming with
its countless lights, pouring out floods of exultation
from its nameless burning splendours into angels and
men, beautiful beyond all dreams, so beautiful that he
who sees it cannot sin.—*Sancta Trinitas, Unus Deus,
miserere nobis.*

Part Seventh.

THE LAST THINGS.

SECTION II.

PURGATORY.

I.

OUR DEAD.

It is a wonderful thing to be a Christian. The world of the saints in heaven is all ours. So also, though in another way, is the world of the dead—of those who are one day to be saints, with new glories, new delights, new jubilees in heaven.

I. We each of us have our own treasures among the dead.

   1. Some who have shared the joys of our past years, and some who have shared their sorrows.

   2. Some whom we have not loved as we could now wish we had loved them—some whom we have loved too much, and perhaps harmed by doing so.

   3. Some whom we have injured by example, scandal, harshness, or indulgence—some whom we have done good to, and perhaps converted.

   4. Some who have gone too soon, some mature and old, yet even then too soon.

   5. Some whose deathbeds have left scarce a doubt upon our minds, some whose deaths have been sudden, overclouded, or distressingly uncertain.

II. Our feelings about them all.

   1. We grudged them to God—but we do not do so now.

   2. We would have them back to behave differently to them : yet, no ! for their own sake we would not have them back for worlds.

3. We envy them the certainty of their glory, and perhaps its nearness; it is hard to think without a thrill of a soul very near its release.

4. Yet we pity them because of the extremity of their sufferings.

5. And some perhaps died in such a state that we may fear their sufferings will be unusually terrible, and their absence from God unusually long.

III. Conclusion.

1. God loves them with an unspeakable yearning love

2. Yet He has, in the case of the dead, made His love depend on ours—we are to them somewhat like what the saints in heaven are to us on earth.

3 Their state is one of incomparable, unimaginable pain.

4. And our hands are full of the most wonderful and most powerful means to help them.

5. What then must be our devotion for the dead? A little or a passing thing? Need I answer this? Have you not echoes in your own hearts that are answering it even while I speak? Oh think, dearest Brethren, of your past years, and of your past loves, of those old faces, of those unforgotten eyes, and of those well-remembered voices, that are silent now.

II.

THE SEVERITY OF PURGATORY.

We think of lands we shall never see—we picture them to ourselves out of books of geography, with their

animals, and plants, and scenery—can we think of
purgatory as a land below our rocks and mines and
subterranean rivers, as a land whose gloomy fire-
illumined corridors we shall never see ?

I. Severity of its punishments.

  1. The time when they come, just when we hoped
to rest.

  2. The intolerable delay of the sight of God.

  3. Their severity in themselves.

    (1) The fire.

    (2) The soul the part tortured, so that *all* suffers
at once, and penetratingly.

    (3) Worse than all martyrdoms.

    (4) No parallel to them in earthly suffering.

  4. Long endurance, because there is no merit to
shorten them.

  5. So far as pain goes, they are a participation of
hell, and in awful vicinity to it.

II. What sends us there ?

  1. We might almost say that that land is the creation of venial sin.

  2. Cowardice in the matter of penance.

  3. Want of perfect sorrow for mortal sin.

  4. Slovenly confessions and examens of conscience.

  5. Being comfortable, which makes the soul sickly.

III. How then to avoid going there.

  1. Recollection, which is the grand impossibility of
lukewarmness.

  2. Manful, discreet, habitual penance.

  3. Carefulness about the sacraments.

  4. A devotion to Indulgences and the Precious Blood.

  5. Charitable devotion to the holy souls.

  6. Aiming at perfection.

7. Fervour, which is a more effectual fire than those of purgatory.

Oh, it is really anything but a hopeless thing to hope to escape purgatory. I can hardly think all is quite right with us in the spiritual life, if we have not that humble hope.

III.

THE CONSOLATIONS OF PURGATORY.

I. The entrance into purgatory.
  1. The moment of death.
  2. The act of renunciation of sin,
  3. The sight of Jesus in the particular judgment.
  4. The voluntary flight into purgatory : no conveying angels needed. Beautiful worship of God's purity : His love of the soul at that moment.
II. The consolations of purgatory.
  1. The soul is in unbroken union with God.
  2. Conformity to the Divine Will, so that they abide their purification with the most perfect contentment.
  3. They are not teased with any vision of self or sin, according to St. Catherine of Genoa.
  4. They are impeccable, and cannot commit the slightest imperfection or have the least movement of impatience.
  5. They love God above everything with a most pure and disinterested love.
  6. They are consoled by angels.
  7. They are in confirmed assurance of their salvation.
  8. Their bitter agonies are accompanied by a profound peace.

III. Why, then, have such devotion for their sake ?

   1. Chiefly for the sake of God's glory.

   2. Because their pains are extreme.

   3. Because, like Mary in her Compassion, we often feel more for a sufferer than he feels for himself.

   4. Because they are helpless.

O beautiful region of the Church of God! O lovely troop of the flock of Mary! The beauty of those souls—the loveliness of their patience—the majesty of their gifts—the dignity of their solemn and chaste sufferings—the eloquence of their silence—the moonlight of Mary's Throne lighting up that empire—silver-winged angels voyaging through the deeps of that mysterious pain—sinless purity of the worship it all gives to God. O world—O weary, clamorous, sinful world! who would not break away, if he could, like an uncaged dove, from thy perilous toils and unsafe pilgrimage, and fly with joy to the lowest place in that most pure, most safe, most holy land of suffering and of sinless love ?

IV.

DEVOTION TO THE PASSION.

Pain is a desperately difficult thing to bear; is bodily or mental pain worst ?

But the soul made miraculously to feel the pain of sense, and this by God—this must be terrific. Will it ever happen to us ? Yes, to most of us, probably to all, for a long time, and to such a degree that the very angels shudder at the vision of it. Let us think of this.

I. Of course the great thing is to be saved: yet purgatory presents most serious reflections.

  1. Any terrible punishment hanging over us is a fear.

  2. Its uncertain severity: yet all *divine* punishments are necessarily severe.

  3. Thus death is not a rest, but the beginning of a punishment.

  4. All little carelessnesses are laying up more fire for us.

  5. Our own experience of the little charity there is for the Holy Souls: it is astonishing how little.

II. It seems from revelations as if the length of purgatories were increasing. Why?

  1. From want of bodily penances.

  2. From the increase of comforts and luxuries.

  3. From the worldliness of modern devout people.

  4. From the quickness, multitude, and variety of occupations.

  5. From a singular want of discernment of God and His claims, brought about by the atmosphere of heresy and unbelief.

III. The Carmelite revelation about Purgatory and Devotion to the Passion.

  1. The passion obviously the standing, unintermitting devotion.

  2. Only from it can true contrition come, because only from it comes a real understanding of sin.

  3. From it also comes the spirit of mortification and robust piety.

  4. It supplies instincts and principles of a Christian sort more than any other devotion.

  5. It is the best protection against the self-indulgent and self-dispensing spirit of worldliness.

6. How acceptable to our Lady.

(1) Because it is the tenderest worship of Jesus and so most like her own.

(2) Because it roots the love of Him most deeply in us—which is her grand joy, her double love, yet single love, of Him and of us.

(3) Because it is the continuation of her own Dolours, and of the worship they were to Jesus.

(4) Because it best enables us to understand her.

(5) Because her Maternity of us came out of it.

The heart can have tears even when the eyes have none. One tear of the heart over the Passion of our Blessed Lord! how much of the cruel fire beneath the earth has it the power to quench—and how piercingly we shall one day moan for ever so little a quenching!

V.

THE LOVE OF JESUS FOR THE HOLY SOULS.

No life would be long enough for us to find out the wonders there are in the grand mystery that God loves us. Nothing about us is so wonderful, neither our creation, nor our redemption, nor our glorification. It is wonderful to think of all the scenes ewe shall pass through at the end of the world: y t not so wonderful as to think that at this very moment the great God loves us, that we have actually each of us a distinct place in the Heart of Jesus. This also is one of the wonders of purgatory.

I. The wonder of the love of Jesus for the Holy Souls.

1 The immense sea of pains and torments in which they lie.
2. Their utter inability to merit anything.
3. The fact that they are there simply for lack of generosity to Him.
4. That in life they had graces far more than sufficient to avoid all purgatory.
5. Yet Jesus looks upon them with a most special and peculiar love.
   (1) Because they are actually saved, and can never belong to His enemy, or fall from Him.
   (2) Because they are in such intolerable sufferings.
   (3) Because of the beautiful holiness with which they suffer.

II. Description of the love of Jesus for the Holy Souls.
1. He looks at their long lives of virtue, grace, conversion, perseverance.
2. He thinks of those mysteries of His own to which they had, or spread a special devotion.
3. He looks at His Mother and thinks how they loved her; how she loves them, and how He loves her.
4. He loves them, out of the amazing generosity of His Sacred Heart, just because they are drawing so largely on the treasures of His Precious Blood, and the alms of the Communion of Saints.
5. He measures all His great Passion, and how it was all for them.
6. He measures all their pains, so beautiful, so holy, so full of sweet desire for Himself,—and only for Himself.

7. He looks at their vacant place in Heaven, and longs to see it filled.

8. He looks at us whom He has made so powerful to help these suffering souls, looks with an affectionate reproachfulness, as if we might console His Sacred Heart more plentifully by doing more for those His Spouses in the flames.

9. He looks at the Eternal Father, and kindles with love of His glory, and sees how the souls will increase it, and rises from His Throne, I think I see Him now—and, like thick silent falls of dew, sheds His Precious Blood over those vast fields of fire.

VI.

THE QUEEN OF PURGATORY.

I. God's judgments on forgiven sin, in this world and the next.

  1. Purgatory, its sufferings.

  2. Who the sufferers are—Spouses of Jesus Christ, who have had final perseverance.

  3. How they suffer—in stillness, love, and conformity.

  4. How God loves them—as the fruit of His Son's Passion.

  5. Mary the crowned Queen of purgatory—Jesus looks at her.

II. Mary's love for the Holy Souls in that realm of sacred suffering.

  1. Because of God's glory.

  2. Because of the remembrance of the Passion of Jesus.

3. Because she remembers her prayers for them when they were alive, and their devotion to her.

4. Because of their guardian angels and patron saints.

5. Because of her delight in exercising her powers, specially as they are powers of mercy.

6. Because of her mother's instinct, for she is their real Mother.

III. The Queen of purgatory bends from her throne over that abyss of pain.

1. She adores the justice and awful purity of God.

2. She magnifies His love in providing this semblance of baptism after death.

3. She aids the souls
   (1) By prayers.
   (2) By sending angels.
   (3) By having her feasts kept in heaven.
   (4) By bidding guardian angels put prayers into the hearts of their clients.
   (5) By the sweet worship of the voiceless yearnings of her own heart, which constrain God.

Oh, solemn and subduing the thought of those souls—that realm of pain—no cry, no murmur—silent as Jesus before His foes. We shall never know how we really love Mary till we look up to her out of those deeps, those vales of dread mysterious fire.

VII.

THE DELIVERANCE OF A SOUL.

Make a composition of place—flames sobbing on the shore of purgatory, like the chafing of the tide upon the rocks—awful dreary light of the far-stretching land of fire—angels white as fallen snow when the sun shines on it winging their way about—in all that land no sin, nothing but heroic virtues and beautiful tranquillity.

I. Of the souls who are in that land to-night, some have been long there; men have forgotten them through ingratitude, or worldliness, or false thoughts of their goodness, or low views of the exceeding holiness of God.

Some are just arrived there, with all yet to go through.

Some are just ready to come out.

All know that they are saved: all know when their punishment will end: but oh! the wearying, lagging lapse of time, which seems so long.

II. But we will take one soul—a London soul: he was poor, had difficulties in keeping the faith, fought for fifty years with this hard-hearted city, alas! not without sin—but had faith, sacraments, perhaps attendance at church, great devotion to mass anyhow—he is gone to purgatory—his hour is at hand: it is depending on *our* prayers, on the prayers of some one of us, on the ending of this octave, on the procession of this night. Oh how he yearns to see God!

III. A growing light—a silentness—one comes, whom all see, beautiful exceedingly, more radiant than a thousand suns—loveliness gleaming from him like a divine vision—his presence seems to shed light and fragrance on every soul—he descends to the level of the fire, embraces—he the beautiful one —that pining soul, lifts it out of its bed of suffering—it grows beautiful in his embrace—he leaves purgatory: we see nothing, but through the still and gloom of night, St. Michael and the soul rise and rise with exceeding swiftness—come within sound of the harps of Heaven—and enter there. St. Peter welcomes his child—St. Michael takes him through astonishing ranks of saints and angels to our Lady's throne, and leaves him there —he has done her bidding—she is the Queen of that dear soul—she rises from her throne—presents the soul to Jesus—and He to the Eternal Father. Oh happy soul—it would be bewildered were it not immortal—the music of Heaven sounds louder; and the choirs of the angels wax stronger, while the new saint is set upon his throne, and crowned by God with the crown which he won in the dark streets and dull traffic of London, but which his Heavenly Father had prepared for him before the world began. Oh happy, happy soul, happy beyond all words, happy now for evermore. Thou wilt think of us to-night, and thy thoughts of us will be blessings and graces in the morning. We too love Jesus, we too prize our faith, we too will fight our fight —and then our turn will come at last, our entry into Heaven, our marvellous coronation, our first sight of the Ever-blessed God, the beginning—oh! who can think of it without trembling with nervous delight?—the beginning of our beautiful eternity.

INDEX.

———◆◆———

BURNS AND OATES, LIMITED, LONDON.

SELECTION

<small>FROM</small>

BURNS & OATES'

Catalogue

<small>OF</small>

PUBLICATIONS.

LONDON: BURNS AND OATES, L<small>D.</small>

ORCHARD ST., W., & 63 PATERNOSTER ROW, E.C.

NEW YORK: 9 BARCLAY STREET.

1889.

NEW BOOKS.

A New Volume of Miscellanies (being the third). By His Eminence the Cardinal Archbishop of WESTMINSTER. Price 6s. The three Volumes can now be obtained at 6s. each.

The Holy See and the Wandering of the Nations. By THOMAS W. ALLIES, K.C.S.G. Demy 8vo, cloth, 10s 6d.
"We give it as our deliberate and carefully formed judgment that Mr Allies' great work on the 'Formation of Christendom' stands simply unrivalled and alone in its own department of English literature '—*Tablet*

The Haydock Papers. A Glimpse into English Catholic Life under the shade of persecution, and in the dawn of freedom. By JOSEPH GILLOW. Demy 8vo, half bound, gilt top, 7s. 6d.

Characteristics from the Writings of Archbishop Ullathorne, together with a Bibliographical Account of the Archbishop's Works. By the Rev. M. F. GLANCEY. Crown 8vo, cloth, 6s.

Leaves from St. John Chrysostom. By Miss ALLIES, Author of "Leaves from St. Augustine." Crown 8vo, cloth, 6s.

Records of the English Catholics of 1715. Edited by JOHN ORLEBAR PAYNE, M.A. With a complete index. Demy 8vo, half-bound, gilt top, 15s.

Spiritual Retreats. Notes of Meditations and Considerations given in the Convent of the Sacred Heart, Roehampton, by the Most Rev. GEORGE PORTER, S.J., Archbishop of Bombay. Second and enlarged Edition. Crown 8vo, cloth, 6s.
(To the Notes of the three Retreats contained in the first Edition have now been added those of a fourth).

Eucharistic Jewels. By PERCY FITZGERALD, Author of "Jewels of the Mass," &c. Fancy cloth, 2s. 6d.

Sermons on the Seven Penitential Psalms. By the Blessed JOHN FISHER. Edited by the Rev. KENELM VAUGHAN. Crown 8vo, cloth 5s.

Mary of Nazareth. A Legendary Poem. In three Parts. By Sir JOHN CROKER BARROW, Bart. Part I Cloth, gilt, 2s.
"Magnificent in its sublimity of thought, yet full of a simple pathos and beauty entirely its own."—*Kent Coast Times*

" Jesu's Psalter :" What it was at its origin. and as consecrated by the use of many Martyrs and Confessors With Chant, for its more solemn recitation. By the Rev. SAMUEL HEYDON SOLE, Priest of Chipping Norton. Cloth gilt, 3s. 6d
" An exquisite reproduction of an exquisite work "

The Wandering Knight: His Adventurous Journey. A Mediæval Pilgrim's Progress By JOHN DE CARTHENY, Brother of the Religious Order of Mount Carmel, and Canon Theologian of the Diocese of Cambrai. Newly translated into English, under Ecclesiastical Supervision, from the Edition of 1572. Cloth, 2s. 6d

SELECTION

BURNS AND OATES' CATALOGUE
OF PUBLICATIONS.

—→+→+ +←+←—

ALLIES, T. W. (K.C.S.G.)

See of St. Peter.	£0	4	6
Formation of Christendom. Vols. I , II., III. . each	0	12	0
Church and State as seen in the Formation of Christendom, 8vo, pp 472, cloth	0	14	0
The Throne of the Fisherman, built by the Carpenter's Son, the Root, the Bond, and the Crown of Christendom. Demy 8vo	0	10	0

"It would be quite superfluous at this hour of the day to recommend Mr Allies' writings to English Catholics Those of our readers who remember the article on his writings in the *Katholik*, know that he is esteemed in Germany as one of our foremost writers."— *Dublin Review.*

ALLIES, MARY.

Leaves from St. John Chrysostom, With introduction by T. W. Allies, K.C.S G. Crown 8vo, cloth .	0	6	0

"Miss Allies ' Leaves' are delightful reading, the English is remarkably pure and graceful page after page reads as if it were original No commentator, Catholic or Protestant, has ever surpassed St John Chrysostom in the knowledge of Holy Scripture, and his learning was of a kind which is of service now as it was at the time when the inhabitants of a great city hung on his words."— *Tablet*

ALLNATT, C. F. B.

Cathedra Petri. Third and Enlarged Edition. Paper.	0	5	0

"Invaluable to the controversialist and the theologian, and most useful for educated men inquiring after truth or anxious to know the positive testimony of Christian antiquity in favour of Papal claims "—*Month*

Which is the True Church ? New Edition . .	0	1	4
The Church and the Sects.	0	1	0

ANNUS SANCTUS :

Hymns of the Church for the Ecclesiastical Year. Translated from the Sacred Offices by various Authors, with Modern, Original, and other Hymns, and an Appendix of Earlier Versions. Selected and Arranged by ORBY SHIPLEY, M.A.

Popular edition, in two parts . each	0	1	0
In stiff boards	0	3	6
Plain Cloth, lettered	0	5	0
Edition de luxe	0	10	6

ANSWERS TO ATHEISTS: OR NOTES ON

Ingersoll. By the Rev. A Lambert, (over 100,000 copies sold in America). Ninth edition. Paper. . . . £0 0 6
Cloth 0 1 0

B. N.

The Jesuits : their Foundation and History. 2 vols. crown 8vo, cloth, red edges 0 15 0

"The book is just what it professes to be—*a popular history*, drawn from well-known sources," &c —*Month.*

BACQUEZ, L'ABBE.

The "Divine Office" · From the French of l'Abbé Bacquez, of the Seminary of St. Sulpice, Paris. Edited by the Rev Father Taunton, of the Congregation of the Oblates of St Charles. Cloth . . . 0 6 0

"The translation of this most edifying work from the walls of St Sulpice, the source of so much sacerdotal perfection, comes to us most opportunely, and we heartily commend it to the use of the clergy and of the faithful " THE CARDINAL ARCHBISHOP OF WESTMINSTER
"A very complete manual, learned, wholesome, and devout "— *Saturday Review*

BORROMEO, LIFE OF ST. CHARLES.

From the Italian of Peter Guissano. 2 vols . 0 15 0

"A standard work, which has stood the test of succeeding ages, it is certainly the finest work on St Charles in an English dress "— *Tablet*

BOWDEN, REV. H. S. (of the Oratory) Edited by

Dante's Divina Commedia : Its scope and value. From the German of FRANCIS HETTINGER, D D. With an engraving of Dante. Crown 8vo . . 0 10 6

"All that Venturi attempted to do has been now approached with far greater power and learning by Dr Hettinger, who, as the author of the 'Apologie des Christenthums,' and as a great Catholic theologian, is eminently well qualified for the task he has undertaken "— *The Saturday Review*

BRIDGETT, REV. T. E. (C.SS.R.).

Discipline of Drink 0 3 6

"The historical information with which the book abounds gives evidence of deep research and patient study, and imparts a permanent interest to the volume, which will elevate it to a position of authority and importance enjoyed by few of its compeers "—*The Arrow*

Our Lady's Dowry ; how England Won and Lost that Title. Popular Edition 0 5 0

"This book is the ablest vindication of Catholic devotion to Our Lady, drawn from tradition, that we know of in the English language "—*Tablet*

Ritual of the New Testament An essay on the principles and origin of Catholic Ritual in reference to the New Testament. Third edition . . . 0 5 0

The Life of the Blessed John Fisher. With a reproduction of the famous portrait of Blessed JOHN FISHER by HOLBEIN, and other Illustrations. Cloth 0 7 6

BRIDGETT, REV. T. E. (C.SS.R.), Edited by.

Souls Departed. By CARDINAL ALLEN. First published in 1565, now edited in modern spelling by the
Rev. T. E Bridgett £0 6 0

CASWALL, FATHER.

Catholic Latin Instructor in the Principal Church
Offices and Devotions, for the Use of Choirs, Con-
vents, and Mission Schools, and for Self-Teaching.
1 vol., complete 0 3 6
Or Part I , containing Benediction, Mass, Serving at
Mass, and various Latin Prayers in ordinary use . 0 1 6
May Pageant . A Tale of Tintern. (A Poem) Second
edition 0 2 0
Poems 0 5 0
Lyra Catholica, containing all the Breviary and Missal
Hymns, with others from various sources. 32mo,
cloth, red edges 0 2 6

CATHOLIC BELIEF: OR, A SHORT AND

Simple Exposition of Catholic Doctrine. By the
Very Rev. Joseph Faà di Bruno, D.D. Seventh
edition . . . . . Price 6d.; post free, 0 0 8½
Cloth, lettered, ... 0 0 10
Also an edition on better paper and bound in cloth, with
gilt lettering and steel frontispiece . . . 0 2 0

CHALLONER, BISHOP.

Meditations for every day in the year. New edition
Revised and edited by the Right Rev. John Virtue,
D.D , Bishop of Portsmouth. 8vo 5th edition . 0 3 0
And in other bindings.

COLERIDGE, REV. H. J. (S.J.)

(See Quarterly Series)

DEHARBE, FATHER JOSEPH, (S.J.)

A History of Religion, or the Evidences of the
Divinity of the Christian Religion, as furnished by
its History from the Creation of the World to
our own Times. Designed as a Help to Catechetical Instruction in Schools and Churches.
Pp. 628 . . . . net 0 8 6

DEVAS, C. S.

Studies of Family Life : a contribution to Social
Science. Crown 8vo 0 5 0

"We recommend these pages and the remarkable evidence brought
together in them to the careful attention of all who are interested in
the well-being of our common humanity "- *Guardian*
" Both thoughtful and stimulating "- *Saturday Review*

DRANE, AUGUSTA THEODOSIA.

History of St. Catherine of Siena and her Companions
A new edition in two vols. £0 12 6

It has been reserved for the author of the present work to give us
a complete biography of St. Catherine. . . Perhaps the greatest
success of the writer is the way in which she has contrived to make
the Saint herself live in the pages of the book "—*Tablet*

ENGLISH CATHOLIC NON-JURORS OF 1715.

Being a Summary of the Register of their Estates, with
Genealogical and other Notes, and an Appendix of
Unpublished Documents in the Public Record Office.
Edited by the late Very Rev. E. E. Estcourt, M.A..
F.S.A., Canon of St. Chad's, Birmingham, and
John Orlebar Payne, M.A   1 vol., demy 8vo.   .   1   1   0

"This handsomely printed volume lies before us   Every student
of the history of our nation, or of families which compose it, cannot
but be grateful for a catalogue such as we have here "—*Dublin
Review.*
"Most carefully and creditably brought out. . . From first to last
full of social interest, and it contains biographical details for which
we may search in vain elsewhere "—*Antiquarian Magazine.*

EYRE, MOST REV. CHARLES, (Abp. of Glasgow).

The History of St. Cuthbert   or, An Account of his
Life, Decease, and Miracles   Third edition.   Illustrated with maps, charts,   &c , and handsomely
bound in cloth   Royal 8vo   .   .   .   0 14   0

"A handsome, well appointed volume, in every way worthy of its
illustrious subject. . . . The chief impression of the whole is the
picture of a great and good man drawn by a sympathetic hand "—
Spectator.

FABER, REV. FREDERICK WILLIAM, (D.D.)

All for Jesus	0	5	0
Bethlehem	0	7	0
Blessed Sacrament	0	7	6
Creator and Creature	0	6	0
Ethel's Book of the Angels.	0	5	0
Foot of the Cross	0	6	0
Growth in Holiness	0	6	0
Hymns	0	6	0
Notes on Doctrinal and Spiritual Subjects, 2 vols. each	0	5	0
Poems	0	5	0
Precious Blood	0	5	0
Sir Lancelot	0	5	0
Spiritual Conferences	0	6	0
Life and Letters of Frederick William Faber, D.D., Priest of the Oratory of St. Philip Neri. By John Edward Bowden of the same Congregation	0	6	0

FOLEY, REV. HENRY (S.J.)

Records of the English Province of the Society of
Jesus. Vol. I., Series I . . . . net £1 6 0
Vol. II., Series II., III., IV. . . . net 1 6 0
Vol. III., Series V., VI., VII., VIII. . net 1 10 0
Vol. IV. Series IX., X., XI. . . . net 1 6 0
Vol. V., Series XII. with nine Photographs of
Martyrs . . . . net 1 10 0
Vol. VI., Diary and Pilgrim-Book of the English Col-
lege, Rome. The Diary from 1579 to 1773, with
Biographical and Historical Notes. The Pilgrim-
Book of the Ancient English Hospice attached to
the College from 1580 to 1656, with Historical
Notes . . . . net 1 6 0
Vol. VII Part the First : General Statistics of the Pro-
vince ; and Collectanea, giving Biographical Notices
of its Members and of many Irish and Scotch Jesuits.
With 20 Photographs . . . . . net 1 6 0
Vol. VII. Part the Second : Collectanea, Completed ;
With Appendices. Catalogues of Assumed and Real
Names : Annual Letters, Biographies and Miscel-
lanea. . . . . net 1 6 0

"As a biographical dictionary of English Jesuits, it deserves a
place in every well-selected library, and, as a collection of marvellous occurrences, persecutions, martyrdoms, and evidences of the
results of faith, amongst the books of all who belong to the Catholic
Church "—*Genealogist.*

FORMBY, REV. HENRY.

Monotheism : in the main derived from the Hebrew
nation and the Law of Moses. The Primitive Religion of the City of Rome. An historical Investiga-
tion. Demy 8vo. 0 5 0

FRANCIS DE SALES, ST. : THE WORKS OF.

Translated into the English Language by the Rev.
H. B. Mackey, O.S B., under the direction of the
Right Rev. Bishop Hedley, O S.B. . .
Vol. I. Letters to Persons in the World. Cloth . 0 6 0

"The letters must be read in order to comprehend the charm and
sweetness of their style "—*Tablet*

Vol. II.—The Treatise on the Love of God. Father
Carr's translation of 1630 has been taken as a basis,
but it has been modernized and thoroughly revised
and corrected. 0 9 0

"To those who are seeking perfection by the path of contemplation
this volume will be an armoury of help "—*Saturday Review.*

Vol. III. The Catholic Controversy. . . . 0 6 0

" No one who has not read it can conceive how clear, how convincing, and how well adapted to our present needs are these controversia¹
'leaves '"—*Tablet*

FRANCIS DE SALES, ST.: WORKS OF.—*continued.*

Vol. IV. Letters to Persons in Religion, with intro-
duction by Bishop Hedley on "St. Francis de Sales
and the Religious State." £0 6 0

"The sincere piety and goodness, the grave wisdom, the knowledge
of human nature, the tenderness for its weakness, and the desire for
its perfection that pervade the letters, make them pregnant of instruction for all serious persons The translation and editing have
been admirably done."—*Scotsman.*

₊ Other vols. in preparation

GALLWEY, REV. PETER (S.J.)

Precious Pearl of Hope in the Mercy of God, The.
Translated from the Italian With Preface by the
Rev. Father Gallwey. Cloth. 0 4 6
Lectures on Ritualism and on the Anglican Orders. 0 8 0
2 vols.
Or may be had separately.

GIBSON, REV. H.

Catechism Made Easy. Being an Explanation of the
Christian Doctrine. Fourth edition. 2 vols , cloth 0 7 6

"This work must be of priceless worth to any who are engaged in
any form of catechetical instruction It is the best book of the kind
that we have seen in English "—*Irish Monthly*

GILLOW, JOSEPH.

Literary and Biographical History, or, Bibliographical
Dictionary of the English Catholics. From the
Breach with Rome, in 1534, to the Present Time.
Vols. I., II. and III. cloth, demy 8vo . . each. 0 15 0

₊ Other vols in preparation

"The patient research of Mr. Gillow, his conscientious record of
minute particulars, and especially his exhaustive bibliographical information in connection with each name, are beyond praise "—*British
Quarterly Review.*

"No such important or novel contribution has been made to English
bibliography for a long time "—*Scotsman*

The Haydock Papers. Illustrated. Demy 8vo. . 0 7 6

HEDLEY, BISHOP.

Our Divine Saviour, and other Discourses Crown
8vo. 0 6 0

"A distinct and noteworthy feature of these sermons is, we certainly think, their freshness—freshness of thought, treatment, and
style, nowhere do we meet pulpit commonplace or hackneyed phrase
—everywhere, on the contrary, it is the heart of the preacher pouring
out to his flock his own deep convictions, enforcing them from the
'Treasures, old and new,' of a cultivated mind '—*Dublin Review*

HUMPHREY, REV. W. (S.J.)

Suarez on the Religious State . A Digest of the Doctrine contained in his Treatise, "De Statû Religionis."
3 vols., pp. 1200. Cloth, roy. 8vo . . . 1 10 0

"This laborious and skilfully executed work is a distinct addition
to English theological literature Father Humphrey's style is quiet,
methodical, precise, and as clear as the subject admits Every one
will be struck with the air of legal exposition which pervades the
book He takes a grip of his author, under which the text yields
up every atom of its meaning and force "—*Dublin Review.*

LEE, REV. F. G., D.D. (of All Saints, Lambeth.)

Edward the Sixth : Supreme Head. Second edition.
Crown 8vo . . . . , . . £0 6 0

"In vivid interest and in literary power, no less than in solid historical value, Dr Lee's present work comes fully up to the standard of its predecessors, and to say that is to bestow high praise The book evinces Dr Lee's customary diligence of research in amassing facts, and his rare artistic power in welding them into a harmonious and effective whole "—*John Bull*

LIFE OF FATHER CHAMPAGNAT

Founder of the Society of the Little Brothers of Mary.
Containing a portrait of Fr. CHAMPAGNAT, and four
full page illustrations. Demy 8vo . . . 0 8 0

"A work of great practical utility, and one eminently suited to these times "—*Tablet.*

"A serious and able essay on the science and art of the Christian education of children, exemplified in the career of one who gave his life to it "— *Dublin Review*

LIGUORI, ST. ALPHONSUS.

New and Improved Translation of the Complete Works
of St. Alphonsus, edited by the late Bishop Coffin :—
Vol. I. The Christian Virtues, and the Means for Obtaining them. Cloth elegant 0 4 0
Or separately .—
   1. The Love of our Lord Jesus Christ . . . 0 1 4
   2 Treatise on Prayer. *(In the ordinary editions a
   great part of this work is omitted)* . . . 0 1 4
   3. A Christian's rule of Life 0 1 0
Vol. II. The Mysteries of the Faith—The Incarnation ;
containing Meditations and Devotions on the Birth
and Infancy of Jesus Christ, &c , suited for Advent
and Christmas. 0 3 6
   Cheap edition 0 2 0
Vol. III. The Mysteries of the Faith--The Blessed
Sacrament 0 3 6
   Cheap edition 0 2 0
Vol. IV. Eternal Truths—Preparation for Death . 0 3 6
   Cheap edition 0 2 0
Vol V. Treatises on the Passion, containing "Jesus
hath loved us," &c. 0 3 0
   Cheap edition 0 2 0
Vol. VI. Glories of Mary. New edition . . . 0 3 6
   With Frontispiece, cloth . . . 0 4 6
   Also in better bindings.

LIVIUS, REV. T. (M.A.,C SS.R.)

St. Peter, Bishop of Rome , or. the Roman Episcopate
of the Prince of the Apostles, proved from the
Fathers, History and Chronology, and illustrated by
arguments from other sources. Dedicated to his
Eminence Cardinal Newman. Demy 8vo, cloth . 0 12 0

LIVIUS, REV. T. (M.A., C.SS.R.)—*continued*.

Explanation of the Psalms and Canticles in the Divine Office. By St. ALPHONSUS LIGUORI. Translated from the Italian by THOMAS LIVIUS, C.SS R. With a Preface by his Eminence Cardinal MANNING Crown 8vo, cloth £0 7 6

MANNING CARDINAL.

Blessed Sacrament the Centre of Immutable Truth. Second edition	o	1	o
Confidence in God. Fourth edition .	o	1	o
England and Christendom	o	10	6
Eternal Priesthood. Seventh Edition .	o	2	6
Four Great Evils of the Day. Fifth Edition. Paper	o	2	6
Cloth	o	3	6
Fourfold Sovereignty of God. Third edition Paper	o	2	6
Cloth	o	3	6
Glories of the Sacred Heart. Fourth edition. .	o	6	o
Grounds of Faith. Seventh edition. . . .	o	1	6
Holy Gospel of our Lord Jesus Christ according to St. John. With a Preface by His Eminence .	o	1	o
Religio Viatoris. Third Edition. Wrapper. .	o	1	o
Cloth.	o	2	o
Independence of the Holy See. Second Edition.	o	5	o
Internal Mission of the Holy Ghost. Fourth edition	o	8	6
Love of Jesus to Penitents. Seventh edition .	o	1	6
Miscellanies. 3 vols. . . . . each	o	6	o
Office of the Holy Ghost under the Gospel . .	o	1	o
Petri Privilegium	o	10	6
Praise, A Sermon on ; with an Indulgenced Devotion.	o	1	o
Sermons on Ecclesiastical Subjects. Vols. I. II. and III. . . . . each	o	6	o
Sin and its Consequences Sixth edition . .	o	6	o
Temporal Mission of the Holy Ghost. Third edition .	o	8	6
Temporal Power of the Pope. Third edition . .	o	5	o
The Office of the Church in Higher Education . .	o	o	6
True Story of the Vatican Council. Second Edition .	o	5	o

MANNING, CARDINAL, Edited by.

Life of the Curé of Ars. New edition, enlarged. .	o	4	o

MIVART, PROF. ST. GEORGE (M.D., F.R S.)

Nature and Thought. Second edition . . .   o 4 o
"The complete command of the subject, the wide grasp, the subtlety, the readiness of illustration, the grace of style, contrive to render this one of the most admirable books of its class "—*British Quarterly Review*

A Philosophical Catechism. Fifth edition .   o 1 o
"It should become the *vade mecum* of Catholic students "—*Tablet*

MONTGOMERY, HON. MRS

Approved by the Most Rev. George Porter, Archbishop of Bombay.

The Divine Sequence A Treatise on Creation and Redemption. Cloth	£0	3	6
The Eternal Years. With an Introduction by the Most Rev. George Porter, Archbishop of Bombay. Cloth	0	3	6
The Divine Ideal. Cloth	0	3	6

"A work of original thought carefully developed and expressed in lucid and richly imaged style "—*Tablet.*

"The writing of a pious, thoughtful, earnest woman."—*Church Review*

"Full of truth, and sound reason, and confidence."—*American Catholic Book News*

MORRIS, REV. JOHN (S.J.)

Letter Books of Sir Amias Poulet, keeper of Mary Queen of Scots. Demy 8vo	0	10	6
Troubles of our Catholic Forefathers, related by themselves. Second Series. 8vo, cloth.	0	14	0
Third Series	0	14	0
The Life of Father John Gerard, S.J. Third edition, rewritten and enlarged	0	14	0
The Life and Martyrdom of St Thomas Becket. Second and enlarged edition. In one volume, large post 8vo, cloth, pp. xxxvi., 632,	0	12	6
or bound in two parts, cloth	0	13	0

MURPHY, J. N.

Chair of Peter Third edition, with the statistics, &c., brought down to the present day 720 pages. Crown 8vo	0	6	0

"In a series of clearly written chapters, precise in statement, excellently temperate in tone, the author deals with just those questions regarding the power, claims, and history of the Roman Pontiff which are at the present time of most actual interest "—*Dublin Review*

NEWMAN, CARDINAL.

Annotated Translation of Athanasius. 2 vols. each	0	7	6
Apologia pro Vitâ suâ	0	6	0
Arians of the Fourth Century, The	0	6	0
Callista. An Historical Tale.	0	5	6
Difficulties of Anglicans. Two volumes—			
Vol. I. Twelve Lectures.	0	7	6
Vol. II. Letter to Dr. Pusey and to the Duke of Norfolk	0	5	6
Discussions and Arguments	0	6	0
Doctrine of Justification	0	5	0
Dream of Gerontius .	0	0	6
Essay on Assent	0	7	6
Essay on the Development of Christian Doctrine	0	6	0

NEWMAN, CARDINAL—*continued.*

Essays Critical and Historical. Two volumes, with Notes . . . . . each	£0	6	0
Essays on Miracles, Two. 1. Of Scripture. 2. Of Ecclesiastical History	o	6	o
Historical Sketches Three volumes . . each	o	6	o
Idea of a University Lectures and Essays . .	o	7	o
Loss and Gain. Ninth Edition	o	5	6
Occasional Sermons	o	6	o
Parochial and Plain Sermons. Eight volumes. . each	o	5	o
Present Position of Catholics in England. .	o	7	o
Sermons on Subjects of the Day. . . .	o	5	o
Sermons to Mixed Congregations . . .	o	6	o
Theological Tracts	o	8	o
University Sermons	o	5	o
Verses on Various Occasions.	o	5	6
Via Media. Two volumes, with Notes . . each	o	6	o

NORTHCOTE, VERY REV. J. S. (D.D.)

Roma Sotterranea; or, An Account of the Roman Catacombs New edition. Re-written and greatly enlarged. This work is in three volumes, which may at present be had separately—			
Vol. I. History	1	4	o
Vol. II Christian Art. . . .	1	4	o
Vol. III Epitaphs of the Catacombs .	o	10	o
The Second and Third Volumes may also be had bound together in cloth . . .	1	12	o
Visit to the Roman Catacombs: Being a popular abridgment of the larger work. . .	o	4	o
Mary in the Gospels	o	3	6

POPE, THOMAS ALDER, M.A. (of the Oratory.)

Life of St Philip Neri, Apostle of Rome. From the Italian of Alfonso Capecelatro. 2 vols . .	o	15	o

"No former life has given us so full a knowledge of the surroundings of St Philip .   To those who have not read the original we can say, with the greatest confidence, that they will find in these two well-edited volumes a very large store of holy reading and of interesting history,"—*Dublin Review*

QUARTERLY SERIES (Edited by the Rev H. J. Coleridge, S.J)

Baptism of the King Considerations on the Sacred Passion. By the Rev. H. J. Coleridge, S.J . .	o	7	6
Christian Reformed in mind and Manners, The. By Benedict Rogacci, of the Society of Jesus The Translation edited by the Rev. H. J. Coleridge, S.J.	o	7	6
Chronicles of St Antony of Padua, the "Eldest Son of St. Francis.' Edited by the Rev H J. Coleridge, S.J.	o	3	6
Colombiere, Life of the Ven. Claude de la .	o	5	o

QUARTERLY SERIES—*continued*

Dialogues of St. Gregory the Great : an Old English Version. Edited by the Rev. H. J. Coleridge, S.J. £0 6 0

During the Persecution. Autobiography of Father John Gerard, S.J. Translated from the original Latin by the Rev. G. R Kingdon, S.J. . . . 0 5 0

English Carmelite, An. The Life of Catherine Burton, Mother Mary Xaveria of the Angels, of the English Teresian Convent at Antwerp. Collected from her own Writings, and other sources, by Father Thomas Hunter, S.J. . . . 0 6 0

Gaston de Ségur. A Biography. Condensed from the French Memoir by the Marquis de Ségur, by F. J. M. A. Partridge 0 3 6

Gracious Life, A (1566--1618); being the Life of Madame Acarie (Blessed Mary of the Incarnation), of the Reformed Order of our Blessed Lady of Mount Carmel. By Emily Bowles . . . 0 6 0

History of the Sacred Passion By Father Luis de la Palma, of the Society of Jesus. Translated from the Spanish. With Preface by the Rev H. J. Coleridge, S.J. Third edition 0 5 0

Holy Infancy Series. By the Rev. H J Coleridge, S.J. Vol I. Preparation of the Incarnation . 0 7 6

,, II. The Nine Months. Life of our Lord in the Womb 0 7 6

,, III. The Thirty Years. Our Lord's Infancy and Hidden Life . . . 0 7 6

Hours of the Passion. Taken from the Life of Christ by Ludolph the Saxon 0 7 6

Life and Teaching of Jesus Christ, in Meditations for every Day in the Year By P. N. Avancino, S.J. 2 vols. 0 10 6

Life and Letters of St Francis Xavier. By the Rev. H. J. Coleridge, S.J. 2 vols. 0 10 6

Life of Anne Catherine Emmerich. By Helen Ram. With Preface by the Rev. H J. Coleridge, S.J. 0 5 0

Life of Christopher Columbus. By the Rev A G. Knight, S.J. . . . 0 6 0

Life of Henrietta d'Osseville (in Religion, Mother Ste. Marie), Foundress of the Institute of the Faithful Virgin. Arranged and edited by the Rev. John George M'Leod, S J. . . . 0 5 6

Life of Margaret Mostyn (Mother Margaret of Jesus), Religious of the Reformed Order of our Blessed Lady of Mount Carmel (1625-1679). By the Very Rev. Edmund Bedingfield Edited from the Manuscripts preserved at Darlington, by the Rev. H. J. Coleridge, S.J . . . 0 6 0

Life of our Life : The Harmony of the Gospel, arranged with Introductory and Explanatory Chapters, Notes and Indices. By the Rev. H. J. Coleridge, S.J. 2 vols. (out of print) 0 15 0

QUARTERLY SERIES—*continued.*

Life of the Blessed John Berchmans. Third edition.
By the Rev F. Goldie, S.J. £0 6 0
Life of the Blessed Peter Favre, First Companion of
St. Ignatius Loyola. From the Italian of Father
Boero. (Out of print). 0 6 6
Life of King Alfred the Great   By Rev A. G. Knight,
S.J. Book I. Early Promise ; II. Adversity ; III.
Prosperity ; IV. Close of Life. . . . 0 6 0
Life of Mother Mary Teresa Ball. By Rev. H. J.
Coleridge, S.J. With Portrait . . . 0 6 6
Life of St. Jane Frances Fremyot de Chantal. By Emily
Bowles. Third Edition 0 5 0
Life of St Bridget of Sweden. By the late F. J. M
A Partridge 0 6 0
Life and Letters of St. Teresa. 3 vols. By Rev. H.
J Coleridge, S.J. . . . . each 0 7 6
Life of Mary Ward. By Mary Catherine Elizabeth
Chambers, of the Institute of the Blessed Virgin.
Edited by the Rev. H. J. Coleridge, S.J. 2 vols.,
each 0 7 6
Life of Jane Dormer, Duchess of Feria. By Henry
Clifford. Transcribed from the Ancient Manuscript
in the possession of the Lord Dormer, by the late
Canon E.E. Estcourt, and edited by the Rev.
Joseph Stevenson, S.J. 0 5 0
Mother of the King, The. By the Rev. H. J. Cole-
ridge, S J. 0 7 6
Mother of the Church. "Sequel to Mother of the King." 0 6 0
Of Adoration in Spirit and Truth. By the Rev. J. E.
Nieremberg. S.J. Old English translation. With a
Preface by the Rev. P. Gallwey, S.J. A New
Edition 0 6 6
Pious Affections towards God and the Saints. Medi-
tations for every Day in the Year, and for the
Principal Festivals. From the Latin of the Ven.
Nicholas Lancicius, S.J. With Preface by Arch
bishop George Porter, S.J. 0 7 6
Prisoners of the King, a book of thoughts on the doc-
trine of Purgatory. By the Rev. H. J. Coleridge,
S.J. New Edition. 0 5 0
Public Life of our Lord Jesus Christ. By the Rev.
H. J. Coleridge, S.J. vols 1 to 9 . . . each 0 6 6
Vols 10 and 11 . . . . . each 0 6 0
Return of the King. Discourses on the Latter Days.
By the Rev. H. J. Coleridge, S.J. . . 0 7 6
St. Mary's Convent, Micklegate Bar, York. A
History of the Convent   Edited by the Rev. H.J.
Coleridge, S.J. 0 7 6
Story of St. Stanislaus Kostka. With Preface by the
Rev. H. J. Coleridge, S.J. 0 3 6

QUARTERLY SERIES—*continued.*

Story of the Gospels, harmonised for meditation. By the Rev H. J. Coleridge, S J. £0 7 6

Works and Words of our Saviour, gathered from the Four Gospels. By the Rev. H. J. Colendge, S.J. . 0 7 6

Sufferings of the Church in Brittany during the Great Revolution. By Edward Healy Thompson, M.A. 0 6 6

Suppression of the Society of Jesus in the Portuguese Dominions. From Documents hitherto unpublished. By the Rev. Alfred Weld, S.J. 0 7 6
[This volume forms the First Part of the General History of the Suppression of the Society.]

Teaching and Counsels of St Francis Xavier Gathered from his letters. Edited by the Rev. H J. Coleridge, S J. 0 5 0

Three Catholic Reformers of the fifteenth Century. By Mary H. Allies. 0 6 0

Thomas of Hereford, Life of St. By Fr. Lestrange . 0 6 0

Tribunal of Conscience, The. By Father Gasper Druzbicki, S.J. 0 3 6

RAWES. THE LATE REV. Fr., Edited by.

The Library of the Holy Ghost :—
Vol I. St Thomas Aquinas on the Adorable Sacrament of the Altar. With Prayers and Thanksgivings for Holy Communion. Red cloth . . . 0 5 0
Little Books of the Holy Ghost :—(List on application.)

RICHARDS, REV. WALTER J. B. (D.D.)

Manual of Scripture History. Being an Analysis of the Historical Books of the Old Testament By the Rev. W. J. B. Richards, D.D., Oblate of St. Charles ; Inspector of Schools in the Diocese of Westminster. Cloth 0 4 0
"Happy indeed will those children and young persons be who acquire in their early days the inestimably precious knowledge which these books impart "—*Tablet.*

RYDER, REV. H. I. D. (of the Oratory.)

Catholic Controversy A Reply to Dr Littledale's "Plain Reasons." Sixth edition 0 2 6
"Father Ryder of the Birmingham Oratory, has now furnished in a small volume a masterly reply to this assailant from without The lighter charms of a brilliant and graceful style are added to the solid merits of this handbook of contemporary controversy "—*Irish Monthly.*

SOULIER, REV. P.

Life of St. Philip Benizi, of the Order of the Servants of Mary. Crown 8vo 0 8 0
"A clear and interesting account of the life and labours of this eminent Servant of Mary "—*American Catholic Quarterly*
"Very scholar like, devout and complete "—*Dublin Review*

STANTON, REV. R. (of the Oratory.)

A Menology of England and Wales ; or, Brief Memorials of the British and English Saints, arranged
according to the Calendar   Together with the Martyrs of the 16th and 17th centuries   Compiled by
order of the Cardinal Archbishop and the Bishops
of the Province of Westminster.   Demy 8vo, cloth   £0 14 0

THOMPSON, EDWARD HEALY, (M.A.)

The Life of Jean-Jacques Olier, Founder of the
Seminary of St. Sulpice. New and Enlarged Edition.
Post 8vo, cloth, pp. xxxvi 628   .   .   .   .   0 15 0
" It provides us with just what we most need, a model to look up to
and imitate ; one whose circumstances and surroundings were suffi-
ciently like our own to admit of an easy and direct application to our
own personal duties and daily occupations "—*Dublin Review*
The Life and Glories of St. Joseph, Husband of
Mary, Foster-Father of Jesus, and Patron of the
Universal Church   Grounded on the Dissertations of
Canon Antonio Vitalis, Father José Moreno, and other
writers.   Crown 8vo, cloth, pp. xxvi., 488,   .   .   0 6 0

ULLATHORNE, BISHOP.

Endowments of Man, &c. Popular edition. .	0	7	0
Groundwork of the Christian Virtues : do. .	0	7	0
Christian Patience, do. do	0	7	0
Ecclesiastical Discourses . .	0	6	0
Memoir of Bishop Willson . .	0	2	6

WARD, WILFRID.

The Clothes of Religion. A reply to popular Positivism   0 3 6
"Very witty and interesting "—*Spectator*
"Really models of what such essays should be "—*Church Quarterly
Review*

WATERWORTH, REV. J.

The Canons and Decrees of the Sacred and Œcumenical
Council of Trent, celebrated under the Sovereign
Pontiffs, Paul III., Julius III., and Pius IV., translated by the Rev. J. WATERWORTH.   To which
are prefixed Essays on the External and Internal
History of the Council. A new edition. Demy,
8vo, cloth 0 10 6

WISEMAN, CARDINAL.

Fabiola.   A Tale of the Catacombs. . . 3s. 6d. and   0 4 0
Also a new and splendid edition printed on large
quarto paper, embellished with thirty-one full-page
illustrations, and a coloured portrait of St. Agnes.
Handsomely bound. 1 1 0